Is It Jook Yet?

Comfort Food From Faraway Places

By Lenny Karpman

Author, and Emeritus Cook & Caterer **Lenny Karpman**

Chief Comfort Food Guru and Chef de Cuisine **Matt Karpman**

Patisserie Head Chef, Artist, and CEO **Erin Keebler Karpman**

Comfort Food Taster, Sous Chef, and Baker **Lily Karpman (10 years old)**

Comfort Food Taster and Assistant Baker **Jack Karpman (7 years old)**

Senior Taster and Guest Chef **David Karpman**

Wife, Artist, Writer, Cook & Caterer, Soul Mate, Editor **Joan Hall**

Comfort food has been around forever despite the notion that the moniker arose in the mid 1960s in a Florida newspaper article. Any food that makes the eater feel better fits the bill. The sensation varies with the beholder, and all are equally justifiable. The defining quality may be texture, taste, aroma, appearance, nostalgia, pain relief, history, family, utility, culture, or mythology.

Even in my ninth decade, I remember the comfort that popsicles brought to my sore throats in early childhood. Hot tea and honey also worked despite opposite temperature and texture. In our home, any illness or emotional stress engendered chicken soup with noodles or dumplings of one kind or another. My family's roots were Ashkenazi Jewish from Belarus and Poland. So the dumplings tended to be beef or mushroom filled kreplach, rather than pork or cheese filled pierogi or pelmeni. The Ashkenazi noodle of choice was a broad flat egg noodle.

No less comforting was the chicken soup given to cure me of a minor cough in Guilin, South China, although the chicken had to have black skin and white silky hair-like feathers, ginger the dominant the flavor, and the noodles made from rice. Local beliefs were that without the black skin chicken and the ginger, chicken soup had no healing powers. That eliminated wonton or egg flower soup in ordinary chicken broth.

Rest assured that Mexican caldo de pollo would have been as beneficial and as comforting in the eyes of native beholders, even with pieces of corn on the cob, chayote, and zucchini floating in it.

The purpose of these comparisons? To make the simple point that the number of foods qualified to be called comfort foods, are enormous. Any collection cannot be comprehensive. The objective of this grouping is to inform, entertain, and demonstrate how culture-dependent all edibles are in a few hundred or so examples. The bias is arbitrary, a personal preference jaded by many decades of travel by an admitted compulsive food explorer, with a cast iron stomach, and many predilections born in the childhood poverty that I never recognized as such at the time. They account for selections that no affluent family member might have known about, let alone have made. Are there qualifiers other than the author feels good when he eats them?

Yes, of course. The ease of preparation matters. Simplicity may be a factor. Flexibility counts. Can the dish serve as a snack, appetizer, or main course with little or nothing more than adjusting quantity?

If so, it is more comforting. Little dishes earn points for between meal taste treats. Groupings of small plates create variety as in Chinese dim sum, Turkish mezze, or Spanish tapas.

And leftovers matter. If the dish in question helps strip the fridge of bits and pieces of leftovers, that is a big plus. Soups, stews, casseroles, frittatas, omelets, pizzas, and assortments of pasta dishes and rice bowls are havens for leftovers, particularly as belly warmers in winter. The same principal fits cold platters in hot climes. Texture and aroma may be disqualifiers in our eyes, but not in the eyes of diners born and raised in a different culture. Egyptians and North Africans love soup made with either molukhia or puree of okra. Many Westerners consider both too slimy. Few of us would choose to gnaw on a duck head or chew pig's ear in a bar. We, not they, maybe the outliers. Cost is also a consideration. I am blessed to be quantum leaps beyond the poverty I experienced during childhood, but a dish that costs much more than an average wage earner can afford, forfeits its designation as comfort food from my perspective. No accounting for my myopic personal taste and lack of objectivity. Mea culpa. Smiles count.

My wife and I have been blessed to visit more than a hundred countries. Our intent has always been to immerse ourselves into the lives, culture, history, hardships, happiness, and hopes of local people, respectfully.

Food exploring offers a bridge to understanding roots, geography, agriculture, beliefs, health, and nostalgia. We are both experimental cooks with unfettered curiosity. She has a more sophisticated palate. I have greater tolerance of the bizarre.

Both sons are fine cooks. Matt is a career food and wine maven. His kids appear to be foodies in the making. Tradition will survive us.

The giants won and Barry Bonds homered,
as he did every time Erin went to a game.

Karpman Family Maryland crabfest.
L-R Wife Joan, Son David, Daughter-in-law Erin, Son Matt,
Grandson Jack, Granddaughter Lily, Old Man Lenny

Table of Contents

A

Ackee and Saltfish. Jamaica's national fruit, the ackee, is the star of ackee and saltfish, the island's national dish, a salty and savory sauté that's often served with fried plantains and rice. The tree that grows scrambled eggs …. Do you remember the lyrics to the popular Calypso song, "Akee rice and the fish is nice?" I thought akee was a kind of rice until I ate it in Jamaica. Ackee is a fruit tree in the same soapberry family as lychee and longan. The fruit is poisonous uncooked, particularly when unripe. As the oblong size-of-a-small-fist fruit ripens, it turns red and finally divides into three segments, each partly enclosing a black seed and yellow pulp called the aril. Only the aril is edible and then only after a five-minute bath in boiling water. It then has the appearance and consistency of scrambled eggs. Ackee fruit together with salt cod, vegetables, and rice comprise the standard Jamaican national dish. The ackee is mild, buttery, and delicate, but the flavor is often masked by the diced Scotch bonnet chili peppers added to the boiled fruit and then lightly fried together. I suggest that you finely dice just a very small slice off the bottom of the red pepper to avoid the ribs and seeds. Canned Jamaican ackee fruit is exported far and wide, but it doesn't compare with the fresh dish. It is often used as a matter of convenience but must be rinsed under a gentle stream of fresh water to remove any hint of the brine from the can.

Açorda Alentejana is from the Portugal's southern region of Alentejo, that stretches along the Spanish border to the Atlantic. The area is predominantly farm country. This rustic farmhouse dish is dirt cheap, recycles stale bread, and is simple to make. The cook drops enough slices or pieces from stale crusty peasant loaves into the boiling water to thicken the liquid into a hearty nearly stew-like consistency. Cilantro, olive oil, salt and pepper follow. The cook breaks raw eggs over the pot and they poach. Voila.

Using stale bread to thicken soups is a trait probably borrowed from Moorish tradition. The simplicity vanishes when açorda Alentejana transforms into an upscale restaurant dish. The addition of costly seafood is the culprit.

Äggakaka is a fluffy tasty egg pancake, cooked and often served in the same skillet. If it is transferred to a dinner plate, it covers nearly the entirety of the plate. Atop the pancake, sliced crisp pork belly or bacon stretches out under a sprinkling of bright red lingonberries. It is appealing to view and marvelous to taste with balanced sweet and salty elements, and crisp, soft, and chewy textures. The dish provides comfort to the people of the Scania region in southernmost Sweden.

Aji de Gallina Most easily translated as "creamy chicken", aji de gallina is the comfort food of Peru with a subtle sophistication in its flavor. Shredded chicken is cooked down with a rich sauce of cream, cheese, walnuts, and chili, served alongside a generous ladling of rice, a hard-boiled egg, and an olive.

Albondigas or polpettes are meatballs in tomato sauce. You might expect them to appear atop a plate of spaghetti in Italy. But not likely. The combination of spaghetti and meatballs in tomato sauce is really an American comfort food dish designed to conflate the attraction to spaghetti with the love of hamburgers of any size. Meatballs in tomato sauce apart from pasta may appear in Italy at times, but ground zero for albondigas is Spain. The meatballs and sauce appear as common comforting tapas all over the country combined with crusty bread to soak up the leftover sauce.

Alheira de Mirandela Historians suggest that many, if not most, of the crewmen that sailed with Columbus in 1492 were Jews fleeing the Spanish Inquisition and its implementation in both Spain and Portugal. Their options were to flee Greater Iberia, convert to Christianity, go underground, or die. Some appeared to convert, but upheld their religious beliefs in secret. They, the Marranos, in order to survive, had to appear Christian. Pork sausage was a basic food in Portugal. Marranos created a look-alike sausage devoid of pork. Alheira de Mirandela included veal, chicken, duck and/or rabbit with bread filler.

It might have been a love for fried food, but fried alheira faux pork sausages with fried potatoes topped with a fried egg outlasted the Inquisition and remain a Portuguese comfort trio to people of all religions.

Aligot from the south of France adds even more comfort to mashed potatoes with the additions of butter, crème fraiche, garlic, milk curds, tomme or Cantal cheese, and lots of elbow grease to whip the fondue-like mixture into silken ecstasy.

Ameijoas a Bulhao Pato During my mid-teens, my dad qualified for a number of weekend insurance company conventions designed to mix work with pleasure in resort settings. Mom went with him. I often cooked for a girlfriend when I had home to myself. My signature dish was linguini with clam sauce. I put washed cherrystones in a pot with a few tablespoons of olive oil, a mashed and diced garlic clove, and ground pepper. After a few minutes of heat, the clams opened and juices mixed with the olive oil, garlic, and pepper. If there were a corked bottle of white wine in the fridge, a splash of it joined in. A scattering of minced parsley for the final two minutes and my clam sauce was born. Tossed with al dente linguini, the food elevated my shaky status more than my shyness and pubertal bumbling deserved.

Bulhao pato style Portuguese clams are quite similar, albeit without pasta. Cooks in Lisbon use cilantro instead of parsley; they serve crusty bread to mop up leftover sauce and they use local clams, that are harder to rid of sand and mud, from the estuary of the Tagus river.

Angel Hair Pasta Like spaghetti, angel hair is long, thin, and the strands are round. Since the 14th century, capellini has been Italy's standard skinny round pasta. Even skinnier, capelli d'angelo emerged in the 18th century. It is a perfect mate for delicate seafood, light sauces, and pestos. Its most comforting quality is that it cooks quicker than other dry pastas and a little goes a long way. Functionality wins. Home cooks use it often for quick kids' lunches.

Angel wings are scrumptious Thai boned stuffed chicken wings fried golden brown. One needs patience. There are several steps, but none requires much talent. The challenge is boning the wings. Step one is to slice open the skin on top (farthest from the wing tip) of the drumette. Next, place a finger between the meat and skin and run it all around the drumette. Snap the joint in two between the drumette and the rest of the wing without damaging the skin. Then twist and remove the skinless drumette.

Stuff the space vacated by the drumette with a mixture of diced cilantro, garlic, white onion, and soaked bean thread noodles. Close the top. Season the skin. I like to use a mix of turmeric and paprika, hardly Thai. Steam the wings for about thirty minutes to cook the chicken and filling. Dip it in beaten egg, coat it with flour, and fry the wings until golden brown. The wing tips become a handle. The plump stuffed part may be sliced on an angle or simply bitten off a bite at a time. The lovely tastes, textures, and contrasts are well worth the prep time to provide a satisfying snack or first course. They can also be an appetizer for meals that are neither Thai nor even Asian.

Anticuchos are an appetizer or a part of an Argentinian or Peruvian mixed grill. They are cubes of roasted beef heart served on skewers or toothpicks. After soaking in a marinade of garlic, vinegar, cumin, and chili paste, they land on oversized grills called parrillas. They become roasted meats, asados, skillfully prepared by asaderos, Latin American grill masters. The pieces are kept small and diamond shape to make them seem more tender than they are. They are very tasty, spicy, and quite chewy. I like them a lot more than most of my gringo compatriots.

Most other beef heart preparations require lengthy stewing to achieve tender texture. Other components of mixed grills, parrilladas, include sweetbreads, steak, blood sausage, ribs, chicken, and lamb. Presentations may include, corn on the cob, potatoes boiled or baked, and bread.

The rust color of Peruvian anticuchos and other grilled meats comes from the paste of an Andean brownish pepper called aji panca.

Aranchini. These "little oranges" are fried stuffed rice balls Sicilian style, colored orange by the addition of saffron to short grain cooked rice.

They are a lot of work, but not if you start with quality leftovers. Many decades ago when I was single, I had a hard time cooking my favorites without preparing more than I needed for a single serving. The two red sauces that I purposely made in excess were meaty Bolognese ragu and spicy arabiatta. Single portion size small bags of both sauces lived in my freezer. When I made risotto with short grain Arborio rice, leftovers didn't do well in the fridge for more than a day. The rice hardened. So I planned, whenever I could, to combine the risotto for arancini by adding saffron to the rice, and cheese and ragu filling with the spicy red sauce as dip the next day. A smallish handful of the rice was rolled into the size of a golf ball. Into a thumb indentation went my filling of parmesan and mozzarella, and a teaspoon of the ragu. I closed the opening securely, rolled each ball in flour, egg wash, and finely, crushed panko. Then into the fryer until orange colored. Done. Always enough for a dinner guest to join me.

Arepas A common first course or snack in Colombia and Venezuela, these cornmeal cakes or buns are topped or cut open and filled with either sweet or savory goodies. The cook stirs masarepa, special corn flour, with warm salted water to make dough, rolls enough to make a ball the size of a golf ball, flattens the ball into the shape of a hockey puck, browns top and bottom in an oiled skillet, then bakes them to finish the insides. Of all the types of corn flour in Latin America, only masarepa begins with precooked kernels of corn. They are larger than most and contain more starch. Depending on the color of the corn, the flour may be yellow or white. An even mix yields a lovely light golden color.

Uncut and topped with runny white cheese, many Colombianos eat this type of arepa for breakfast. The most popular fillings for partly cut Venezuelan aprepas are these: black beans and cheese, chicken and avocado, chicken salad, plantains and cheese, shredded chicken with tomato sauce, shredded beef, spicy pork and avocado, and tuna creamy salad.

Arroz con Pollo How simple is it to prepare rice with shredded chicken in it? A pretty mundane dish one might think. To my surprise, arroz con pollo is the standard featured main dish at just about every communal event of importance in my current home country of Costa Rica. I have had it at weddings, graduations, christenings, milestone birthdays, and anniversaries. The ingredients are only a little different from what they might be anywhere. Long grain rice from an electric cooker often colored with a bit of red achiote paste or oil, and at times steamed with chicken broth instead of water; already cooked rotisserie chicken, skinned, deboned, and shredded, or boneless skinless chicken breasts poached and shredded; diced sweet red pepper, celery, onion, garlic, and cilantro leaves, plus optional peas, corn kernels, diced tomato or carrot; and the seasoned herbal binder of Salsa Lizano (Costa Rican preferred quasi equivalent of Worcestershire sauce), soy sauce, and tomato sauce or catsup. Throughout Latin America, recipes for the same dish vary a little, but the basics are the same. Mexican and Peruvian cooks tend to add some chili pepper heat.

Before I came to Costa Rica, I made arroz con pollo with a recipe from a Cuban neighbor. It was so easy. First I browned salted chicken thighs in oil, removed them, and sweated onion, red and green bell pepper, and garlic in the same frying pan. Into a heavy duty pot with a tight-fitting cover, I put thighs, garlic, onion, pepper, a little tomato paste, cumin, oregano, ancho oil, chicken broth, long grain rice, and let it simmer without ever lifting the lid for an hour. Depending on whim, I added frozen corn kernels and/or peas at the end, just long enough to heat them through.

Other variations include oven baked rice and chicken with crisp rice on top, paella de pollo with crisp rice socarrat on the underside, and additional meats or seafoods. The origins of the dish appear to be in Spain during Moorish rule.

Arroz de Pato Another variation on arroz con pollo is Portuguese duck rice. The two part preparation simmers the duck meat until tender in red wine, then puts the duck and cooked rice in an oven to crisp the rice on top. Sounds perfect, but in Portugal, so many casseroles receive a gratuitous topping of sliced smoked sausage. So does arroz de pato. Comfort food in spades.

Asheh Reshteh. Farzad was from Iran. His wife Fatima from Azerbaijan. He was a surgical resident in an off-the-beaten-path smallish Brooklyn hospital that had a hard time attracting top American trained residents. After med school in Iran, he had done an internship in a small Texas city. I chose the hospital for my OB-GYN clerkship for the opportunity to do more and watch less than I would have at a university hospital. He and I became friends. We had lunch together at a neighborhood Italian hole-in-the-wall eatery. After a satisfying bowl of minestrone soup on a cold February day, he offered to invite me to his apartment to try his wife's asheh reshteh, "an even better soup like this. My wife makes it the same way my mother does, even though she is not Iranian. It is the same in both of our countries."

I could hardly refuse. When might I ever get to taste Azerbaijanian authenticity again? Well, she was a charmer, and answered all of my dozens of questions about this most flavorful and tart, bean, lentil, noodle, greens, and cooked yogurt rich soup. The beans were dry kidney beans, small white beans, and garbanzos all presoaked. She used brown lentils but said any kind except red ones would work. The noodles, reshteh, were unique. She bought them at a Middle Eastern market in her neighborhood. They were long, white, starchy, and salty. She broke them in half and only added them to the gently boiling bean, lentil, and greens a few at a time. She couldn't explain why except to say that her mother always did it that way "because of the starch."

The greens were a mélange of spinach, dill, parsley, mint, and garlic chives. Towards the end of cooking she added kashk when she could find it in the same market. When they didn't have any, she "cooked" yogurt instead. She said that real kashk was like creamy feta.

An average Italian or an American might prefer less salty and less sour minestrone, but to me the ash reshteh's flavor and almost gumbo consistency was perfection. Farzad shared that this soup was the most enjoyable part of traditional Iranian New Year dinners.

He promised me a return invitation to taste his wife's ash-e anar, Iranian pomegranate soup, but she had to go home to Azerbaijan when her mother was diagnosed with cancer.

Ayam Goreng I thought fried chicken was solely American. Southern style marinated in buttermilk before coating and fried in lard was my measuring stick. I was wrong. Several countries share the honor, but with distinctive variations.

We were driving in Indonesia near the international airport when we saw a fried chicken venue with a nearly full parking lot and about a dozen trucks too large for the lot, parked along the road.

"For hearty, affordable, good comfort food, follow the truckers," my dad always said. So, we did. Amazing! What a spice mixture. We could identify garlic, ginger, and lemongrass by flavor, shallots by sight, and turmeric by color. We asked the waiter if we were missing any. "About six more," he answered. He mentioned coriander, galangal, curry leaves, cumin, and fennel seed as he hurried away to transport more delightfully aromatic, crunchy, juicy plates full to the appreciative masses. In addition to the great taste, texture, and aroma, crunchy crumbs of flour mixed with herbs and spice were retrieved from the fryer with a mesh strainer and tossed over the plate. Unique in my experience. Yummy.

See Taiwanese fried chicken for my second favorite.

B

Bacalhau a Bras There are reputedly 365 fine ways to prepare dried salted cod, one for each day of the year. I have yet to find one that uses an entire large piece and appeals to me more than a good, moist, firm, white fleshed, fresh fish. The repeated soaking in milk or fresh water to rehydrate the cod and lessen the salt load requires more time and effort than most comfort foods demand. Yet it is among the most popular in Portugal and in any part of the world where Portuguese colonialists, explorers, and ex-pats have ever dwelled; even places surrounded by seas teeming with fresh fish such as Barbados, Brazil, Italy, Jamaica, Macao, Morocco, Mozambique, Norway, Spain, Trinidad, Uruguay, and Zanzibar.

We scheduled a month driving north from Madrid across Spain and into Portugal.

I am not much of a drinker, but I planned for a long weekend in Oporto to visit the aging caves for my favorite alcoholic beverage, port. Who knew? That entire three-day weekend, all of the caves were closed because of a national holiday – Columbus's birthday. Surprise. One evening we ate at a small tapas bar rather than having to wait hours for late night dinner houses to open. Because of the holiday, they were short staffed and their tapas options were quite limited. I ordered bacalhau a bras by default at the recommendation of the waiter. He extolled, "It is my favorite and probably the favorite bacalhau dish in this part of Portugal."

To my surprise, I liked it. It didn't pretend to be a thick fillet of fresh fish. It was not too salty and it was simple, affordable, appealing to the eye, moist, and tasty. Locals loved it. It was traditional. Battered and fried bacalhau was flaked into thumbnail size pieces, tossed with fried thin potato strips and browned onions, simmered with beaten eggs, and topped with olives and diced scallion. It fulfilled all of my criteria for comfort food. I had a glass of port after, the same brand I could have gotten at my local grocery at home. With the port, I swallowed my pride and gave the dish a three-star comfort rating.

Baeckeoffe is a perfect Alsatian stew readily available in beautiful Strasburg. The slowly cooked rich, warming, tasty treat is named after the large baker's oven that it simmered in for three hours, and the name of the dish itself. The one pot medley contains many different types and cuts of meat augmented by collagen donated from pig's feet. Meats usually include lamb and beef as well. The veggie list starts with carrots, followed by celery, leeks, onion, and ends with potato all cooked in goose fat. The pot and cover are sealed with flour paste that is not broken for all three hours. Add French bread and local white wine and savor slowly.

Bagels Where to start? New York? Montreal? Krakow? Historians disagree. Hieroglyphics from ancient Egypt in the Louvre depict rolls with a hole in the middle. From Egypt to Mediterranean countries came two types; taralli fennel flavored crackers along the Adriatic coast of Italy's boot in Puglia; and bagele, a softer variety known along the west coast of what now is Israel, and ka'ak a similar soft roll in Syria with a hole in it.

Wheat cultivation dates back thousands of years. Poland emerged as a Slavic country in the tenth century. Despite the absence of geographic protective barriers and relentless political instability, it became the breadbasket of Central Europe. From the 1490s, white bread and preboiled bagel facsimiles could legally be baked only by the Krakow Bakers Guild that excluded Jews. The next chapter in the bagel story may be mythological, but it has been told and retold throughout bagel history. In 1683, King Jan Sobieski saved Poland from Turkish invasion. As part of the victory celebration, the bagel became a symbol of the victory honoring the king. He revoked the exclusivity rule of the Krakow Bakers Guild. Jews could make bagels legally. And they did with a vengeance. To this day, Krakow claims to be the original home of the bagel as we know it.

From Central Europe, the bagel seems to have migrated both east and west. To the east, they traveled the Silk Route to Western China. In Xinjiang Province, Uyghur flatbreads, nang or nan, are large round rings or solid wheat flour loaves sprinkled with sesame seeds and/or spices, sold from street carts, in store fronts, or on table tops in night markets, usually adjacent to the wood-burning tandoors in which they baked. They sport crisp golden brown crusts that contrast with soft chewy centers. The seller may decorate the tops with piercings made with a nail-like tool. In the central plains of Inner Mongolia, nang are called hubing, foreign bread, reflecting their Silk Route origins west and south of China. Uyghur bagels, girde nang, look like smaller ring loaves, baked over hot coals or wood in tandoors. They look just like bagels until you notice that the central hole is actually just a membranous dent. They are similar in taste, texture, size, and shape to good old New York bagels. The batches from wood-burning tandoors, have the additional quality of smokiness, which makes them even better. Often dusted with white sesame seeds, they go from grate to plate while still warm to be paired with hot tea, or to be dipped in mutton soup in a Muslim meat market. In recent times, these girde nang have begun to appear in Muslim markets in other parts of China as far away as the southern metropolis of Guangzhou.

Bagels have become common in Japan for about the last about thirty years. They tend to be softer, less chewy, and a little sweeter than New York bagels. They frequently appear to be green tinged from the infusion of green tea into the batter. Most remind me of the prepackaged bagels that American bread companies sold in chain supermarkets in the 60s. Their similarity to authentic bagels stopped at the shape. But the Japanese ability to reproduce anything with near authenticity has begun to create fine artisanal traditional bagels in recent years.

Traveling west, Turkey has had round rolls called simit since the 16th century. They are often promoted as bagels, but only the shape is bageloid. Modern actual Turkish bagels called açma, are saltier and greasier than our New Yorkers.

In Russia, bagels are bubliks. They are made from yeast and wheat flour that is preboiled and baked. Along with Ukranian, Lithuanian, Belarusian, and Polish bubliks, they are larger, denser, and more chewy than American bagels. The addition of butter, milk, and egg whites to the batter increases the density. Sushki are very small sweet dessert bagels in Russia, about a quarter the size of bubliks. The boiling water used in the first stage of preparation is sweetened with sugar. They are either uncoated or coated with poppy seeds.

In Finland, *Vesirinkeli* are boiled in water before being baked. Their holes are larger and they are virtually never served without being toasted and buttered first. These Finnish specialties are very similar to generic bagels, except their holes are a bit wide.

Actual bagels reached the shores on our side of the Atlantic in the 1800s.

They were beigels in London and became known as bagels when they crossed the Atlantic with hordes of immigrants to New York city and Montreal. To this day, proponents of New York bagels and Montreal bagels joust for bragging rights as the world's best. In fact both exemplify the fine qualities of good flour and yeast, crispy brown crust, chewy soft interiors, and the compulsory hole in the middle. Montreal or Canadian bagels are a little smaller, thinner, and have a larger central hole. They are also sweeter. Honey is added to the pre-baking boiling water bath. Wood fueled ovens may add a hint of enhancing smokiness and create a crisper crust. The thinner periphery and larger hole interfere with the ease of sandwich making. Both styles now come covered with an ever-expanding choice of toppings and new different types of flour. Mechanical mass production has yielded a process wherein boiling and baking become one by steam baking.

One might surmise that Israeli bagels mirror New York bagels. They do not. They are not preboiled, hence not chewy. They are skinny and oval rather than round. The only topping is sesame seeds. To my palate, they were disappointing.

Food historians agree that the hole in the middle emerged to assure even baking, ease of transportation, on display in carts with dowels, on poles on the shoulders of street venders, and on tall pegs in bakery display cases and windows.

Baloutes are fertilized duck eggs that are incubated for 18 or 21 days. They are boiled for about 20 minutes, and sold from straw baskets by vendors at basketball and baseball games in the Philippines. They are peeled and salted like regular hard-boiled eggs but they combine egg yolk and white, the duck embryo, and a strong fetid, rancid aroma.The 21-day variety has a larger embryo. Bony body parts are starting to show. They are believed to be aphrodisiacs, otherwise I can't believe that they would be so popular. I guess the power of suggestion works for believers. Viagra please.

Baloutes in Manila

Bangers and Mash Brits like it a lot as an unpretentious affordable comforting lunch. Just sausage and mashed potatoes made simply or exotically according to site – pub or gastropub. The mythology of the name may be related to the pop or bang made by a lesser quality sausage bursting its skin in boiling water. It dates back to the end of WWI. I like it with spicy sausage and onion gravy. Woefully bland bangers are far too common.

Bebek Betutu Bali is a marvelous place to visit, feast, and forage, particularly inland away from the beaches that tend to be cookie-cutter playgrounds for hard drinking young people. It is a Hindu oasis in a vast Muslim nation. The cuisine is mostly Indonesian, Indian, and Chinese. Because it is Hindu, its roast suckling pig dishes are famous, outstanding, but not unique. One of the few uniquely Balinese dishes is bebek betutu, smoked duck wrapped in palm leaf or betel-nut bark, which contains natural oils to further enhance the flavor. Seasoned with betutu spices that are heated in coconut oil, they include candle nuts, chili peppers, garlic, ginger, galangal, peanuts shallots, shrimp paste, turmeric, and wild ginger, all finely ground using mortar and pestle. It takes several hours to prepare, so it must be ordered in advance. Hardly a fast food like most comfort foods. Hailed as among the very best duck preparations anywhere, the meat is very tender, aromatic, tasty, turmeric yellow on top and nearly black inside. Rice hull smoking darkens the meat.

Beef Empanadas are ubiquitous fried or baked pastry packets of meat throughout Latin America. There is no question that Argentinian beef is as good or better than any. Cooked until tender in stock, the packets have more layers of flavor and are among the juiciest of the competition. In addition to typical empanada seasonings, Sao Paolo cooks add cumin, olives, raisins, sweet red peppers, and modest amounts of heat.

Beef Noodle Soup, no kidding. Too mundane to be special? Not in the eyes of Taiwanese cooks and beholders. It is Taiwan's national dish despite the fact that pork and seafood are so much more common than beef. The island nation (Republic of China), has a central spine of nearly uninhabited mountains. The remainder of the country is too densely populated to make room for lush livestock pastures.

The finished product is fabulous. Hurdle number one, using the perfect cut of beef. Cognoscenti choose chuck, but not any chuck.

They go to great lengths to find the fattiest pieces. Most are too lean and risk becoming dry. Then they red braise the meat until tender. Red braising is simmering in soy sauce. If cooks choose fattier beef shanks, the cooking time lasts for up to three hours. The meat joins fresh bok choy, pickled mustard greens, white noodles, and herbs and spices in a beef broth bath to simmer to perfection. Dry red chili peppers adds moderate but not uncomfortable heat. Ginger, garlic, tomato paste, onion, quartered tomatoes, spicy bean paste, rice wine, star anise, sugar, and soy sauce balance every element of taste. Fresh scallions and cilantro go in last. The noodles of choice are fresh opaque white flour noodles. The result is a perfection itself, not at all mundane.

Taiwanese beef noodle soup

Origins of beef noodle soup in a land where cattle are work animals? When too old to pull plows, or turn milling grinders, they were roasted whole to feed a small village or large family. But after the civil war in the 1940s, veterans of Kuomintang who fled Mao's forces on the mainland, brought beef noodle soup with them, a vestige of their homeland and history.

Beet Borsht When most people talk about borsht, they describe a Russian or Ukrainian version of sweet and sour beef bone stock seasoned at times with toasted caraway seed, onions and lemon juice in which red or green cabbage, potato, tomatoes, carrots, and a few diced beets are cooked. Some add apple cider vinegar or fermented beet juice. The meat can be either beef or pork.

That is nothing like the Ashkenazi meatless beet borsht that is probably the most satisfying strange cold soup that I have ever eaten. The way that Grandma, Mom, and I made it changed little over the decades. And the specifics may even be unique to my family's recipe. I have never had anything quite like it outside my family.

Beet borscht

For starters, it is cooked in water seasoned only with salt, sugar and lemon juice. The main ingredient is a large bunch of beets, rendering it more sweet than sour, and almost iridescent magenta. Some like it hot. Not the Karpmans. After cooking the inch-long thick matchsticks of peeled and cut beets for about an hour, the embryonic soup cooled, then moved into the fridge to be chilled

It came in a tureen to the middle of the round dinner table for a milchik (meatless) meal. Surrounding the tureen were the following: a pot of peeled boiled potatoes, still hot, sitting on a heatproof pad; a bowl of sour cream from the fridge; a few quartered hard-boiled eggs; cucumber pieces peeled, halved lengthwise into logs, rendered seedless by a swipe of a melon baller, and cut across into half-inch segments; diced scallions; and lemon wedges. No milk vs. meat conflict here. We ladled elements into our individual bowls. The cold soup followed by sour cream received a whisking. Next came cukes, egg quarters, and scallions, and finally a tennis ball size hot potato in the middle of the bowl like the rock of Gibraltar in the Mediterranean at red sunset. What a fabulous mix of flavors, textures, colors, sweet and salty, hot and cold.

We ate the soup with pulled pieces of fresh baked challah except on Passover when we settled for matzo. So sorry that all but a few Ashkenazim among you have ever shared a similar extraordinary vegetarian treat.

If you want to try a simplified quickie version to see if you like it enough to follow the directions above, buy Manischewitz beet borsht in a jar, mix it chilled with sour cream and a few chunks of cucumber. Try it for taste even though it has too few pieces of beet in the mix. If you like the simplified sample, go for the real thing.

To my surprise, I found borsht mixed with sour cream like Grandma's but with boiled potatoes next to rather than in the soup, in Vilnius, Lithuania.

Beggar's Chicken Over 55 years ago, when I tasted beggar's chicken baked in clay for the first time, it was a brand new sensation in San Francisco courtesy of Cecelia Chang. When I rhapsodized about it to my friend Chung, he corrected me. "It, jiaohua tongzi ji, is a Hangzhou dish copied by the chefs of Shanghai. My parents are from a town on a beautiful lake near Hangzhou. Many other wonderful dishes that Americans think of as Shanghai-style are really from the Hangzhou region of Zhejiang Province. Do you know about Dongpo pork belly stewed in wine and soy sauce — named after a poet Dongporou; Westlake fish braised in sweetened vinegar, xihu cuyu; fresh water shrimp in Longjing green tea leaves; and pork wrapped in lotus leaf? All from Hangzhou. Because so many of the country's best authors, artists and poets lived there, chefs catered to very sophisticated diners and responded with the best cuisine anywhere. As you know, Shanghai is more of an international city than a traditional Chinese city. Its history only goes back to the nineteenth century when the British built it as a port for their ships. The culinary tradition in Hangzhou goes back more than a thousand years!"

"Thanks for the lesson, Chung. How did you get so smart?"

"Blame my parents. The name they gave me means intelligent boy."

Jiaohuaji is now quite common. In Zhejiang's capital, Hangzhou, it is no longer an expensive item served only in fine restaurants. Without its clay coat, the succulent chicken still wrapped in leaves, appears as an affordable take-out food in markets.

The folktale tells of a poor beggar who acquired a chicken but had neither pots, nor condiments, nor knives. Versions of the tale vary. He either captured a wild chicken or stole a domesticated one. He didn't want the aroma of roasting chicken to draw attention to him. He therefore coated the chicken in clay from the riverbank and baked it over an open fire. After the clay had hardened and the embers faded, he cracked open the clay with a rock. Then the aroma escaped. The feathers had become imbedded in the clay and fell away. As he tore into the wonderfully aromatic flesh, a scholarly passerby, drawn by the scent, meandered closer. The beggar supposedly gave the impressed scholar a taste. He sent his servant back to get the recipe. Its fame spread all the way to the 17th century Imperial Court.

The chicken I ate in San Francisco back then was also baked in clay, but it was fabulously seasoned and layered with lotus leaves between the bird and the clay. I have since had it stuffed and baked in pastry and foil. In all cases, the enclosed bird remains juicy and the intoxicating aroma explodes when the package is opened. In Hangzhou, our waiter ceremoniously cracked open the baked clay vessel at our table and engendered applause from adjacent diners.

Beouf Bourguignon can be an expensive dish in a fancy French restaurant, but in a blue collar bistro or homemade, it is an economical hearty comforting stew. The two ingredients that can save the cook many euros are the meat, chuck, and the wine, a dark red vin ordinaire from Burgundy. None of the steps require special skills. But the prep time is a little long, and the cooking time includes a three-hour simmer.

Step 1, Dice a few strips of bacon, thick cut if possible, in a little oil. Render the fat and remove the bacon.

Step 2, brown cubes of chuck dusted with ground pepper in the drippings and oil. Remove the meat.

Step 3, cook carrots and onions in the same pan, stirring to liberate tasty bits.

Step 4, deglaze the pan with red wine and beef broth.

Step 5, put the meat back in and sprinkle a thin coat of flour over the top, enough to caramelize the surface of the meat and ultimately thicken the broth.

Step 6, toss halved cremini mushroom in butter for a few minutes.

Step 7, add enough beef broth to nearly cover the meat and veggies, add a few teaspoons of tomato paste, peeled pearl onions, thyme, minced garlic, mushrooms and bay leaves. Cover and simmer for three hours. Strain the ingredients to reduce the liquid by about a quarter. Recombine everything.

Step 8. Call me to join you as you serve the Beouf Bourguignon with a side or on a bed of mashed potatoes. I'll bring a fresh baguette to sop up the juices at the bottom of the plate.

Bi For many years, my clerical assistant in the medical office was a young woman who had escaped from Vietnam on a boat with her family. Miraculously, they all survived a storm at sea and nearly three days without food or water. One day she brought me a plastic container with lunch. "Guess what it is." she beamed. I guessed wrong. It looked like thin rice noodles with brown matchsticks that I thought might be mushroom and a tan fine powder on top, which was not the ground peanuts that I presumed. When informed that I was wrong on all counts, I changed my noodle guess to jellyfish strands. Wrong again. "OK. What is it?"

"Bi."

"Just bi?"

"Yes, just bi."

The white strands were fine threads of pork skin no thicker than angel-hair pasta. She bought them frozen, soaked them in warm water and patted them dry.

The brown matchsticks were leftover sliver cuts of pork roast. The powder was broken rice flour toasted in a dry pan. From a tiny jar, she dressed it with garlic-flavored nuoc mam. I have been to Vietnam twice since then, but have never had better bi.

Bibimbap Many countries feature a bowl of white rice topped with assorted goodies as a catch all comfort receptacle, often for leftovers. Versions from Latin America, to North Africa, to Mexico, to Thailand, and to Japan all satisfy. My favorite is the Korean version, bibimbap. The platform, a bowl of short or medium grain white rice, receives a topping of vegetables, meat, marvelous sauce with a bit of a kick, and a fried egg. The underside is also special. More so in Korea than in Korean restaurants abroad, the cooking bowl for the rice is made of chiseled stone or oven-proof ceramic. The rice that abuts the heated bottom browns and crisps like soccarat in the bottom of a paella pan. The meat of choice is marinated ground beef, cooked separately. The marinade typically mixes soy sauce with garlic, sugar, and a splash of sesame oil. Kicking it up a notch, I prefer bulgogi strips. The usual veggie combo aligns spinach, bean sprouts, carrots, and shitake mushrooms cooked separately but sparingly. The carrots and shitakes are sliced thin and long to approach the shape of the bean sprouts. Dried sheets of seaweed, scissor cut into strands, maintain the pattern. The egg on top is sunny side up with congealed white and runny yolk. If this were all, bibimbap would be a decent rice bowl. No kimchi? Yes, some diners ask for and receive a little kimchi to add to the artistic arrangement on top of the rice. I like kimchi, but prefer it separately plated so it doesn't overwhelm the other flavors in the rice bowl. What elevates bibimbap over the top for me is the final ingredient, the sauce. Gochujang, fermented chili pepper paste, has moderate kick, complex flavor, some sweetness, and hint of smoke. Straight out the jar, it works well. Many Korean cooks enhance it a little with garlic, sesame seeds, vinegar, and sugar. You, the diner get to admire the artistry of the decorated toppings, and then mix it and devour it.

Bistec á la pobre. Every South American country has its own version of the "poor man's dinner." In Colombia, it's the bandja paisa, a huge plate of pork, red beans and rice, fried plantains, and avocado. In Brazil, it's feijoada, a stew made from black beans, veggies, sausages, and offal. And of course, in Chile, it's the bistec á la pobre. This hearty meal is comprised of grilled beef, fried potatoes, onions and a fried egg. Not only will this keep you going for a long day of work, but it's the ultimate hangover dish when you've been out late. So I have been told.

Blanquette de Veau Breast of veal was quite inexpensive when I was young. Mom prepared in two ways . She cut a pocket into the meat, stuffed it and roasted it, or made a white stew out of it that I only learned a decade later, was a traditional French comfort ragu called blanquette de veau. Neither meat, butter, fats, nor diced vegetables are allowed to brown and caramelize. The technique bore the name en blanquette in French cookbooks. The cookbooks made a light roux to thicken the white sauce. Mom relied on egg yolks and cream. When I studied at a French restaurant many years later, the chef opted for my mother's approach.

To blanched cubes of meat, add carrots, celery, garlic, onions, leeks, and shallots, all peeled and diced plus a bag of herbs and spices, a bouquet garni. Mom added homemade broth. I use white wine. Cover and simmer for about an hour and a half. Drain off excess liquid, add sautéed mushrooms, egg yolks, cream, a squeeze of lemon plus some zest, serve with white rice and garnish with chopped parsley.

Blood Sausage. We Americans constitute a small minority of international diners who don't adore blood sausage. Forgive me for offending so many of you, but I actually like blood sausage in moderation.

Blood sausage is best when fresh and maintained at a cool temperature from a newly slaughtered animal before it has clotted. Left uncooked, fresh blood sausage has a short shelf life of only a few days. Enter black pudding or blood pudding. It is made by cooking blood or dried blood with a filler until it is thick enough to congeal when cooled.

Cooked blood sausage has a longer shelf life and is a staple in numerous cultures from Asia to Africa to Europe and the Americas. Blood from pig, cattle, sheep, duck, goat, horse, buffalo and dog, end up as human food. In Europe and the Americas, typical fillers include meat, fat, suet, bread, cornmeal, white potato, yam, sweet potato, yuca, onion, chestnut, barley, kasha, millet and oatmeal. In Spain, Portugal, Brazil, Central America and Asia, potato is often replaced by rice. Prepared to be bored by long lists? I won't be offended if you skip this long alphabetically organized list of common varieties of blood sausage:

Biroldo is the Italian name for blood sausage from the part of Tuscany around Lucca. Tuscan ex-pats also add pine nuts, raisins, fennel seed, or cinnamon.

Black pudding is a synonym for blood sausage, an integral part of the so called English breakfast. It is made from oats and pig's blood.

Blodkorv is Swedish blood sausage that differs from generic blood pudding by the addition of any combination of applesauce, dark beer, pork fat, raisins, and rye flour.

Bloedworst is Belgian blood sausage made from beef blood, cinnamon, dried bread, onions, pepper, pork fat, and salt. It is purple and moist unlike the British black, drier link.

Blood tongue sausage is called Zungenwurst in Germany. This large head cheese roll is made primarily of pig's blood, chunks of vinegar pickled tongue, and small cubes of ham fat augmented by bread crumbs and oatmeal. The precooked variety has the color of nearly black eggplant skin. In Nancy, the menu labeled it boudin de langue. I ate it cut thick and browned in butter.

Blóðmör is Icelandic sausage made from lambs blood, oats, rye flour, and suet. The mixture gets stuffed into pouches sewn from quarter parts of the lamb's stomach or standard sausage casing. The sausages are pickled. In *Reykjavik*, we had them served boiled with mashed potatoes.

Blutwurst comes from the Rhineland and resembles French boudin noir. It's likely to come to the table sliced, revealing a cross-section of speckled chunks of meat suspended in dried blood. Add applesauce and mashed potatoes to a plate with fried blutwurst - blood sausage, and onions – himmel un aäd. In the Rhineland, it is fried and made from horse meat.

Tote oma, dead grandmother, is a macabre named hot dish of loosely minced and mixed blutwurst, liverwurst, and potatoes common to Berlin.

Boudin du Béarn from Aquitane, the coastal region in southwest France from Bordeaux to San Sebastian, is a type of *boudin à la viande,* blood sausage with head meat. It is either sliced and eaten cold, or fried as intact links, often in the company of apples, onions, or chestnuts.

Boudin noir is the generic name for dried, precooked black blood sausage in France. As described above, it may have added small cubes of cooked head meats, vegetables or chestnuts. Typically it contains apple. Served heated or cold, it is a mainstay on charcuterie platters.

Buristo is southern Tuscan winter sausage cooked in pigs' stomachs and made with pork blood and fat.

Cháo Lòng is the Saigon version of pork parts in jook. Offal and congealed pig blood add to the mystery of pig tongue, heart, liver and even uteri. I liked it but seldom were any of my western compatriots even willing to taste it.

'Dồi tiết' is boiled or fried Vietnamese blood sausage made from pork blood and fat and seasoned with basil. It is spelled a little differently in Ho Chi Min City – 'dồi huyết'.

Drisheen is Irish blood sausage unique to County Cork. All over Europe the filling for boudin is basically pig's blood and fat. In Cork, in addition to pig's blood black pudding, putoga fola, they use sheep's blood or a mixture of blood from sheep and pig. The blood mixed with fat and breadcrumbs is seasoned with tansy, a roadside wild herb.

Karvavitsa is Bulgarian pig pluck and blood sausage made especially for Christmas. Pig pluck is larynx, trachea, lung, heart, and liver, taken from young pigs. Herbs, spices, and lard complete the sausage filling. Although I only had in Sofia, we also saw it on menus in Bosnia, Croatia, and Serbia.

Kaszanka is Polish sausage made with pig's blood, fat, and starch with variable additions of pork shoulder or offal stuffed into inverted segments of intestine, sewn closed and roasted. Non-kosher kishka. It is typically served hot with boiled potatoes and sauerkraut, but can be eaten as a cold snack or appetizer.

Moronga is primarily Mexican blood sausage also found in Cuba, Nicaragua, and Puerto Rico. It has a little chili pepper kick to it explaining why it is rarely seen in Costa Rica, Guatemala, and Panama where locals are intolerant of hot spicy foods. The blood itself is usually seasoned with diced chili peppers or chili powder, plus oregano, mint, and onion. Encased in pig intestine, it is boiled for hours and then usually sauced with additional jalapeños and onions, chili verde or chili rojo on a plate with beans and tortillas. It may also be fried and packed into tiny taquitos or fatter gorditos.

Mustamakkara is rye flavored Finnish blood sausage pancake traditionally eaten with lingonberry jam or beets.

Sanguinaccio, derived from the Italian word for blood – sangue, is sausage made of pig's blood, or, less commonly cow's blood, similar to French boudin noir. In the Piemonte region of Northern Italy, cooks use mashed potatoes as the filler. Links can be grilled, fried or boiled. Throughout the Piedmont, a winter boiled meat extravaganza called bollito misto is very popular, particularly in the cold Alpine winters. The mixed boil has a number of different meats in it, one of which is usually sausage. The sausage of choice may be cotechino – standard Italian sausage, zampone – stuffed pig's trotter or sanguinaccio.

Spanish morcilla has many variants. The basic form features pig blood and rice. Other regions mix in mashed potatoes and onions, or replace the rice entirely with either the potatoes or onions. Less often breadcrumbs and/or nuts enter the fray.

Sundae is Korean blood sausage made of cellophane noodles, barley, and pig's blood with host of other possible ingredients including bean sprouts, shiso leaves (screw pine), fermented bean paste, the ubiquitous kimchi, scallions, and glutinous rice; all stuffed into cow or pig intestine. Near the university in the Sillim neighborhood of Seoul, students jam multiple restaurants specializing in sundae. Though it is traditionally steamed or boiled, I had it grilled from the back of a tented truck that appeared on a side street after dark near our hotel. With smoky red chili paste, gochujang, and cold beer it was fabulous.

Véres hurka is Hungarian sausage made with rice, pig's blood, lung meat, onions, lard, and marjoram. Amazing! No paprika! Hurka is Hungarian for sausage. The more common variety of Hungarian sausage substitutes liver for blood and does indeed include a generous amount of sweet smoky paprika. Both are tasty, but the bloodless variety is more popular. Either is available with a slab of fresh baked bread and mustard at Central Market Hall, Vásárcsarnok, at the southern end of famous Váci utca, the most famous walking street in Budapest. The magnificent pedestrian-friendly shopping street parallels the Danube on the Pest side of the Elisabeth Bridge. It is a must visit when in Budapest.

Verivorst, blood sausage, is traditional Estonian Christmas food. It is far more popular than the local blood dumpling, verikäkk. The sausage comes in many sizes and shapes and is usually baked or fried and served with butter, lingonberry jam, or sour cream. Estonia and Finland are far more similar than Estonia is to either of the other two Baltic countries – Latvia or Lithuania. Not surprisingly, we found verivorst with lingonberry jam to be as popular in Helsinki as it was in Tallinn.

Bobootie is South Africa's national dish. This ground meat and fruit well-seasoned casserole topped with béchamel/custard is a bit like comforting Greek moussaka or British cottage pie. It can be plain or fancy. It usually comes with a local favorite, Mrs. Ball's Chutney. It is pronounced bo BOOR tee.

Bolinhos de Bacalhau My preference for bacalhau is to skip it entirely or to serve in a fritter or fried first then minced in salad. This fritter combines shredded rehydrated cod fish, with potatoes, eggs and parsley, coats hand-formed balls with breadcrumbs, and fries them crisp and golden outside and creamy soft inside. Like all bacalhau preparations, tedious soaking and desalting comes first.

Bottarga Salt cured, pressed, and dried eggs from gray mullet, are also called Sicilian caviar. The process preserved some seafood in the days before refrigeration. Bottarga is now considered one of the most sought after and luxurious foodstuffs in Italy and Sardinia. During the mullet spawning season in August and September, Sicilians, Sardinians, and Southern Italians take the roe from gray mullets, salt it, press it, and then leave it to air dry for six months. The result is a solid hunk of eggs the color of amber and blood oranges, that when sliced and eaten or grated over pasta, blossoms into a gloriously savory, smoky and briny bouquet. Much more affordable than

Caspian caviar, they were originally used as a poor man's answer to roe. While on the subject of caviar, there are shops in Kiev that offer you free tastes of the Caspian stuff.

Besarabsky Market, Kiev, Ukraine.

Braised Beef Cheek Spanish Stew Beef cheeks are tough, but braised slowly over time, they become deliciously tender and moist. A proper braising liquid combines beef broth, robust red wine, a mixture of diced carrots, celery, and onions, and a medley of garlic, thyme, salt and pepper. My preference is to pair the tender moist cheeks and their generous thick sauce with mashed potatoes. These very strong masseter muscles of a cow were once very cheap cuts for bargain hunters. Gourmets have changed their tariff by upscale butchers of these and of sweetbreads for the same reason. Properly prepared, they are fabulous.

Bratwurst is the name given to as many as forty regional variations of a sausage that dates back to 1313 in Nuremberg. It is most common in northern Bavaria where it appears pan roasted on a plate with sauerkraut or potato salad. Street vendors sell the sausage in a bun with mustard. The ingredients begin with ground pork alone, or mixed with lesser amounts of veal or beef. Seasonings include marjoram, caraway, and garlic.

Brik a l'oeuf In Tunisia, it is sold on the streets and served in the finest restaurants. Whenever miles of walking and the heat of the midday sun sent us under the shade of a tree with a cold drink, we enhanced our respite with one of these each. So too did innumerable locals. Although it is strictly Tunisian, it is such an unusual delight that it is beginning to appear as far away as Marrakesh and Paris. It is clearly not a health food. Warka is an unsweetened pastry made in sheets that are thicker than filo and thinner than commercially prepared wonton skins. The cook folds a single sheet to form a central well into which he/she carefully breaks an egg. Then the well is seasoned with salt, cumin, and chopped parsley, and/or the egg is surrounded with any combination of canned tuna, vegetables, herbs, potato, capers, scallions, meatballs, or sardines. The filling is no bigger than a ping pong ball. The sides of the pastry sheets are folded together in a rectangle, semi-circle, or triangle and pressed together to extrude the air from around the filling. The sides may be bonded with an egg white wash. The brik is then carefully lowered sideways into an inch of hot oil and the oil is spooned over the brik. In the short time it takes to make the outside crispy and golden brown, the egg white cooks firm inside but the yolk remains runny. The finished product gets gently blotted of its surface oil, drizzled with a squirt of lemon juice from a fresh wedge, and eaten as soon as it is not too hot for the lips. The trick is to avoid having the yolk run down your chin. To make it at home, warka is not likely to be available, but wonton skins are a fair substitute. Filo is too fragile for frying unless you use multiple sheets.

B'steeya. After three enchanting days in Fez, I learned to navigate the grand souk without a map.

Horace from New Bedford was obviously lost. He asked if I could help him and his entourage find their way out of the souk. We followed the foul sulfurous breezes back to the tannery and exited together. They invited me to join them for dinner. They reserved a table in an old royal household with fountain, mosaic blue and white tile, waist-high brass candelabras, and overstuffed silk pillows around a dark wood low table elaborately carved and inlaid with delicate mosaics. A bilingual cook was hired to demonstrate the step-by-step creation of Morocco's beloved b'steeya. She told us that eating a b'steeya was like being embraced by a lover. We shared a huge b'steeya, a phyllo wrapped pigeon meat pie made with eggs, almonds, saffron, cinnamon, butter, and sugar. We each followed our share of the pie with a separate dish. I had tender juicy rabbit braised in chicken stock, paprika, ginger, cumin, coriander, cinnamon, garlic, and preserved lemon served aside couscous. Dessert was kanefa, a Napoleon facsimile of layers of slightly thicker than phyllo warka pastry, interspersed with sugared, fried almonds and crème anglais, perfectly scented with rose flower water. Some menus call it milk b'steeya.

B'steeya

At home, two weeks later, I invited three couples and woman friend to come to dinner, ready and willing to help make it. I prepared chicken, not pigeon, poached in herbs and butter; beaten eggs barely cooked in the poaching liquid and saffron, toasted ground almonds tossed with cinnamon and sugar; a stack of phyllo sheets under a damp towel; a pair of pastry brushes and a bowl of melted butter; and scissors, aluminum foil and more cinnamon sugar. Lamb shanks baked in the oven, instant couscous sat in a steamer and Casablanca carrot salad waited in the fridge. One of the guests made and brought baklava for dessert. The invited stacked individual sheets of phyllo slathered with butter across a paella pan about eight deep; layered on the other parts of the filling – chicken, egg, sweet ground nuts –twice each; brought the ends together sealed shut; carefully flipped over using a platter; and decorated the top by cutting an elaborate snowflake from the foil and dusting on the cinnamon sugar. They cheered in unison as our b'steeya went into the oven. The meal surpassed any in Morocco.

Burrata is hand crafted buffalo mozzarella filled with the richest cream imaginable. It needs to be fresh to be perfect. And perfect it is in the heel of Italy's boot. We immersed in Lecce, Apulia, for several days and successfully sought out and devoured fresh burrata daily.

C

Cabbage Rolls. When my sister and I were young kids, the only meats we ate besides offal were breast of veal and cheap fatty ground beef. The beef came to our table four ways, meatloaf with mashed potatoes and gravy, spaghetti and meatballs, porcupine meatballs, with rice in the meatballs or stuffed rolled cabbage leaves. The cabbage rolls enclosed ground beef seasoned with just salt and pepper, expanded with uncooked rice, rolled in blanched green outer cabbage leaves, and baked on a bed of chopped inner whiter leaves in a sweet and sour tomato sauce seasoned with lemon juice and sugar. We thought that all of the dishes were prototypically American. As we aged we learned otherwise.

The game is called cabbage roll geography.

"What do you call stuffed cabbage rolls?"

"Well, we call them mahshi koromb."

"Oh, you are from Egypt."

"Yes. That's right."

From Central Europe to the Pacific Coast of China, and south to North Africa, cabbage rolls are cooked cabbage leaves wrapped around a variety of fillings. Various meats, many different grains, all sorts of vegetables, potatoes, and mushrooms in any combination show up unexpectedly. Among the grains are white and brown rice, millet, barley, corn grits, and buckwheat groats.

Even the cabbage varies from blanched in water, to fermented, to pickled, from ordinary green, to curly savoy, to Napa or Chinese, to purple, and to bok choy. Purple and bok choy are outliers for this dish. Once rolled and aligned in oven proof containers, the rolls may be steamed, baked, or simmered covered.

With or without the tomato based sauce, they often receive a dollop of sour cream except in Kosher kitchens that won't mix milk and meat.

The smallest ones are cigar shaped from Lebanon and come with a yogurt dipping sauce. The largest are Grandma's recipe for Belarusian Jewish holishkes. She use the largest whole leaves.

On occasion, she skipped the usual sauce and dressed them with savory mushroom gravy. Romania is home to pickled instead of blanched cabbage leaves.

Coriander, onions, garlic, mint and/or dill may flavor the filling. For crunch, pork skin cracklings may join the mix. Bits of pork fat or rib may bring in a hint of smoke. Sauerkraut is a common passenger.

So what are they called in your ancestral homeland?

Cabrito en Sangre. "Baby goat in a bowl is like a culinary loving hug, to be savored," he explained. In a suburb of Monterrey in northeastern Mexico. I received an invitation to a baby goat feast by a man I just happened to sit next to on the way to an international medical conference.

We dined on bowls of cabrito en sangre, a ten-pound month-old kid slaughtered for the occasion. I asked about the word sangre, blood. Pablo told me that the head, tail, skin, denuded carcass and lower legs bones were saved for another purpose, but that everything else went into this feast – blood, tongue, intestines, stomach, lungs, heart, kidneys, liver and meat. First they were all boiled in seasoned water. The meat was cut into roughly half-pound chunks. All the organs were coarsely diced except the stomach and intestine, which were cut in thin strips, and the caked blood, which was forced through a sieve. The boiled meat was fried in fat and dressed in a sauce made from cooking juices, blood, the diced and cut offal, a heap of garlic, ancho chili peppers, roasted tomatoes, onion, oregano and Tabasco. It was more than just a stew. It was an adventure and competition of savory tastes and different textures that made taste buds giggle.

In Salamanca, Spain, Joan and I dined adjacent to a kindly man who looked like he was eating Mexican cabrito en sangre with rice added to the stew making it look like a paella. He had a plate of chanfaina in front of him and his description of the ingredients sounded identical to my Monterrey feast, except baby lamb was substituted for kid. He, too, compared eating the dish to a loving hug.

Cacio e Pepe American comfort food mac and cheese Italian version. Literally cheese and pepper in Italian. It was a Roman dish first. The pasta can be any of a number of skinny egg noodles including spaghetti and bucatini. The pepper is cracked black pepper. The cheese? Probably grated Parmigiano-Reggiano.

But it isn't macaroni sayeth the quibbler. So cross the mountain border into Switzerland and order Älplermagronen, herdsmen's macaroni with melted gruyere, potatoes, and perhaps some tiny pancetta cubes home-style.

Two other close, but no macaroni, are Käsespätzle in Germany and pastitsio in Greece. And for dessert? Grandma's Ashkenazi lokshon kuggle with wide egg noodles, cinnamon, cream cheese, cottage cheese, milk, eggs, and raisins, and friend Fadya's Syrian kunafeh made from semolina, string cheese, sugar syrup, rosewater, milk, and butter. Move over Kraft. While we may think of it as an American favorite, this dish is actually European in origin.

After a visit to France, president Thomas Jefferson fell in love with macaroni pasta dishes. He bought himself a pasta machine and copied some European recipes. He served mac and cheese at state dinners. Today, the most luxurious recipes are made with no fewer than four different types of cheese, and are slowly cooked in the oven until bubbling, hot and oh, so creamy.

Caldo de Albondiguillas de Pollo is an unusual soup from Uruguay. We had been dining almost exclusively on seafood in Montevideo in the ancient wrought iron palace of the old fish market on everything from mouth-watering congrejo to paella. Time for a change. I tried this soup. It is chicken stock with leeks, potatoes, carrots, celery and little chicken meatballs. The meatballs are made from ground chicken, pine nuts, pancetta, eggs, flour, and breadcrumbs, suggesting that the recipe is partly the product of Italian immigrants. Adding the bacon-like salt and flavor of pancetta, chew of pine nuts, to airy chicken meatball/ dumplings, to hearty chicken stock with potatoes and leeks, titillated my food explorer genes. So nice. Such an unusual and satisfying rarity this most traditional of Portuguese soups.

Caldo Verde This green soup is as simple as it gets: broth, onions, potatoes, and kale, cooked with "garlic and olive oil. Nothing says winter comfort food like a good serving of caldo verde in a traditional clay pot. This soup would normally be served with a slice of linguiça, typical smoked pork sausage, on top and crusty bread alongside. Enjoy!

Cannoli. Since we can't travel to Sicily as often as we crave cannoli, we find a Sicilian bakery in our hometown or vacation city and indulge. Then we trundle off to an 8 a.m. cannoli 12-step meeting. Cannoli are tubes of flaky pastry stuffed with sweetened ricotta cheese, candied fruits and optional chocolate bits. They are dusted with a little powdered sugar and consumed rapidly before anyone can ask for a bite. The dough is rolled and wrapped around hollow shiny metal cylinders before deep frying that look like hair curlers from the fifties.

Carpetbag Steaks marry tender beef fillets with freshly shucked oysters in Australia. Pockets cut into the sides of the beef receive a pair of oysters salted and peppered. Pockets sewn or tied shut, the steaks are seared for just a few minutes on each side in parsley butter, then cooked over low heat for about ten more minutes to reach medium rare status. The pan drippings and parsley butter dress the steaks for serving.

Cassoulet The first time I had this marvelous stew of sausages, beans , and poultry pieces, the waiter in the French café in Queens, New York, told me it was the equivalent of the comfort food, good old American franks and beans. Indeed, although the beans were small white navy beans and the franks were Polish kielbasa, it was hardly franks and beans.

In the spring of 2006, Joan had a milestone birthday. Our plans for the celebration incorporated two themes: romantic travel and new sausages. Our destinations were Barcelona, Toulouse, and Berlin where we had not been; Vienna, Frankfurt and Venice where she had not been; and Paris, which we both knew but had not visited together. In Barcelona, in addition to a romantic birthday dinner and miles of exploring on foot, we sought and found butifarra amb mongetes, a stew of local Catalan pork sausage and white beans. The stew, escudella, is most often eaten at Christmas. It begins with the same butifarra de pages (Catalan sausage). The other ingredients are tangerine-size pork meatballs, noodles and garbanzo beans and chicken feet on occasion. Butifarra is made from ground pork, seasoned with nutmeg, clove, thyme, Cayenne pepper and white wine. It is stuffed into hog casing, braised and usually fried. After a spectacular train ride through the Pyrenees, we disembarked in the home of cassoulet, Toulouse. Toulouse sausage is the only variety natives would consider in their signature white bean casserole. French chefs too remote to get the real thing, often substitute sweet Italian sausage or Polish kielbasa. Blasphème! Toulouse sausage is another pork wurst, coarser and firmer than most, seasoned with red wine, pepper, smoked bacon, garlic, and parsley.

Have you ever made cassoulet in the traditional manner of Southwestern France? The process requires several hours, spread over two or three days. It is not the fast food prep of typical comfort food. If you are a glutton for punishment, I personally like Paula Wolfert's recipe from her book, *The Cooking of Southwest France.* The basics are white cannellini beans, duck confit, various cuts of pork, Toulouse sausage, tomatoes, garlic, onions, carrots, broth, and breadcrumbs, baked slowly after many preliminary steps. My home version was less than classical by necessity, but satisfied all ten guests. What Joan and I ate in Toulouse was better, at least in part because of tantalizing aromas from ours and other diners' plates, superior sausage, crusty warm bread, and robust local red wine. Dining in the "Pink City" along the banks of Canal du Midi or the Garonne River also had its pluses. In retrospect, my central tureen and serve yourself bowl presentation was also second class by comparison.

Causa One of Peru's best dishes, causas come in every shape and size. Imagine a small cake made of various layers. The top and bottom layers (and usually several in the middle) are made of potato mashed with lime, salt, and mild chili sauce. Between these potato layers you'll find a plethora of other ingredients. One layer may be avocado, another shredded crab meat or chicken, another hard-boiled eggs and mayonnaise. No two causas are exactly the same. You'll find this dish as a dainty appetizer on most menus, sometimes served up in heartier portions as main courses in restaurants, at markets, or in family homes.

Century eggs Nearly black aged Chinese duck, quail, or chicken eggs may be called hundred-year-old, thousand-year-old, century eggs, or pidan. The dark green yolk and dark brown jelly-like outer layer result from aging in ash and salt that raises the pH to alkaline levels causing a change in the proteins. In China, comfort and balanced body heat go hand-in-hand. The young are considered overly hot and the elderly overly cold. Quarters of these black eggs appear commonly on cold appetizer plates for hot summer days or to cool the young, and in hot jook on a cold winter's day or to warm up the elderly. They have a mildly sulfurous and salty flavor. They do have to age, but not for a century. They transform over a few weeks to a few months.

Cha gio Vietnamese spring rolls wrapped in rice paper and fried, come filled with cellophane noodles, crab meat, ground pork, shredded carrots, and shrimp.

You can also wrap the cha gio in fresh lettuce leaves and herbs such as mint leaves and cilantro. Bun cha gio mixes segments of chia gio logs with salad, noodles, and nuoc chom.

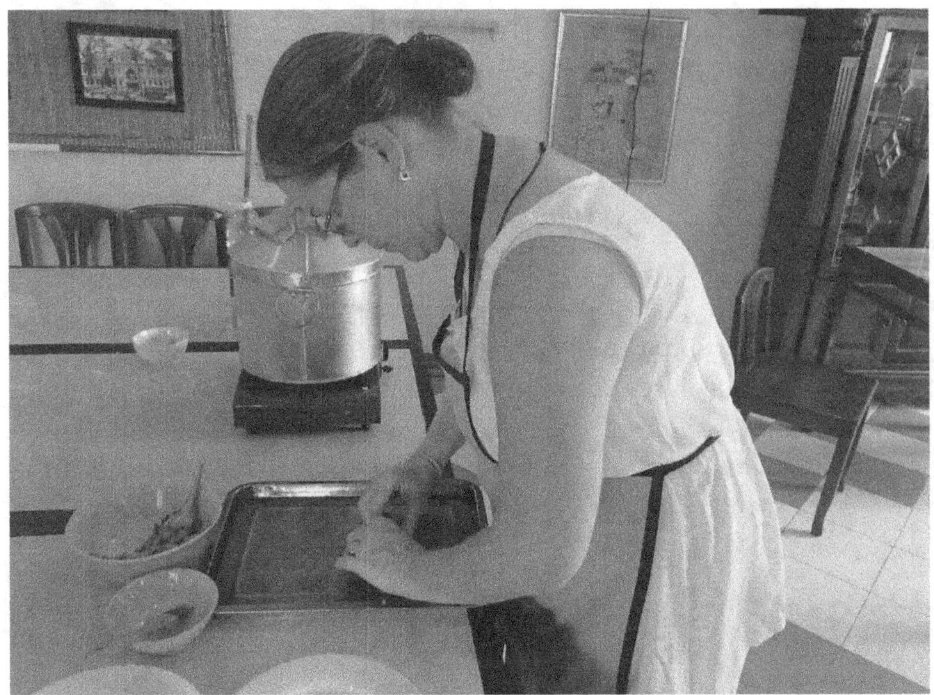
Here they are being made by Joan Hall, my wife.

Cha siu bao Steamed stuffed buns, baozi or bao. Bao rhymes with cow. Zi sounds like dsuh. Known worldwide by their shortened name, bao, these leavened buns come in two sizes, 4-5 inches wide called dabao and 2-3 inchers called xiaobao. They are Cantonese standards at every dim sum place in South China. They also come baked with the browned surface slightly sweetened.

Cha siu pork The red shiny strips of meat hanging on hooks along-side roast ducks in the windows of Cantonese markets worldwide are cha siu pork. The pork is any cut of relatively lean boneless meat taken from ribs, belly, shoulder, or tenderloin. Strips or rectangles need be butchered along the grain. The pork pieces marinate refrigerated for 24 to 48 hours in sealed plastic bags containing brown sugar, dark soy sauce, five-spice powder, hoisin sauce, honey, minced garlic, red coloring agent (red food coloring or red fermented bean curd), Shaoxing rice wine, and star anise. Just as spice rubs on American barbeque create a dark smoke ring under the surface, the marinade creates a marinade ring under cha siu's surface.

Maltose, a sugar commonly used as a glaze in China, brushed over the surface, makes it shiny as it does on the surface of Beijing duck.

Translating cha siu, describes the process - pork burn roast. The seasoned meat roasts over indirect heat, usually in a closed oven. Low and slow. It takes hours, but the pork ultimately reaches an internal temperature of 150 F. That is when the cook transfers the strips to the hooks. Self basting fat drips down onto a tray. When a customer orders one or more strips, the cook slices them across the grain and puts them in a take-out container that seldom stays closed in the car. They go well into soups, on noodle dishes, as they are as an appetizer or side dish, or between fingers, trying not to make the steering wheel of the car too sticky. Rule of thumb: don't eat all of them on the way or you will be busted.

Cha Siu Pork

Chalupas Chalupa means "boat" in Spanish. This first course or light main course is an underlying fried corn tortilla "boat" upon which are layered chicken, beef or pork, an optional cheese layer, and a topping of fresh green salad or cooked vegetables dressed with lime juice and/or mayonnaise.

Cherry cheesecake. I was 16 in 1954, and new to New York. One Friday night that winter, I rode the subway alone and went to Madison Square Garden to see my first National Basketball Association game. The Knicks beat Philadelphia. Afterwards I headed to Times Square. A school friend told me that the cherry cheesecake at Lindy's was "to die for." I arrived in sneakers, chinos, a t-shirt, and a black shiny cloth jacket with my first name in pink script over the left breast. The maitre'd shooed me away from the front door. "Sorry sonny, we're full." I scanned the large room of better-dressed patrons then stopped and pointed to a table for four occupied by a solo middle-aged man near the back. "How about that table?" I pleaded. The man saw me point and the maitre'd shake his head NO. He smiled and waved us over. "Have a seat, my boy. Be my guest." Hank Greenberg, one of the greatest baseball players of all time, a Hall-of-Famer, a team owner, a famous businessman, and philanthropist invited me to join him at his personal table. I had chocolate milk and cherry cheesecake with my idol and happy memories that never wane. What made that cherry cheesecake an indelible source of comfort was the company.

In subsequent years, I enjoyed cheesecake in New Zealand, Australia, Japan, South Africa, Germany, France, Philippines, Italy, and England, that I can recall. There may have been more. None matched my Lindy's experience.

Chicharrones Tiny played right defensive tackle on our football team at the air force base. I literally played in his shadow, linebacker behind him. He had been morbidly obese as a teen. Then he discovered ketogenic diets ala Atkins. He shed 70 pounds and became a mobile 265 pound six footer with no visible body fat. Other teams routinely double or triple teamed him out of survival necessity. It created the opportunity for me to appear much better than my meager talents deserved. He carried all fat and protein snack food with him to avoid being tempted by carbs. He shared bags of pork skin cracklings often. I accepted unabashed. One day he brought homemade cracklings, thick, greasier, skin, fat and half an inch of meat attached.

"My wife gave in and made them like she had them at home as a kid. They are called chicharrones."

"Wow." My one word answer. After the Air Force, I looked for and found them in Latino markets in San Francisco. For the past 17 years, a great chicharronera has been open four days a week less than a mile from my Costa Rican home. Into a vast caldron, the cook dumps alternating batches of cubes of meaty skin or separate skin only over a hot wood-burning flame and ember bed. The pork skin renders its own fat. Salt alone seasons both kinds. No comment on health concerns. When I succumb, I usually order two thirds with the meat attached and a third skin only.

Making a comeback in Denmark, flæskesvær, crunchy, salty pork cracklings are again served in bars and appear on restaurant menus after a long hiatus.

Chicken feet There is no twelve-step program for my addiction to Chinese style chicken feet. They are euphemistically called feng zhao, literally translated as phoenix or peacock claws. In typical dim sum emporia they are de-clawed, patted dry, dropped in hot oil and dunked in ice water to loosen up the skin, then steamed in fermented black beans, bean paste, and a little sugar. The results are tender paws of fluffy succulence loaded with savory goodness. The skin and tendons fall off the little bones with a minimum of sucking. Many fellow diners simply spit out the bones onto a plate. I learned to transport them blindly from lips to plate with chopsticks. My inner child could all but hear my mother saying "Oh what a good boy."

When I took my two young sons (now 50 and 53) to their first dim sum foray, I ordered steamed in black bean sauce chicken feet per usual. They looked at me, whispered to each other and broke out in song.

"Dirty, stinky chicken toes,
Daddy sticks them up his nose."
"Where did you learn that?"
Together, "In preschool."

On a recent trip, we wandered the streets of Manila. There we encountered an assortment of curbside foods served on Styrofoam plates or in Styrofoam cups. One bore the inscrutable name, Addidas. Yes it had an extra D, but how or why these sweet and spicy cold chicken feet got named after a shoe brand is beyond me. Imelda Marcos? Who knows?

The boiled feet are served in a tasty sauce of balsamic vinegar, soy sauce, hoisin, and sugar, tossed with slivered scallions and ginger, plus red hot chili pepper slices.

Chicken feet and peanut soup A bizarre-sounding but delicious marriage between Grandma's chicken soup and steamed "peacock claws" is a common Chinese soup, usually made at home, and seldom seen on restaurant menus. It has a third ingredient completing the requisite triumvirate — Chinese red dates or jujubes. My friend Lilly Fan had the smoothest wrinkle-free skin I ever encountered in an eighty-year-old. She shared her secret. After her first pregnancy, she ate this soup regularly to fortify her system and remove her stretch marks. She was so pleased that she did the same with her subsequent two pregnancies and at least once per cycle at the time of her subsequent menses. She continued the regime monthly after menopause. "It's the jujubes and the collagen from the feet," she explained. "Anyone can make this soup. It's easy and keeps your skin beautiful." Like so many Chinese soups, the broth begins with pork ribs or other pork bones along with chicken, in this case the feet. The broth simmers for hours. Most folks constantly remove scum from the surface and the bones before serving. I leave the bones in because I enjoy gnawing on them after they have become soft. Some cooks skip the bones and enrich the broth with dried cuttlefish or dried black mushrooms. The peanuts are raw and skinless. Leaving the skins on darkens the soup but doesn't change the flavor. After hours of cooking they become soft. They are actually not nuts, but are members of the pea family. Some cooks use black-eyed peas along with or instead of peanuts. I like to add a little black fungus (wood ear) to give it a chewy crunch for contrast. To add another dimension, cooks often include a leafy vegetable or salted preserved veggies before serving. Cheap ingredients, easy to make, healthy, tasty, and a source of cosmetic beauty — not a bad combination. I had it first in Hong Kong, and made it at home when I spotted packages of feet in the markets in my Chinese neighborhood in San Francisco.

Chicken-in-the-pot is a staple in old fashion Jewish restaurants from New York City to Miami;

Ajiaco is chicken-in-the-pot in Colombia. We ate bowls to overcome the cold and damp of a rainy day in Bogota at high altitude. It was indeed a variety of chicken in the pot. The primary starch was an assortment of different kinds of potatoes. The soupy stew included onions and an herb that was new to me. Guasca gave the dish a bright kick similar to citrusy oregano. It was garnished with elote (logs of corn on the cob) and slices of avocado. In the US, we call guasca potato weed and don't eat it. Ajiaco had its origins in Spain.

The same dish has siblings and cousins all over the world, including sancochos from Panama, Venezuela, and Bolivia; and cazuela gaucho in Argentina.

One pretentious deli on New York's Lower East Side, called their version of chicken-in-the-pot, poulet pot au feu.

At home, three generations of us used to brown seasoned and lightly flour-dusted boneless chicken thighs in a little oil in a Dutch oven, crisp the skin side, and remove them from the pot, leaving residual oil, rendered fat, and caramelized bits behind. We then added about a quart of chicken stock, carrot, potato, celery, and onion and simmered until the potatoes were tender. The browned chicken pieces went back in, only to be reheated. The soup/stew, seasoned with salt and pepper, went into bowls, accompanied by fresh rye bread. We added pearl barley, garbanzos, lima beans, zucchini, turnips, or parsnip at times. Simple, straight forward, and soothing.

In Peru, it is a meatless potato stew. In both Mexico and Cuba, the stew adds other proteins beyond chicken in the preparation of puchero estilo Mexicano and fricasé de pollo alcaparrado Cubano.

Coq au vin was indeed the epitome of stove top chicken-in-the-pot when I started to cook beyond simplicity in the mid 1960s. Watching Julia Child on TV helped. The star, a flavorful old rooster, cleaned and prepped, bathed in the fridge for 24 hours in red wine. I couldn't afford a Bordeaux so I chose a California pinot. I made stock from wings, back, neck, heart and gizzard plus roasted celery, onion, carrot, and parsnip. I patted dry the wine off the bird, and browned the legs, thighs, and breast pieces skin side down in rendered bacon fat and a few splashes of corn oil in the only large heavy duty pot with a cover that I owned. The bacon pieces waited in a cup. After the skin crisped, the pieces flipped over for less color than the skin. Salt and pepper rained over the chicken. Next came the liquid, a quarter cup of cognac, and enough of the stock to almost cover the chicken pieces. Added flavor came from minced garlic, quartered small white onions, the red wine that soaked the chicken, and dried thyme. On went the cover for about 15 minutes with care to avoid boiling over. Cover off, pot off the heat. After sprinkling a few tablespoons full of all-purpose flour over the chicken pieces and gently mixing it in to thicken the liquid, into the mix went tomato paste and the bacon pieces. Back on a low heat to simmer covered for another half hour. Chicken pieces cooked through, removed to a platter.

Sauce reduced on medium heat without the cover. When ideal consistency reached, added back the chicken pieces and sliced raw mushrooms for final five minutes of cooking. Patience is not one of my strengths. From pot to the table while hot it went. Wiser cooks let it cool and refrigerate overnight. They removed the hardened fat from the top, reheated the coq au vin, and served it the next day. Great result with total loss of humility until I ventured deeper into Julia's *Joy of Cooking*. Humility returned repeatedly.

Coq Riesling is a first cousin. In this creamy take on coq au vin, the chicken is braised in dry Riesling and silky-rich crème fraiche. It is stirred in at the end, making it extra-decadent. In addition to the Riesling, chicken thighs, and standard cut up vegetables, thyme, lemon juice, and shallots add depth of flavor.

Jollof African chicken and rice is a popular one-skillet dish in West Africa. Every time we schedule a West African trip, a kidnapping, coup, or revolution forces a change in plans, so forgive me. I have eaten Nigerian Jollof chicken only once and in America. It was in a modest café with an open little kitchen. The cook sweated onions, red and yellow bell peppers, tomatoes and hot chili peppers including seeds and ribs in a large skillet. She then poured the contents into a blender and pulsed it into a red sauce. In the same skillet, she browned small chicken chunks sprinkled with curry powder, added the red sauce back in, and simmered it to thicken the sauce by reduction and completely cooking the chicken. To finish the dish, she added some dried herbs that I couldn't identify, and she wouldn't, together with parboiled long grain rice. A tight fitting cover did the trick. She served me hot, spicy chicken mixed with fluffy rice, and a nice layering of flavors.

In Cairo, we ate koshari. Bites of seasoned browned chicken thigh and breast mixed in a tomato based rice pilaf with almonds, lentils, garbanzos, celery, carrots, and sautéed broken pieces of thin pasta cooked in a single pot. The seasoning remained a mystery but we thought we detected cumin, garlic, chili peppers, sumac, cilantro, something citrus, salt, and pepper. Hearty, flavorful, and hot. Unusual mix that really works and is unlike any other chicken-in-the-pot.

Greek one-pot chicken and rice had to be dominated by lemons. It was. It was a simple dish by Greek standards in a hole-in-the-wall at the far end of the swarm of waterfront bars in Thessaloniki. White rice cooked in chicken broth seasoned with lemon juice, zest, and even roasted lemon halves, tasted of garlic, oregano, drops of olive oil afloat on top, salt, and pepper. The olive oil probably browned the chicken thighs. It was quick, simple, popular, and far less expensive than the drinks served to the young people in the bars in the time of an imploding economy. Our lunch was the special of the day. All of the other diners (three couples) were eating the same thing. I asked the waiter how the young people could pay for their drinks when the unemployment rate was astronomical in their age group. He shrugged and said that they use credit cards, and never pay them off.

We stayed in Tallinn, Estonia's capital, for just four days. The cuisine, as expected, mixed heavy meats, lots of potatoes including potato pancakes, crusty dense breads, pickles, cabbage, caraway seeds, stews, hearty soups, sour cream, and all goodies that we had eaten in Lithuania and Latvia, with treasures of the sea and myriad lakes, including a fabulous assortment of smoked fish. One unexpected dish was one-pot chicken that included Greek Kalamata olives, Italian pancetta, Spanish red wine, and more heat, presumably from chili powder, than any other Baltic dish. Browned boneless chicken thighs, garlic, fennel, tomatoes, and onion completed the dish. Crusty, dense rye bread obviated the need for potatoes, rice, or noodles. It seemed as foreign to Estonia as I was, but it really hit the spot.

ANON: A chicken in every pot? What else?

Chicken livers and asta soup Gizzards, necks, feet, hearts, and backs of chickens are universally recommended to enhance the flavor of chicken soup or stock. There is nearly always a coincident admonition to remove the liver lest the stock turn sour. Many faux factoids become so entrenched that they take on a life of their own. Yes, it is true that improperly cleaned livers may have appended gallbladders with enough internal bile to sour a pot. A cold water rinse and simple inspection make that result nigh on to impossible.

My habit is to dice the gizzard and heart and leave the liver whole. They go into the pot with the chicken, vegetables and spices at the outset of the boil. After only ten or fifteen minutes a bubble, I fish out the liver and reward the cook (me) with it as a snack. Left in the soup too long, the livers become dry, hard, and less flavorful.

In a number of cuisines, most notably Southern European, chicken broth, chicken livers, and pasta are combined in soup. An Easter version of Greek egg-lemon soup adds sautéed chicken livers to the usual mix for the last ten or fifteen minutes in the pot. In Italy, hard cheese gets grated over the top as it is served. The French add white wine, the Spanish add sherry.

To avoid over-boiling the livers, they are usually gently cooked in a skillet and transferred to the soup in the final stages of preparation. Also in the skillet may be onions, garlic, a diced apple, an alcoholic beverage, or enough flour to make a roux with the oil in the pan. I like to add a few tablespoons of cream to a skillet of sweated garlic and onion, an ounce or two of tawny Port, salt, and pepper, and gently cook halved livers until light on the outside and still a little pink in the middle. In a pot of chicken broth, pasta spirals or shells should have been cooked al dente and the skillet mixture added only a few minutes before serving with a grated pecorino cheese, parsley and/or lemon slice garnish.

Chicken offal My father's family had a flock of black and white speckled chickens on their small farm in Belarus. Grandma Khana used every part other than the head and the blood. Feathers went into comforters and pillows. Diced bits of fat and skin became cracklings called gribines. Fried up and salted, they were eaten atop soup or potatoes, in stuffing, in matzo balls or out of hand. The rendered fat was schmaltz, the traditional butter, lard, and shortening equivalent in the Ashkenazi (Northern European) Jewish diet.

Chopped chicken livers, g'hakte leber, became coarse pâté. The other giblets, backs, and feet flavored the soup. Tiny egg yolks contained in membranes within the hens, devoid of shell or white, went into the soup bowls of the youngest children or grandchildren. They were accompanied by such fanfare that little hands clapped for them. They tasted like creamy ordinary hard-boiled yolks, but were nonetheless received as if they were treasures. Similar in size and taste, rooster testicles were something Grandma never made. I had them once in chicken soup in Hong Kong. They were creamy, almost pasty, like yolks that were not quite hard-boiled.

Gizzards, the muscular part of the stomach, have always been a favorite if simmered long enough to become tender. They match well with Chinese five spice, Hungarian gulyas, or chicken stock seasonings. Tiny chicken hearts usually go along for the ride with gizzard preparations.

Chicken soup In Jewish folklore, chicken soup is a symbol of hope, health, prosperity, fertility, and new beginnings. Thus, no traditional wedding or Jewish New Year celebration would be complete without it. Thoughts and feelings that waft up from this golden broth are tradition, nostalgia, comfort, family, security, spirituality, survival, stability, and life itself. It spans the gamut from purest simplicity to regal transcendentalism. Mom launched her famous ship, Ess Ess Mein Kind, at least three times a day, every day. Translated from the Yiddish, its name was "eat, eat my child." What we ate more than any other single dish was hot, steaming, golden chicken soup, served more ways than I can remember. Her mother, Fannie Rosen and Dad's mom, Khana Karpman had done the same. Some of the chicken-soup occasions were to usher in the Jewish Sabbath. Others were to begin any holiday feast, or as a stand-alone lunch on blustery days, or as a vehicle for kreplach (wonton like pasta packets) and knaidelach (matzo balls) or to help heal all ailments from a runny nose to a broken heart.

When Dad lived in a tenement in Hartford as an adolescent, he raised Rhode Island Red chickens on the roof and hatched fertile eggs on bags of warmed salt. His mom turned extra roosters into manna called chicken soup.

He turned 33 in 1944 and fulfilled a life-long dream. He bought a farm in Bloomfield, Connecticut, with chicken coops endowed with hot and cold running water and electricity. Before we moved in, he was drafted into the navy. He sold the farm. When the draft age for married men with children went from 34 to 32, he landed in the interspace and was discharged before he was ever deployed. The new owner wouldn't sell. Dad couldn't buy the farm back. After retiring, he and Mom moved to Northern California near my home. Nearly every summer, we went to Petaluma, "The Chicken Capitol of the World" so he could admire dozens of varieties of prize chickens at the fairgrounds.

In his 92nd year, he was suffering from advancing dementia. His ramblings often included images of baby chicks, egg gathering, and Grandma's chicken soup. My wife Joan and I decided to become Costa Rica residents. We moved him out of his assisted-living quarters in California and brought him with us to our small farm in Costa Rica's

Central Valley. We fenced off an area outside his bedroom, built a coop and adopted a small flock of poultry. They included reds, blacks, a pair of white Chinese silkies, a pair of guinea fowl and a lone rooster. He approved.

Ancient Egyptians ate chicken soup as a remedy for the common cold. Ibn Sina, a Persian doctor in the tenth century, wrote about the curative powers of chicken soup. Two hundred years later, the Egyptian Jewish philosopher, rabbi and physician, Moses Maimonides, hailed chicken soup as a means for "rectifying corrupted humours" and suggested that it be given to lepers early in the disease, people suffering from hemorrhoids, and to patients convalescing from a host of ills. When he immigrated to Spain, he brought along his all-inclusive liquid pharmacopeia.

By the seventeenth century, chicken soup made with parsley, thyme, spearmint, lemon balm, and onion was reputedly a cure for nearly everything.

During my surgery rotation in medical school in Brooklyn, at one of dozens of hospitals named after Maimonides, I witnessed the magic. The first nutrient given to patients after surgery was chicken broth followed by generic red or orange gelatin. The hospital cafeteria was like none other in my travels. It served chicken soup with matzo balls. Two blocks away, chickens were slaughtered under rabbinical supervision and the scrutiny of orthodox Jewish women shoppers.

Ancient remedies for respiratory infections included pepper and garlic. They do their work by thinning mucous secretions and allowing the sufferer to clear them and breathe with less difficulty. Vaporizers work the same way. The vapors rising from a hot bowl of chicken soup undoubtedly are similarly beneficial. It may explain the admonition that even in a hospital bed; chicken soup should not be ingested through a straw, bypassing the chance to inhale the steamy curative vapors.

Pulmonary specialist and professor at the UCLA School of Medicine, Irwin Ziment, M.D., has shown that an amino acid released from chicken during cooking chemically resembles the drug acetylcysteine, prescribed for bronchitis and other respiratory problems and found in some cold medications. It is not an antibiotic, thus the nature of "Jewish penicillin" in chicken soup remains a mystery.

Dr. Stephen Rennard of the University of Nebraska showed that all forms of chicken soup, even when made from cubes or powder packets decrease the ability of neutrophils, from going to the site of the problem. Neutrophils are the most common kind of white blood cell and first responder to tissue injury or infection. They are potent fighters against bacteria, but useless against viruses. By retarding this response, chicken soup, he suggests, reduces inflammation, the cause of many symptoms of viral upper respiratory infections.

Bubbe or bubbi is the Yiddish word for grandmother. The fabulous comforting effect of Grandma's essence is universal in Jewish mythology. Mystery solved. By releasing endorphins, allaying anxiety or by placebo effect alone, the bubbe-mycin exuded from golden broth is the cure-all. It's just an old wives' tale to some. But by coincidence, bubbe-miser, the Yiddish term for wives' tale, sounds like a first cousin to bubbe-mycin. So, in Yinglish, enough already.

CNN reported before the COVID 19 pandemic, that over-stressed pandas at the Wuhan Zoo in central China were being fed "home-cooked chicken soup twice in a month to reduce stress and give them a nutritional boost."

Q: Is chicken soup good for your health? A: Yes, unless you're the chicken.

Chicken tikka masala One of the most popular Indian dishes in the world originates not from the subcontinent. It is British, using Indian ingredients and techniques from the days of the Raj. Delicious, light, creamy, it adds yogurt and cream to garam masala.

The meat and marinade: Cubes of skinned and boned chicken thigh meat (my preference). Most recipes use breast meat, which can dry out. Toss the cubes with plain yogurt, cumin, garam masala, garlic, ginger, lemon juice, paprika, salt and turmeric. Rest in fridge overnight.

Ignore the common direction to bake in the oven. Use a sturdy frying pan. Mix the chicken with the marinade and brown the pieces in the pan in a mixture of clarified butter and oil. Remove them when the surfaces are darkened. Deglaze with a little more ghee (clarified butter) and a pile of diced white or yellow onion. Let the deglazed brown bits from the chicken and the onions turn brown. Season with repeat aliquots of ginger, garlic, garam masala, and paprika for less than half a minute, just long enough to release their fragrant oils. Add tomato sauce and cream. Simmer until the sauce thickens. Add chili powder to taste, for the last fifteen minutes. Serve with basmati rice and poppadums, and enjoy.

Chifrijo This lunch dish, fast food, comfort food, or bar room snack doesn't reflect an ordinary Spanish name. It is an amalgam or portmanteau of the words chicharron and frijole. There are two kinds of chicharrones, one of fried pork skin cracklings and a second, with chunks of pork with skin still attached that are fried in their own rendered fat. The latter go in chifrijo. Frijoles are standard brown or red beans. Served in a wide mouth cup or small bowl, chifrijo melds the pork and beans in layers with rice, surrounds the combination with crisp corn chips and tops it with diced tomato, sweet red pepper and onion plus cilantro leaves and a squeeze of lime juice. Minus the chicharrones, the dish is a very old Mexican standard, but chifrijo per se seems to have a short two or three decade history only. It reputedly started in Costa Rican bars, but now appears throughout Latin America and has become street fare and a staple at farmers' markets and public celebrations.

Chilaquiles translates as "in a sauce of chili peppers" from the indigenous Mexican Nahuatl language. The dish pairs hot sauce with salty crumbled fresh cheese, natilla (Latino sour cream), and crisp tortilla chips or triangles.

Chili con carne is not foreign born. Despite ancient myths about a blue lady transponder in Spain, red chili with meat came from San Antonio, Texas. And five-way Cincinnati chili, which includes pasta and a meat sauce, somewhat similar to Bolognese-style, is also American. Chili cheese dogs combine American Coney Island style hot dogs with brown, not red, meat gravy seasoned with Greek herbs. These three chili eats are included only to dispel beliefs that they are imports.

Chili verde clearly claims import status from northern Mexico, possibly Chihuahua. The dish combines pork cubes, serrano and jalapeño chilies, garlic, and green tomatillos in a sturdy pot to simmer slowly until the pork is tender.

Chinese broccoli, gai lan or kai lan, doesn't look like broccoli but the flavor is similar, albeit a bit bitter. It is my favorite cooked vegetable anywhere. Whenever three or more of us eat dim sum, I order a large dish of it for the table and consume about half of it. It is the perfectly satisfying counterbalance to small plates of rich steamed or fried goodies. It is a narrow stalked plant with tiny white buds and/or flowers where broad dark green spinach-like leaves attach. The stalks look like the brightest green asparagus spears ever, minus the tips. In stir-fry plates, the stems are usually par-boiled first, and then added with the chopped raw leaves for a quick cook that keeps them a little crunchy. If you order broccoli beef in China, you are most likely to eat gai lan beef. Steamed a little and napped in a little oyster sauce, it rocks. Gai lan is so easy to make at home.

Chiverre The flesh of this Central American huge, white, spaghetti squash gourd, baked, separated from shell and seeds, stripped of a dark bitter internal stripe, mashed, and sweetened, used to fill empanadas year round, as a filling in Easter and Christmas pastries, and as a holiday jam. Look for this very tasty, mahogany colored sweet.

Chocolate truffles, as expected, have their origin in France. Nearly a century ago, a student of Escoffier had an accident. He meant to pour his hot cream into sugar and eggs to make pastry cream, and poured into the wrong bowl on his station. It went into chunks of chocolate, which promptly melted. The misshapen ball that formed left him in a quandary, so he rolled it in cocoa powder. Voila.

Chocolate contains caffeine and is therefore a stimulant. I am among the masses who consume chocolate to counteract stimulation, tension, and anxiety. We turn to chocolate for calming relaxation, for escape from chaos by the change of direction and focus toward chocolate. Of the hundreds of chocolate options available, I chose a frozen Milky Way as a kid. For the last half century, I graduated from dark chocolate bark to truffles. They are expensive, but I require only a single piece and the rest of the box lasts for months in a refrigerator.

Obviously, these goodies contain neither shaved truffle fungus nor truffle oil. The name reflects appearance similar to the balls unearthed by trained dogs or pigs under oak trees in southern Europe.

Chorba de poisson serves as my favorite way to begin a Tunisian meal. The rich red flavorful tomato and pepper pasta soup is made with cumin flavored fish stock instead of typical Tunisian mutton broth. Pieces of fish and/or shrimp, lobster, octopus, or squid are added at the end of the cooking cycle. It is served with a chopped parsley garnish and lemon wedges on the side. Every Mediterranean cuisine has its version of this soup or stew, from bouillabaisse in Marseilles, to cacciucco in Naples, to zuppa di pesce in Palermo, to zarzuela in Madrid, to baliki corbasi in Istanbul. Sfax is particularly famous for its version, chorba bil hout Sphaxiya. The Algerian version omits the peppers and substitutes potatoes and eggs. Did I mention that all of them are excellent?

Clam chowder. Not native American from New England? No. It came aboard ships from France and England. It was basically clam stew thickened with crumbled, otherwise indestructible, seafarer biscuits called hardtack and flavored by bacon pieces. Among coastal Canadian settlers from France, the stew in a bucket was called chaudière. From Maine to Connecticut, it became chowder, except in Massachusetts lingo where it was and is chowda.

Potatoes, bacon, cream, quahog clam pieces, onions, salt, and pepper have weathered the last 200 years without change. In about 1930, tomato rather than cream based clam chowder emerged. Manhattan chowder remains more of a footnote than a true competitor.

Cold snow pea soup   I don't recall where or when I added this recipe to my old hand-written collection. But I made this soup often when lunch was planned for a hot summer day. It is unusual, bright, refreshing, very tasty and easy to make.

To a quart of chicken or vegetable broth and a pint of heavy cream add two pounds of snow peas in their pods, having first removed the stem end and the string that runs along the outer edge. Add about ten fresh mint leaves, a minced onion, a pinch of ground clove, two teaspoons of honey and salt and white pepper to taste. Simmer without boiling for fifteen minutes. Purée with an immersion stick-blender. Chill overnight. Serve with a small sprig of mint and a thin slice of lemon on top.

Colonial goose During Victorian times in England, the centerpiece at Christmastide dinner was roast goose. By the 18th century, turkey dominated. Émigrés from the UK to New Zealand carried memories of roast goose for Christmas dinner into a land of countless sheep and very few prized Christmas geese. No problem. They anointed stuffed leg or boned shoulder of lamb with a new name, colonial goose. The stuffing sewn or tied into the goose cavity contains various mixtures of ground or minced lamb, diced kidneys, bacon, breadcrumbs, egg, honey, onion, and the iconic quartet of parsley, sage, rosemary, and thyme. Goose fat and/or white wine keeps the stuffing moist during oven roasting. Sounds like an affordable, satisfying alternative to me.

Cottage pie Basically shepherd's pie made with beef instead of lamb, most Americans, myself included, mistakenly used the shepherd's pie moniker indiscriminately regardless of the type of meat. It took a Brit to show me the error of my ways. "No lamb, no shepherd," sayeth Brit friend Gary.

Cou-cou Not an eccentric or a bird or clock, cou-cou, but rather the name of three unrelated comfort foods from different faraway places. It is the national dish of Barbados. This okra and cornmeal polenta usually comes to table served with steamed flying fish. When spelled kuku or kookoo with the accent on the second syllable it morphs into an omelet or frittata eaten especially on the first morning of the New Year in Persia. In Peru, cau cau becomes a stew of tripe in milky broth.

Cozido a Portuguesa I ate a large cup of this dish in a small café along a cobblestone side street in Lisbon. It seemed to be a mixture of boiled meat and hearty stew. A workman enjoying a cupful of it sat next to me. He spoke some English. "What do you call this dish?" I asked.

"Cozido a Portuguesa. But we also call a lot of these dishes kitchen sink stew. The cook creates great stuff from everything but the kitchen sink, and helps use up leftovers."

Our dish had pork cubes, ears, liver, kidney, and blood sausage, presumably from the same pig. In addition to pieces beef and chicken, there were also many vegetables.

Crab season for hairy crab from Yangcheng Lake just northeast of Shanghai is August to October. The small crab, also called Chinese mitten crab, is very expensive and prized mostly for its roe, which is believed to cool excess heat in the body and restore balanced health to qi, the life force itself.

My own experience with hairy crab has been underwhelming, but despite the high cost in a famous restaurant, there is no guarantee that I ate the real thing. Estimates are that 90% of all crab sold as hairy crab is counterfeit.

Dungeness Crabs, California

It is best eaten simply steamed and paired with Shaoxing yellow rice wine. For clams, I'll stick with New England cherrystones, steamers and little necks. For crabs, I prefer Maryland blue crabs, Florida stone crabs (claws), or California Dungeness, thank you. The two kinds of crabs in China are fresh water mitten or hairy crabs from lakes in Eastern China, and sea crabs imported from other Southeast Asian fisheries or from our side of the Pacific.

Mitten (hairy) crabs are aggressive mud burrowers that have invaded waterways from the Thames and Clyde in the U.K. to Chesapeake Bay in Maryland and the Hudson River in New York, creating an eco-hazard that destroys fisheries. Their name derives from their furry claws. Their green shells are very hard. They turn red when boiled or steamed. The meat is sweet, but sparse, and hardly worth the effort to extract. Roe and fat delight locals in China. They are integrated into the soupy fillings of Shanghai's xiaolongbao soup dumplings, during the Mid-August Festival. Yes, the dumplings have a lovely sweet taste that joins the savory broth to compliment the inner pork ball perfectly. But the dumplings taste only minimally different from the roe-less dumplings prepared during the rest of the year to my admittedly unsophisticated palate.

Crab lollipops On the beach alongside Ha Long Bay, Vietnam, we snacked on crab legs shelled halfway from their former body attachment toward their tips, and encased in a velvety shrimp paste, browned over charcoal. The tip of the crab leg served as a handle. We dipped the plum sized end in nuoc cham, and nibbled our way to and through the crab. Unfortunately, we had to share them with fellow travelers.

When I first tried to make them at home, I used a mortar and pestle, toasted homemade rice flour, pulverized rock sugar, hand diced boiled pork fat, and I boiled and cracked the crab legs – much too labor intensive.

Short cut time to wow your friends at cocktail parties.

Ingredients:
One pound shelled raw shrimp deveined and blotted dry
An ounce of boiled pork fat or bacon
An ounce of granulated sugar
Either a tablespoon of roasted rice powder, a teaspoon of potato
    starch, or a teaspoon of cornstarch
Half teaspoon each of salt and ground black pepper
    (decrease the salt by half if you used bacon above)
Two small garlic cloves mashed
An egg white
A bag of frozen crab legs, already cooked and peeled, leaving
    only about an inch of intact shell at the tip (available at many Asian
    markets in the frozen seafood section).
A little vegetable cooking oil.

Preparation:
Puree all the ingredients except the crab and oil together in a Cuisinart-style blender until you have a thick paste. Dip your fingers in oil and mold small plum sized balls of the paste over the exposed crab meat. Line them up on a cookie sheet and bake them until golden brown in a 400 degree oven. Turn them once to brown the underside. Serve them warm or at room temperature with either a spicy peanut sauce, a mixture of Hoisin and red chili pepper sauce, or more traditional Vietnamese nuoc cham.

If you can't find crab legs, substitute two-inch sticks of sugar cane and cover one end with balls of shrimp paste. Add chopped shrimp to the paste recipe above after it comes out of the blender.

Don't buy already prepared shrimp paste in a jar. It is a totally different product.

Crayfish xiao long xia. The craze to eat crayfish by Chinese millennials caused a transformation similar to two other scourge-to-prized sea creatures, lionfish and mitten crabs.

We snorkeled among dozens of exotic, gorgeous reef and rocky shore lionfish in the Red Sea. They are an invasive species and have harmed native fisheries from the Sea of Cortez and Florida Keys to the Mediterranean and Indian Oceans. Once the poisonous spines are removed, they are not only harmless, but the firm white flesh achieves excellence. To counter these invaders, fisherman and chefs have joined forces to prepare them for eating and limit their numbers. So far, so good. Gourmets approve.

With invasive infestations of mitten (hairy) crabs worldwide, we need only use the same approach and encourage harvesters and cooks to transform them into a palatable desirable food source for non-Chinese or overseas Chinese to diminish their numbers.

When crayfish invaded Chinese rice fields in the 1920s, they were an intolerable scourge. Only in the last few decades have these mud burrowers emerged as affordable alternatives to lobster. They have been called mini lobsters in China.

Joan and I donned disposable gloves, and devoured a bucket of crayfish alongside hot sauce in the Cajun country of Louisiana. We twisted off the heads, pinched the bodies, and sucked out the amazing lobsteroid flesh. Millions of young Chinese do the same today. They cook the crayfish in chili pepper laden crab boil, not Old Bay. We all drank cold beer with our crayfish. We chose Heineken. In Hubei, they are more likely to favor Tsingtao. There are currently an estimated 18,000 crayfish restaurants in China. The dreaded pests are now inadequate to fill the diners' demands. They import many tons from Louisiana.

Care to pursue a different tourist itinerary? Qianjiang in south central Hubei is clearly the crayfish capital. The city sports a 100 ton, 100 square meter crayfish sculpture, a crayfish festival, and ecological city center. The area devotes more than 60,000 acres to simultaneously growing rice and raising crayfish. The annual crayfish output exceeds 70,000 tons.

I love crawfish boiled in typical Louisiana spice mixtures, served in a heaping bowl with a remoulade dipping sauce. Crawfish in China tend to be boiled in spicy oil rather than seasoned water. The Sichuan variety challenges tongue and lips but is spectacular. The combination of Sichuan peppercorns and chili peppers is called mala or ma la. Chinese crawfish raised in rice fields are the same species as those found in Louisiana. They were actually exported from China into several American southern states before the demand increased exponentially at home. The season is the hot summer months.

One more style of crayfish seems to be unique to two cities, Houston and Ho Chi Minh City. Viet-Cajun, loaded with lemon grass, garlic, and ginger in the boil. With such a large population of assimilated Vietnamese ex-pats in Houston, it makes sense. That the fusion combination made its way back to Ho Chi Minh City is as surprising as the fact that New Orleans, with its large Vietnamese population, serves crayfish only the Cajun way.

Croque monsieur More than a toasted ham and cheese sandwich, this French café or barroom treat lightly toasts thinly sliced white bread, crusts removed. For the inside, béchamel layers smoothly on the toasted surface. A layer of lean Parisian ham slices comes next. Atop the ham, gruyere or Emmental(er) cheese layers to cover. The top slice of bread covers it and a chef's trick is to weigh in down a little in the fridge overnight so it does run all over everything when baked the next day. Final prep – butter the outsides, top the sandwich with more béchamel and/or cheese and bake until brown on top. Add an egg and you have croque madame.

Croquettes Another typical item on tapas menus, croquetas, bites of protein enhanced with béchamel sauce, encase in fried breadcrumbs. Tasty.

Jamón croquetas and salt cod croquetas are common varieties. They're tricky to make and are perhaps best enjoyed at a tapas bar, along with a cold beer.

British cod fish cakes use fresh Atlantic cod, mashed potatoes, salt, pepper, optional onion powder, breadcrumbs to coat and butter to fry them in. Growing up in New England, we thought that they were an American comfort food.

Boring chicken croquettes in Russia, kotlety pozharskie, garner love and comfort. Why? Perhaps because of the pink paprika sauce that tops them or the egg noodles and mushrooms under them.

Cuy We flew to Quito, Ecuador, high in the Andes. At 9350 feet, Quito challenged our respiratory reserve as we trudged up and down quintessentially quaint narrow streets lined with colonial monuments, churches, and government buildings. We drank coca tea every few hours to prevent altitude sickness. It worked. Friends from California were visiting their daughter, an exchange student at the local university, while we were there. We met for a feast of roasted pork loin rubbed in piquant spices, roasted tiny potatoes dressed in a yellow cheese sauce, corn, and chicha morada, a refreshing purple corn drink similar to sangria.

She heartily recommended a visit to an indigenous mountain craft market. We went the following day and hated to leave even after three hours, but the lunch hour was fading and we had a date with a guinea pig. I had asked our driver if he knew a good place for me to try cuy.

He lit up like a Christmas tree. "My favorite food in the world and the best place to eat it is in the next town." The modest house and small eatery belonged to a woman as old as the Andes. She fried up a gutted and skinned guinea pig and served it whole on a platter with fries, a small bowl of hot sauce, and a salad. The outer layer was crispy golden brown and the meat as succulent and as tasty as the best rabbit. The only distractions, the face and teeth, caused Joan to groan and threaten to tell our grandchildren. She never told them.

Roast cuy with yuca chips and cabbage slaw.

D

Dal bhat, a dish made of lentils and rice, is a traditional meal from the Indian subcontinent, popular in many areas of Nepal, Bangladesh, and India. It consists of steamed rice and a cooked lentil soup called dal. It is a staple food in these countries. Bhat or Chawal means "boiled rice" in a number of Indo-Aryan languages

It is considered to be the national dish of Nepal. One can see how this comforting combination of flavors and heat, would be perfect on a cold day. The rice or bhat is either boiled or steamed. It is often served in the middle of the dish and surrounded by the dal/lentils and perhaps some other curries, achars (pickles), or chutneys. Nepalese eat this dish at least once a day. It is considered to be a well-balanced meal.

We were in Chitwan National Park in Southern Nepal. There was a crunching sound off at ten o'clock, distinct from the sound of grass compressing under our elephants' huge padded feet. As our eyes pierced the gloom, we saw a large, nearly white, oval mass more than half the size of one of our mounts. A boulder? No. It moved. The mahouts deftly guided our elephants in closer by maneuvering their bare feet against the backs of the pachyderm's ears. We froze twenty feet away from a solitary, single-horned white rhino, eating his breakfast grass. His small black eyes glanced in our general direction momentarily, without fixing on us. He ate and we stared, with jaws agape for five minutes. When he wandered off, we followed, careful not to disturb him. We reached a crystal clear watering hole imprinted with the tracks of a herd of spotted deer and the fresh large prints of a male tiger. The elephants drank, the mahouts scanned the grass and listened, and the six of us along for the ride, smiled nervously at each other.

Jeetu, our naturalist guide, could hear sounds that we couldn't, and could predict the appearance of birds and animals before they were visible. One of the elephants headed off in a different direction. The two remaining were sisters. Without warning, they began trumpeting loudly, as they pummeled a bare patch of ground at the base of a large sal tree with their trunks. Jeetu dropped to the ground as the mahouts calmed the agitated sisters. He sniffed the bark of tree and caressed it with his fingertips. He squatted and bent at the waist, examining the ground from a foot away. He peered into the branches of every other tree within fifty yards and examined the underbrush in every direction.

"A leopard killed a spotted deer on this spot last night and dragged the carcass into a tree north of us. It is gone now. The elephants don't like the smell of the kill or the smell of the leopard." The elephant extended a back leg. He jumped up on it and pulled himself back up by grabbing the tail. We headed west. Sudden movement in the branches above us scared us to the brink of incontinence. Jeetu never even looked up. "Langurs," he whispered, as a family of black-faced beige monkeys bolted though the branches. We dismounted onto a wooden platform, descended the twenty steps, and scurried down the path to our cabins to empty bladders and wash faces in preparation for 8 o'clock breakfast.

We squealed to one another about the amazing morning and had an English breakfast with black pudding, bacon, sausage, eggs, and beans. Jeetu declined our offer to join us and ate a bowl of spicy lentil gravy over rice, dal bhat. He was a vegetarian and ate the same meal twice a day, the second time, just before sleep. He supplemented it with a few cooked vegetables and an occasional piece of fruit. We thought his eating habits strange. He thought the same about ours. He was puzzled that we spent a small fortune, came to southern Nepal from California to observe the majesty of animals in their natural habitat, and then ate them. He was uncomfortable around meat eaters. He sat in the kitchen with other vegetarians and ate Nepalese dal bhat

Later in the day, Jeeto took us on a nature walk. Suddenly, he raised both arms to stop us in our tracks. He pointed. The rhino was just below us. He smelled us or felt our vibrations above him and crashed headlong through a thicket and out of sight. None of us said, but we wondered in unison what would have happened had we wandered into this living Sherman tank on his path rather than fifteen feet above him.

That night in bed I wondered and dreamed. I could see myself behind my closed lids walking alongside a rhino sharing my gift of sight with him, singing along with the birds, and sniffing the breezes for scents of other privileged creatures. So many images from the past danced before me. Yes, it had been a fine day at Chitwan.

Donkey The story goes that horse soldiers in the Taihang Mountains above the North China Plain in Hebei Province had to slaughter and eat their horses to avoid starvation during a frozen winter. When they tried donkey meat in order to spare their steeds, they found it more tender and very tasty. What evolved was a preference that carried over into cities even during times of plenty. From the city of Baoding in Hebei comes the old saying that "In heaven there is dragon meat, on earth there is donkey meat." Donkey meat remains a favorite in Northeast China. The donkey burger, lurou huoshao, doubles as street snack and menu item in fairly fancy restaurants. The bun equivalent is a flakey flatbread shaped like a pita pocket. Strangely, the flat bread is usually freshly roasted and hot, while the cooked meat is at room temperature. Cilantro leaves or green pepper add color and flavor. China once boasted of having the largest donkey population in the world. Currently the herd is small and dwindling despite full-blown efforts to increase breeding.

China has become the major importer of donkeys from Africa and America's Southwest. The reason goes beyond tasty burgers. E'jiao is the reason. This medicinal miracle made from boiling donkey hides purports to delay the onset of menopause, to enhance male sexuality, cure dementia, help alleviate respiratory distress, and retard aging. It is very expensive and the hide of an adult animal yields only a kilo of e'jiao, a most foul-smelling brown glop. In 2015, we traveled through Shandong Province where donkeys had been most evident in the past. We saw very few.

Gansu donkey meat is special. It tastes like sweeter, more tender, lean horse meat. It is revered for distribution throughout urban Northern China. And it is far more affordable than all other specialty meats. It even ends up in mundane burger patties and in simple sandwiches. Try it on a bed of yellow alkalinized wheat noodles, lurou huangmian. Donkey sandwiches look like pita pockets filled with sweet, tender shredded meat. They are not uniquely Hebei snacks, but they are common. You may see them called donkey burgers.

Donuts Holland appears to be the place of origin of modern donuts. Dutch settlers brought oil cakes, olykoek, to New Amsterdam, which became the Island of Manhattan. They were round but had no central hole. Translated as oily cakes, they were fried sweet dough pastries. These doughnuts closely resembled later ones but did not yet have their current ring shape. They received their central hole to make doneness uniform and to decrease greasiness. From that time on, they were viewed from abroad as American.

Down derry If you were to fry inch-long pieces of pig intestines, stuff them one each into balls of flavored mashed potatoes, cover the spheres with shredded cheese and bake them, what would you call them? Comfort food? Expletive deleted? In the British Isles they are called "down derry".

Doro wat Stewed chicken, doro wat, claims the title of Ethiopia's national dish. It is composed of chicken, hard boiled eggs, onions, tomato, and stock. Fluffy flatbread called injeira serves as fork or spoon. Made from fine fermented millet flour, injera cooks on a flat top. Pieces torn off by diners, serve as a grasping utensils between thumb and forefinger.

Ethiopian tef has made it into trendy U.S. markets. It is a tiny ancient grain, both nutritious and tasty with a nutty flavor. Its iron content exceeds other grains and it is also high in protein. Tef is mixed with water and allowed to ferment for several days. The resultant dough is a little sour and full of bubbles. When baked over a fire on a clay plate, it yields injeira, flatbread that is spongy, nutty, and sour. It has a unique taste well worth getting used to.

The gravies, soups, or stews eaten with it are called wotts or wats. Wats are hot and spicy by all standards. They may contain any combination of ber-beri (Ethiopian very hot red pepper), black pepper, caraway seeds, cardamom pods, cinnamon bark, whole cloves, coriander seeds, cumin seeds, dill seeds, fenugreek granules, mustard seeds, nigella (a black wild onion seed), and grated nutmeg. The spices are toasted together in a hot, dry skillet until aromas rise. Then they are ground and added to the soup or stew pot.

Ethiopian cooks cut a whole fat chicken into serving-size pieces and set them aside. They add to a hot well-oiled deep frying pan two chopped onions, a teaspoon of grated ginger, and three cloves of garlic mashed, followed by a peeled, seeded, and diced pair of tomatoes, and a teaspoon for each diner of berbere, an Ethiopian spice blend that includes ber-beri hot peppers,, or a substitute mixture of cayenne and paprika adjusted to the heat tolerance of the guests. They add two tablespoons of butter and enough water to keep the mixture liquid. After the ingredients have blended, in go the chicken pieces to simmer covered until the meat starts to fall off the bones. The penultimate additions are another two tablespoons of butter and ample spice mix. With the heat turned off, a hard-boiled egg for each diner goes into the stew.

At the table, there are three options. In Addis Ababa, a very large injeira pancake would cover most of the table. A ladleful of doro wat would go on top in front of each diner, along with side mounds of a tongue-cooling mix of yogurt and cottage cheese, cooked green vegetables, and kifto – heavily spiced beef tartar mixed with clarified butter. Option number two is to set individual large pancakes on plates of about the same size and add the same toppings. The third option is to offer the injera in spongy rolls alongside the same stew and sides plated, for the guests to tear off pancake pieces with which the diner grasps the food and mops up the liquid.

Be prepared to serve your guests lots of cold local beer or Ethiopian fermented honey-beer to quell the flames in the mouths of newcomers to the cuisine.

Duck heads In Shanghai, some bars and eateries prepare duck's head snacks stir fried and seasoned with many herbs and spices. They are called yudon. Diners don't really eat them. They nibble off the skin and gnaw and suck a little but the head is mostly discarded.

Duck necks. I have loved to gnaw on the necks of roasted chickens, ducks, and geese since childhood. It frustrated me that Chinese-style roasted ducks in San Francisco were always sold with the head and neck attached until the succulent beast was cleaved into to-go cartons. I could buy tongues, gizzards, and livers, but not my coveted necks. Introducing a chain of 2000 restaurants all over China, thriving for about a decade that features spicy roasted logs of duck necks: Juewei Duck Neck is the name of the chain, Juéwèi yābó in Pinyin. They originated in Hunan Province. At the current exchange rate, I can buy a bag of necks to gnaw on for more than an hour for about $5. Nirvana!

Dumplings Yes, outed again. Another one of my addictions - dumplings, be they fried, steamed, or boiled Even omitting the fillings, describing different combinations of flour, egg, water, and salt can cure insomnia. To maintain wakefulness, skimming the following paragraphs is OK. At home in Costa Rica, when I make dumplings for chicken soup other than matzo balls, I combine equal parts of fresh salty local white cheese crumbled as finely as I can, masa harina, and cornmeal, into twice the volume of all-purpose wheat flour. I season with caraway powder, nutmeg, and black pepper. The cheese contributes sufficient salt. Half as much milk as wheat flour creates the ideal consistency. With oiled hands, I roll walnut-size balls and gently lower them into simmering soup, carefully avoiding overcrowding and cover for six or seven minutes.

Mom mixed together and kneaded into smooth dough, two cups of flour, a quarter cup of oil, a half cup of milk, three eggs and a teaspoon of salt. She dropped teaspoon-size balls into boiling water and, when they were done, transferred them into soup.

Grandma made dumplings she called nockerl. She beat four eggs with a half cup of water and mixed in a cup of flour and a teaspoon each of salt and baking powder. She boiled her nockerl like mom boiled her dumplings.

Dr. Dorothee Perloff turned 80 in December 2008. That year she taught me how to make spaetzle. She learned to make spaetzle from her German pediatrician mother. Her grandmother was also a physician. Her batter was a little thicker and drier than standard dumpling dough. It arose from a similar meld of flour, eggs, milk and salt, albeit with more flour. She rolled the dough into long skinny cigar shapes. With a pair, of scissors, she cut off inch long little logs above a pot of boiling chicken soup. Five minutes later, the dumplings floated to the surface. The spaetzle reduced the temperature of the soup a little. Reheated. Devoured.

We also consumed them as a side dish, similar in taste and texture to Italian gnocchi.

In Vienna, I had spaetzle boiled first, then lightly browned in butter, topped with parsley and served with sour cream. Yum.

In Germany, we had potato dumplings - mashed potato, flour, eggs, salt, pepper, and butter coated with breadcrumbs, boiled and served aside anything that came with gravy. They were creamy and as tasty as mashed potatoes and gravy might have been. On another occasion, accompanying sauerbraten, we had napkin dumplings, Serviettenknödel. No, they were not made of napkins. They were made from chunks of large soft pretzels. The pretzel pieces soaked in milk and bound with eggs, seasoned with nutmeg, onions, and parsley. The moist mixture, encased in plastic wrap, had its ends twisted, forming a sausage shape. To keep the sausage from exploding while being boiled, pinholes pierced the wrap. The unwrapped cooked log yielded slices, dumplings, that achieved perfection in the sauce from the sauerbraten.

While we were eating pelmeni in chicken broth in a Russian restaurant in San Francisco, an Iraqi companion volunteered that his mother made similar meat filled dumplings called koobe when he was a child. Indeed, both are made from small balls of dumpling dough, indented with a thumb, stuffed with savory ground meat, sealed and boiled. In Russia, the meat mixture is usually half pork, half beef – in Iraq, all beef. Pelmeni also contain more pepper and grated onion than koobe. The only paprika–free dish I ate in Budapest was chicken broth and spaetzle made from a kind of cream of wheat called majgombac.

Csipetke are Hungarian-style firmer spaetzle or pinched noodles. They are predominantly served with goulash, more of a soup than a stew in Hungary. They are also served with other soups, including chicken.

In the Czech Republic, we ate liver dumplings in chicken soup. The liver was usually chicken, but duck and beef liver are options. Ground liver is mixed with flour, breadcrumbs, egg, garlic, onion, salt, pepper, parsley, and marjoram. Similar liver dumplings exist all over Central and Eastern Europe. Dense Czech potato dumplings are a side dish only.

In Korea, we ate mandu, marvelous savory meat filled dumplings, by the dozen. They were steamed, not boiled, and came in bamboo baskets with ginger-soy-hot pepper dipping sauce. Generally, Korean cuisine is very much to my liking. Atypically under-seasoned, weak chicken broth with pasty flavorless boiled flour dumplings came as a side dish along myriad delicious side plates at most dinner houses in Seoul. What a disconnect.

Dumplings

Yes, gnocchi are Italian dumplings usually made from potatoes and flour, but also from semolina and ricotta cheese. I have eaten them in chicken broth in the United States, but never in Italy where they are served in red, green, or brown sauces or under melted butter or cheese. The usual ingredients are just flour, mashed potato, egg and water as needed. Oh, so simple, yet very difficult for the neophyte. For starters, you need to select thick-skinned baking potatoes, drier than their trendy cousins - new potatoes or Yukon gold. Next, bake them, don't boil them. Third, mash them smooth and add less flour by about 25% than your recipe requires. Fourth, use egg yolks rather than whole eggs. Fifth, don't freeze them. They become glue-like when defrosted. Last, consider skipping one thru five and buying them fresh from a pasta/ravioli factory or deli.

In sub-Saharan Africa, chicken soup thickened with ground nuts (peanuts) is often served with dumplings made with starch from yam, cassava, taro root, plantain, processed potato flakes or mixed semolina and ground rice. The dumplings vary from culture to culture, but collectively, they are called fufu. They may be poached balls or dishes with the consistency of slightly dry mashed potatoes. In the latter case, the diner picks up a small handful and rolls the fufu, adding it directly into the soup or stew.

In Northern Argentina, ground cooked chicken, eggs, and flour meatball/dumplings go into the soup in which the chicken originally cooked.

Japan is an enchanted land of treats called dumplings – tofu and crab balls, ginger beef gyozas, sweet rice balls, korokke - potato fried dumplings, pickled seaweed wrapped savory meat and root vegetable, dango jiru (mochi flour, miso, dashi and white fish), and one of the world's best desserts, mochi dumplings filled with sweet red bean or lotus paste.

My favorite is a pancake batter round ball surrounding a tender chunk of octopus called tako-yaki. What looks like a heavy metal muffin tin sits over heat. The indentations are hemispheres. Batter goes into the wells and begins to crust golden brown. Precooked octopus is dropped into the center and more batter goes on top. The cook spins each ball in its well with chopsticks until a perfect globe the size of a golf ball is complete. The crispy shell surrounds custard-like batter with the seafood morsel in the center – sweet and savory, crunchy and creamy.

However, none of the Japanese dumplings that I know are boiled and served in chicken soup. They are often sold in orders of eight, more than most couples can consume.

Shandong dumplings defy most standards for excellence in Chinese dumpling hierarchy. The best dumplings in Taipei, Shanghai, and Hong Kong are deemed to be those with the thinnest nearly translucent skin, the exact number of perfect folds, and the finest ingredients. Shandong dumplings wear thick coats, are squeezed imperfectly rather than folded closed, and offer basic pork and cabbage filling. But in typical Chinese fashion, the whimsical eyes of the beholder see a shape that conjures up gold nuggets, and therefore portends prosperity and good fortune.

Durian Throughout Southeast Asia, locals absolutely adore the malodorous fruit of the durian tree. But first, you have to get past the smell. Pardon the crude analogy, but it smells to me as if it had been regurgitated by the family cat. When pressed in a previous publication, I described the flavor as "juicy fruit gum chewed in a dumpster of rotting potatoes."

In a challenging situation in Bangkok, I was honored with an extra-large portion at the table of a friend's family. I barely escaped embarrassment, concealing nausea behind the falsest of smiles. Nearly as nose-unworthy as stinky tofu, durian is a fruit with detectable stench from blocks away that has caused it to be banned in trains, buses, hotels and all of Singapore. It grows in humid hot climes including South China, but the so-called "king of fruits" is cherished more in Thailand, Malaysia, and Indonesia than in China. In recent years, Chinese companies have gained permission to import frozen durian from Malaysia and have been producing durian-flavored puddings, cakes, ice cream, and beverages with some initial success. The flavor outclasses the smell by miles. An estimable author characterized it as "the mix of sour cheese and onion with a little bit of turpentine." Subjectively different. You might want to try durian-flavored mousse cake or cheesecake in Shanghai as a baby step towards understanding why durian is probably the best-loved fruit in Southeast Asia. It looks like a green rugby ball with spikes. A lone durian sapling on my farm in Costa Rica died mysteriously while every other of about a hundred trees survived and flourished. Karma?

"Let's go find some durian, you know – the stinky fruit," she proclaimed with a smile. I returned her smile with a little apprehension. From allergy-related nasal congestion and oversized turbinate bones in my nose, I was usually impervious to all varieties of natural and synthetic aromas. Not so that Sunday in Bangkok. My diminutive soft-spoken friend from San Francisco was on the home turf of her family and her childhood. She was my guide for the day. Her feather-like hold on my arm steered me through the bustle of the Sunday crowds. There, at the weekend market on the edge of the city, thousands of shoppers gathered to buy everything from plaid boxer shorts and eyeliner to hundred kilo live pigs. We were on a durian quest.

Without any warning, she tightened her grip so it felt like an over-inflated blood pressure cuff. Yaowapa erupted in a shrill staccato, "Smell the perfume! Smell it! Smell it!" I inhaled hard, with tightly sealed lips, forcing a jet stream through my nasal resistance and immediately wished I hadn't. The assault on my olfactory sense was worse than a compost heap on a muggy day. Whatever it was, I was sure that it had been regurgitated. My eyes watered. She dragged me headlong into the crowded aisle past the lemongrass and galangal stands, past the caged monkeys, past the chest high pyramid of shallots, to the star attraction that day, the ripe durian.

Yao was only one of a horde of delighted shoppers, who smiled widely and chattered in a cacophony of nasal singsong, so much louder than her usual dulcet tones. We squeezed and squirmed through the throng to the front row. Spread out before us was a fifty foot long display of football sized yellow-green fruit covered with pyramidal spines an inch long, looking like World War I floating mines.

People were caressing the durian, raising them up toward their downward tilted noses to sniff the "perfume" of the individual fruit. It looked as though they were greeting the fruit with the traditional head bow and hands in apposition in front of the face that the greeting, sawadi kah, implied. Durian is thought to be an aphrodisiac.

A saying in Behasa, the native language of Malaysia and Indonesia, suggests that when ripe durians drop down, sarongs rise up. In my hands the fruit was only rough skinned and barbed. My hands had been forewarned by my nose, and were incapable of conjuring up a loving caress. Yao sniffed a few dozen durians – no mean feat – and selected two to bring home with us to her mother's house. I insisted on paying since I had been invited to dinner. They cost as much as my inexpensive hotel room.

"My mother will be so pleased. She asked me to look for some extra special durian during your visit. It is a tradition in our country to honor revered guests with this wonderful delicacy. She was a little hesitant that you might not like it, but I assured her that you eat all kinds of Thai foods in markets here and in restaurants back in San Francisco. You are not squeamish like some Americans. You'll see. It is delicious, even if it does smell spoiled." Yao had tied the first knot in the noose.

Her mother accepted them with a very uncharacteristic giggle of delight, hidden behind her hand. Then, standing on tiptoes, she gave me an even more uncharacteristic hug and kiss on the cheek, as she tied the second knot in the noose.

She led me by the arm to the living room and sat me down between her husband and son, Arun, in a silk cushioned, black lacquered, ornately carved chair. In moments I had a cold beer in my hand, rice chips and molten-spiced dip at my side. Arun sealed my fate, and tied the final knot.

"You are so thoughtful to bring fine durian to my mother's table. It is as a bridge into our family, telling us that you are a kindred spirit, unlike some of the Americans Yao has brought home to visit in the past." His sentiment was genuine and offered in kindness. He could not have known that it had already begun to constrict my throat.

We took our seats along the narrow table. I was assigned a space in the middle of a long side, flanked by Yao and her sister, and across from her niece and nephew who never turned their smiles away from me.

Dinner began with a velvety smooth fish puree wrapped in banana leaf. Next came boned stuffed chicken (angel's) wings, roasted golden brown, filled with yam noodles, ground shrimp, pork, and aromatic herbs. Pad Thai, topped with fresh cilantro, green basil leaves, omelet strips, shrimp, roasted pork, and ground peanuts, followed. A bowl of sticky rice with two dipping sauces and prawns in green curry gravy filled the last remaining spaces on the table.

Reckoning came at dessert. Under the durian's yellow-green skin was a thick white rind. Inside it were sections containing large black seeds surrounded by golf balls of the acrid yellow flesh. It was served as if it were custard. The entire family, Yao's parents, two siblings, sister-in-law, niece and nephew, riveted their beaming eyes on me, proud to honor my presence with an overly large portion of the best ripe durian in the land. There was no escape.

I clenched my left fist in my lap until my fingernails burrowed into the flesh of my palm, and locked my facial muscles in a rigid smile to overcome any other response. On a large spoon that trembled imperceptibly, I hastened the silky custard past my lips and down my throat, shortening the duration of contact with my tongue's taste buds as much as possible. It worked, but barely. I was nauseated for only a moment. To my relief, the durian had a flavor different from its stench. It tasted like mushroom pâté and Juicy Fruit gum. My facial muscles ceased their throbbing and began to relax. The heat of my facial flush began to cool. I had survived this confrontation with a simple piece of fruit without humiliating my hosts or myself. No, I hadn't won. My near defeat had escaped detection.

"Kaup koon mak ka", thank you very much, I blurted aloud. My hosts mumbled pleased you-are-welcomes, not knowing that my thanks were actually intended for the deity of intestinal fortitude. That they were audible was purely an accident of the moment.

Forty years ago, a few years before my durian encounter, this anonymously written limerick appeared in the magazine *Horticulture:*

The durian – neither Wallace nor Darwin agreed on it.

Darwin said: "May your worst enemies be forced to feed on it."

Wallace cried, "It's delicious."

Darwin replied, "I'm suspicious

For the flavor is scented like papaya fermented,
After a fruit-eating bat has pee'd on it."

Two other South Asian fruits worth mentioning are jackfruit and noni. Neither is as prominent in the cuisine in China as they are in neighboring culinary cultures. Jackfruit is a durian look-alike but many times larger. When one ripens on my land in Costa Rica, I sometimes need to enlist the aid of my gardener to carry it to an adoring friend. It has a slightly putrid odor, far less offensive than durian and is quite sweet. You may have it as an ingredient in savory stews or curries, especially in Malaysia, Indonesia, or Trinidad. It has become very popular in North America in the past few years as a steak substitute in vegan recipes.

Noni smells like the shoulder pad after the baby burps. Despite its super-food status as a cure-all, I can't give away the bushels of fruit my lone tree yields all year-round. The horses, ducks and chickens won't eat it. Its taste is bitter. Some folks add it disguised to curries. The one dog of our pack that does eat it has such foul breath, that he alone is not allowed to lick face. The sweetened juice of Tahitian noni sells well in California health food stores. If it really did "cure" arthritis, diabetes and atherosclerosis as claimed by some, it might be worth masking in fruit shakes. So far no quality double blind confirmation exists.

Noni

E

Egg tarts Macau or Macao was once an island off the coast of Guangdong, China, with an intervening sand bar. Forty miles west of Hong Kong, it is actually the main island and there are two lesser islands connected by three bridges. When I first visited Macau forty years ago, it was a drab Portuguese colony, a city with traditional Chinese and Portuguese architecture set on Portuguese tile patios. It was otherwise dusty, and in need of paint and purpose. After more than 400 years of Portuguese colonial rule, it reverted back to Chinese ownership in 1999. Now, the pendulum of glitzy Las Vegas of Asia has swung beyond moderation the other way. The sixteenth century facade of St. Paul's Cathedral, the old wall, and fort draw Western tourists to the old town, while hordes of mostly visiting Chinese head to the casinos. The Venetian is the world's largest casino. It has its own mini Venice replete with gondolas gliding in canals plus Italian opera sung by gondoliers. Another venue offers an amazing floor show in the largest pool in the world. Watch fireworks competitions, Cirq de Soleil-style acrobatics, diamond and ancient jade displays, and a 360-degree movie of underwater scenes of a dragon's playground. Along the narrow streets and alleys in the older areas, little shops sell famous pork chop buns, wonderful clay pot rice meals, sheets of jerky, fabulous egg tarts, and many more oven baked goodies than most other Chinese locations.

Egg tarts

Coloane is one of the two smaller islands. It is a great place to see giant pandas and to visit Lord Snow's original bakery for Portuguese egg tarts. From here, they gained popularity exponentially across the world. The flaky lard crust that exemplifies Chinese egg tarts everywhere give way to layered puff pastry at Lord Snow's. The egg custard filling is as good as the best anywhere.

Original home of egg tarts in Asia

Eggplant parmigiana had humble beginnings. Its debut in print appeared in Ippolito Cavalcanti's *Cucina teorico-pratica,* published in Naples in 1837.

Ignore the claims that the dish came from Parma farther north, and is named after Parma's iconic parmigiana reggiano cheese. The primary cheese in the dish is mozzarella, not Parmesan. Historically, eggplant parmigiana hails from coastal Southern Italy, and Sicily. It arose as an inexpensive belly filler for the poor. In Sicily, a palmagiana is a wooden door or shutter with downward-facing, horizontal slats that resemble the layering of eggplant slices spread out like palm leaves in the dish. A good guess as to the origin of the name. Another educated guess informs us that in the Sicilian language , unlike Italian, the name in parmiciana means Persian. Indeed, eggplant is not native to southern Italy. It arrived with Arab traders from the east in the 9th century. Europeans would not eat it. Even Romans were skeptical. Their name for what Italians now call melanzane was mela insanum in Latin, crazy apple. The inference was that eating eggplant would drive people crazy. Not so the fearless Southern Italians and Sicilians.

Eggplant parmigiana is ubiquitous in Naples, second only to pizza Margherita. It is a simple dish, much lighter than the ooey-gooey American versions that bury the eggplant under so much melted cheese, the flavors of tomato sauce and eggplant virtually disappear. The cheese, rubbery, tasteless American wanna-be mozzarella, is a far cry from the fresh mozzarella balls in Naples or in Palermo.

The recipe advocated by a Michelin star chef just south of Naples in Sorrento, starts with simple fresh marinara sauce in the bottom of a baking dish covered with a single layer of fried fairly thick eggplant slices. Fresh mozzarella slices cover the eggplant. Repeat the addition of tomato sauce and sprinkle with a layer of grated Parmesan cheese. Add another layer of eggplant slices, mozzarella and another layer of sauce. Top with a final heavy dusting of Parmesan cheese. He suggests baking at 355°F for about 35 minutes. The rough ratio of mozzarella to Parmesan is 5 to 1.

Eight ingredient immortal soup In southern China I was on my own. After canvassing both sides of the main street of a Pearl River estuary town, I chose a restaurant that advertised Eight Ingredient Immortal Soup. Eight is a lucky number in China. The bilingual guide next to a tour bus confirmed what I suspected. Those who eat the soup are believed to achieve immortality. She didn't know all the ingredients, but remembered some – snake, cat, turtle, rooster and wild boar. The soup was redolent with chunks of unidentifiable meat, the flavor superb. And so far, for forty-five years, the immortality part has worked as advertised. Survival. Comfort.

F

Fabada A favorite of the northwestern Asturias region of Spain and based around the white fabe bean (broad bean, fava bean), fabada is a one-pot feast usually served with a mixture of pork meats. Any combination of four very tasty meats complete this comfort dish; chorizo, bacon, morcilla (blood and rice sausage), and pork belly.

Fajitas came from Mexico to Houston in the early 70s. Within a decade, they became one of the major standard bearers of the Tex-Mex craze that swept across the U.S. Early on, they came to the table atop a brazier on a metal tray. A bed of caramelized onions supported marinated skirt steaks grilled dark on the outsides and pink inside when sliced against the grain. In time, the braziers gave way to hot metal platters, and the onions mixed with multicolor bell peppers. The marinade of lime juice, garlic, jalapeño, cumin, cilantro, oil, and salt seasoned the meat for an hour or more before the meat received a drying pat down and met the grill or hot frying pan. Diners then rolled the steak and onion mix in corn tortillas.

Skirt steak for fajitas.

Feasting in the Arab world The Arab Muslim world includes the Middle East, Arabian Peninsula, and North Africa. Iran is not Arab, Israel is not Muslim, and Turkey is partly in Europe. We shall include them all in this section, because their cuisines overlap considerably and cause overwhelming confusion unless compared with each other. Many Arab comfort foods are described elsewhere in this volume including e.g. asheh reshteh, brick a l'oeuf, b'steeya, baliki corabisi, koshari, and many more.

People in the Arab world do not just eat, they feast as family. The Arabic greeting, when you arrive at someone's home for dinner, welcomes you as family. The cloak of instant kinship immunizes the guest from all political, religious, cultural, or ethnic animosity. In lands of Arab nations, anger is never brought to the table. Hosts feel compelled to cajole guests to continue to eat past the onset of physical discomfort. To deign to acquiesce is considered ill-mannered. The midday meal often lasts for two or three hours. Breakfast begins early. Dinner may occur as late as midnight. Fresh coffee made with cardamom is brewed all day. Sweet tea flavored with mint or apple is also poured throughout the day. Sweets, nuts, and pastries are offered for snacks at hourly-intervals between meals in homes or shops.

Lunch is a euphemism for a festive gathering that begins between two and four PM. Whichever country you are in, the table will literally be covered with small dishes called mazzas, mezzes, or mezzas. There will be bread and rice or wheat based starch. The meat will most likely be mutton or goat. Seafood is plentiful along the coasts. Poultry is common, including as a base for or as an ingredient in soups and stews.

Supper is often little more than a snack of leftovers, fruit and cheese, or a pastry with sweet tea or coffee.

Combinations of spices vary from household to household, from town to town, and from region to region. Nonetheless, there are certain combinations that are so typical for a given region that they have distinct names and are sold in markets already mixed.

From the Arabian Peninsula, kebsa is the combination. It contains cardamom, cinnamon, clove, coriander, cumin, nutmeg, pepper (both red and black), and sun-dried Basra lemons. Also typical of the regional cuisine are rosewater and orange flower water, saffron or turmeric, and fresh green chilies, rather than the red pepper of other Arab lands.

From Persia comes a similar mixture of cardamom, cinnamon, clove and pepper. Ginger is unique to the Persian mix and the ingredients that make kebsa curry-like (cumin, coriander and turmeric) are eliminated.

From Syria, Lebanon, Palestine, and Jordan, the mixture of allspice, cinnamon, clove, and nutmeg is called bharat. As for the coloring agent, and the prized red pepper from Aleppo, fle fle Halibi, is the pepper of choice.

Ras il hanut, the Moroccan spice mix, contains cinnamon, cardamom, nutmeg, ginger, cumin, coriander, turmeric, rose petals, and pepper.

In Libya, b'zar is similar, lacking only rose petals and cardamom.

From west to east across North Africa, seasonings go from sweet and mild toward sour and hot. Honey, orange flower water and preserved lemons in a stew recipe are giveaways that the chef is Moroccan. Hot green chili peppers and saffron are characteristic of dishes from the Arabian Peninsula. Lots of nuts typify desserts from Syria and Lebanon. Orange and rose flower waters, and ginger, are much more common in North Africa and the Arabian Peninsula than in the Middle East. Allspice is common only in the Middle East. Preserved lemons are standard in Morocco and Algeria, dried limes in Iraq and Kuwait. If green olives in pomegranate molasses are a side dish, you are in Lebanon. A Bedouin lamb dish, maglubah, also known as "upside down" puts you in Jordan. Kushari, a rice, macaroni, and lentil pilaf topped with puree of fresh tomatoes is a Cairo staple. Lamb and chicken are eaten everywhere, but beef is eaten frequently in Iraq. In Egypt, water buffalo is common. Pork products are nonexistent throughout the Muslim world.

Bread is eaten for breakfast, pita stuffed for lunch, bits of toasted or dried flatbread are added e.g. to salads (fatoush in Syria), soups (shorba in Tunisia), stews (tashrib in Iraq), and scrambled eggs (fatut in Yemen).

The standard starch is couscous in North Africa, burghul (bulgar wheat) in the Middle East, and rice in Persia and parts of Iraq. Couscous reaches from Sicily to Syria, but burghul has only crossed the Red Sea to Egypt. Rice has become a specialty item throughout the Arab world, particularly as a substitute for meat stuffing in vegetarian dishes and as fancy centerpiece pilafs for festive occasions, modeled after Persian wedding rice.

Tagine, tajin, or tajeen is both the Moroccan name for slow-cooked stew, and for the clay pot with cone-shaped dome in which it is cooked. Typically, the stew contains lamb or poultry, citrus, fruits, vegetables and olives. The Moroccan version is more likely to be sweeter and contain raisins, quince, apricots, and honey, than the Algerian or Libyan versions. In Tunisia, a great source of confusion may arise when tajine can mean stew or omelet. Stews in Egypt and the Middle East do not contain fruit, and in Syria, the words tagine and tajine are unknown. Strangely, tajin is a common term for lamb chunk and vegetable stew on the West Bank of the Jordan River, just a hundred miles from the Syrian border.

Other sources of confusing food vocabulary are the words for yogurt and okra. Laban is yogurt in the Middle East. In Cairo, coffee, kahwa, comes black, with sugar or bi laban, with milk. The same coffee ordered bi laban in Damascus or Amman elicits strange stares and the coffee arrives with yogurt on the side. Kahwa bi haleeb would get a cup of coffee with milk away from northern Egypt.

Okra is common in North Africa and the Middle East, but it is preferred crunchy and firm, rather than viscous and soft, so it is often treated with vinegar and quickly deep fried, not stewed to the mushy consistency it has in gumbo. In Egypt, okra is called bamiya, but in Morocco it is called malookia. Egyptian malookia (milookhiyya, milukia, malookhiya) is chicken soup made dark green and viscous by the fibrous weed of the same name, also called Jew's mallow, flavored with allspice and cayenne.

Iftar is the word for breakfast except during Ramadan, when breaking of the daylight hours fast occurs at sunset, rather than at sunrise. Shourbat adas and shourbat freekeh, soup made with lentils and with cracked green wheat cooked in chicken broth are common Ramadan fast-breakers.

At an Israeli feast I attended in 1958 to celebrate the young country's tenth anniversary, the first course was like cold vichyssoise spiced up with Tabasco sauce and thickened with red lentils. It was milk-free because the base was made from chicken broth and a white flour and oil roux. The sabra (Israeli born) waiter called it Esau soup.

Shourabat ed djaaj is much more than simple chicken noodle soup in Lebanon. It is a festival dish in which an entire chicken is stuffed, sewn shut and boiled in salted water. The stuffing consists of half a cup each of rice and water, a cup of ground lamb, a quarter cup each of slivered almonds, pistachios, pine nuts, and pinches of salt, pepper, and cinnamon to taste. The stuffed bird flavors the broth intensely. More rice is boiled in the broth and it becomes the first course with a little more cinnamon and some chopped parsley as a garnish. The carved chicken, mounds of stuffing, a cooked vegetable, raw salad and yogurt complete the meal. A little of the broth may be reserved as a gravy for the chicken and stuffing.

From the West Bank and Jordan comes this idea for chicken, fava bean, and chickpea soup with dumplings. Boil a chicken in water flavored with salt, pepper, onion, and turmeric. After forty five minutes, remove the chicken, cool, skin, bone, and cut the meat into cubes. Grind half a pound of chicken dark meat and giblets and two onions and mix with an equal amount of chick pea flour. Season with salt, pepper, a pinch of cardamom powder and enough turmeric powder to turn the mixture yellow. Add enough water to make a thick paste and refrigerate for an hour. Oil your hands and make walnut-size balls. Simmer them covered in chicken stock for twenty minutes. Add back chicken pieces to heat through for the last five minutes. Serve topped with chopped parsley. A common soup in the Middle East, particularly in Syria, is shorba il roz, chicken soup with rice. Chicken pieces and chopped celery are boiled in water seasoned with cinnamon, allspice, salt, and pepper until the meat is tender. The soup is simmered another six or seven minutes to cook the last addition, the rice.

Palestinian egg lemon soup in chicken broth is similar to Greek avgolemono, except that real rice replaces rice-shaped pasta.

In Jewish homes in North Africa, tfaia is the variation on the Greek egg-lemon theme. It is often served the night before Yom Kippur, the Jewish holiday of Atonement. To this chicken-lemon-egg soup, there are no additions of milk or cream because of Jewish dietary law. It is usually augmented with leek, turnip, carrot, onion, and celery. Typical of North Africa, the broth is seasoned with clove and cinnamon in addition to salt and pepper and may be garnished with mint.

Sorda is Moroccan Passover soup with matzo pieces and fresh shelled fava beans and peas that may contain either chicken pieces and chicken broth or beef pieces and beef broth.

Leblebi is the basic belly filler soup of the Maghreb (Arab North Africa). Garbanzo bean purée is seasoned with harissa, lots of garlic, onion, carrot, celery, cumin, and salt. The liquid may be water, chicken, beef, or vegetable broth. Pieces of meat or chicken may be added. Garnishes include lemon wedges, capers, pickled turnips, parsley, scallions, cilantro, cucumber slices, tuna chunks, chopped hard-boiled eggs, olive oil, or extra harissa. The soup is often ladled over large croutons of stale bread. As one heads west from Tunisia, garbanzo soup is likely to have additional beans, lentils, squash, and sugary ingredients and far fewer garnishes. Leblebi, garnished with hard-boiled eggs is sometimes eaten for breakfast.

Algerian luz shorba is chicken broth and heavy cream, ground toasted almonds, chopped onions and a flour and butter roux.

Shorba jazza iriya, another Algerian soup, is a hodge-podge of chicken wings and necks, lamb or beef chunks, noodles, chick peas, zucchini, green peas, potatoes and tomato paste.

Rechta is handmade North African flat spaghetti. It is also the name of a chicken spaghetti dish with a cream sauce and a soup. The soup is chicken chunks and broth, broken pieces of rechta pasta, garbanzo beans, fava beans, grated potato, sliced carrots and celery, onion, tomato paste, cinnamon, paprika, salt, and pepper. Mint, parsley and lemon slices may garnish. It is particularly popular in Algeria and Tunisia.

Herira is a spicy soup thickened with fermented flour and vinegar. It can be made with chicken or lamb and is most popular in Morocco and Algeria. Flour, vinegar and water are allowed to ferment in a warm place for 10 to 24 hours. Chicken parts are boiled in water with garbanzos, lentils, onion, tomatoes, celery, parsley, cinnamon, caraway, cumin, turmeric, anise, chili powder, salt, and pepper. When all the ingredients are tender, the chimera (fermented flour), a little tomato paste, and either pasta or rice are added for a final 15 minute simmer. A splash of lemon juice and a few cilantro leaves are the finishing touches. It is commonly eaten as the daily fast breaker at sundown during Ramadan.

In Libya and Morocco, rashda begins fresh made, forced through a sieve to yield small irregular shapes a little larger and less uniform than couscous. The exotic Libyan soup bearing the same name begins with cut sections of chicken boiling in a quart of water flavored with cinnamon, onion, tomato paste, clove, nutmeg, ginger, harissa, salt, and pepper. When the chicken is tender, it is removed, skinned, boned and shredded. The onions are also removed. Chickpeas and the pasta are cooked separately, mixed with melted butter, flavored with orange flower water, tossed with raisins that have been plumped in hot water, and put into bowls along with the chicken and onions. The hot stock is poured over the dish.

In Lebanon, Jordan, and Palestine, the same dish is made with the addition of allspice. It is called "the Moroccan one," Magrabeeya. Parenthetically, in Morocco, the pasta of choice for this dish is couscous. I once had it made with barley-sized Israeli couscous in the Arab Quarter of Jerusalem, outside the Jericho Gate.

Turkish chicken egg-lemon soup uses vermicelli noodles rather than orzo or rice, but is otherwise identical to Greek avgolemono. From the eastern mountains of Turkey comes yogurt çorbasi. Hulled wheat is cooked until tender in chicken broth. Flour water, egg yolks, and yogurt are mixed together and passed through a strainer into the simmering wheat soup. The options for garnish are cilantro or mint.

While most lentil soups are made with beef or lamb broth, Turkish red lentil soup is frequently made with chicken broth. Cook a cup of red lentils and a cup and a half of diced onions in a quart and a half of stock until the lentils begin to disintegrate. Purée the lentils and onions with an immersion blender or strain and mash them. Mix a cup of milk, two egg yolks, and a few tablespoons of flour. Temper with a little soup and add back into the barely simmering liquid while stirring. Serve this velvet-smooth golden soup with mint, cilantro or croutons.

Shorba ads, ubiquitos lentil soup, is usually made with lamb and beef broth. It is a simple soup made with the addition of red lentils, chopped onion, cumin, lemon juice, salt and pepper. In Egypt, it is common for chicken boiled to make soup to be removed after about half an hour, to be slathered in butter, cardamom, cinnamon, red pepper powder and salt and to be roasted for a second course after the soup.

Hamud, the name for Egyptian chicken lemon soup, doesn't include eggs, but does contain vegetables such as celery, leek, and zucchini. Lots of garlic, salt and pepper add flavor, and rice adds body. It can serve double duty as a sauce to go over a plate of rice and chicken rescued from the soup pot and roasted.

The Tunisian version also omits eggs in its version of Greek avgolemono. True to form, the soup does contain chicken broth, chicken pieces, lemon sections, and orzo. Diced garlic, onion and a little tomato paste spend a minute or two in hot oil before being added to the soup along with salt and pepper.

Yayla chorbashi quite similar, but offers the addition of about ¾ cup of pearl barley for the same amount of soup. The barley is cooked until tender in the flavored broth. A few minutes before serving, the same yogurt mixture or yogurt without flour and egg is added. The garnish may be mint or parsley.

There is a soup on the island of Cyprus that is identical to Greek avgolemono, but for the addition of meatballs made from ground lamb, mint, eggs, parsley, salt, and pepper, it is called yourvarlakia avgolemono.

Hot soup is uncommon in the Gulf States. What there is usually has the distinct flavor of the regional spice mix, baharat, the unusual tartness of loomi, dried limes, or the features of borrowed Indian cuisine.

In Yemen, spicy hot condiments mandate the nature of common soup. Chicken shares center stage with lamb. Turnips, leeks, celery, zucchini, and potato join in. Hawayij and hulba are the typical spice mixes - black peppercorns, caraway seeds, cardamom, saffron threads, and turmeric for the former and a paste of fenugreek, coriander, garlic, and hot chili peppers for the latter. Be prepared to eat soup with bread pieces instead of spoons.

Iran has a refreshing assortment of cold soups made with dried fruit, pomegranate and yogurt. Soup of any kind is uncommon in Iraq.

Sorry for the length and complexity of this segment. Hope it helps circumvent confusion.

Feijoada Lelana was from Brazil. She introduced us to the national dish of her original country. Feijoada fits my comfort food hit parade. Hearty, bursting with flavor, loaded with cheap ingredients, perfect single dish meal for a cold night served with crusty bread and robust red wine. The host or hostess gets to sit with guests the entire mealtime. Her bean stew exuded textures and flavors that we, the offal eating minority, adore. All sorts of pig parts including hocks, ears and knuckles join in. For the majority of you who eschew our offal, neat and tidy pork pieces replace offal in feijoada in Lisbon's upper class restaurants.

Fideuà Less well known to tourists, fideuà denotes a type of Spanish pasta similar to vermicelli. Popular in Catalonia and Valencia in seafood dishes, it rivals paella for their taste and intricacy.

Finnan haddie Dad and I shared a love of smoked fish for breakfast. When I took Mom and Dad to England, we tried every variation of smoked kippers, cod, and haddock. The winner – gently simmered in butter and cream, smoked haddock topped with a poached egg for breakfast, brunch, or high tea.

Fish and chips used to come wrapped in day old newspaper until the health department banned the exposure to lead in newsprint. Trips to England were marked by strangely limited eats sixty years ago: Neighborhood Indian curry houses; pubs serving steak and kidney pie, bangers and mash, Cornish pasties, Scotch eggs, and ploughman's lunch; and then there were the chippies. Not women of the night. Unadorned fish and chips shops. Great fresh cod fillets in beer batter with thick cut twice fried starchy potatoes and a splash of vinegar. Well worth at least two lunches a week. Since those days of simplicity, I have learned that fish battered in flour and fried in oil came to England with Sephardic Jews who fled from Spain and Portugal. The first chippie opened in the early 1860s. It belonged to Joseph Malin a Jewish émigré to London. In a cookbook in 1845, Alexis Soyer, a renowned Victorian chef included a recipe for "fried fish, Jewish fashion." Chips came from Belgium.

Not a fair comparison, but the best fried codfish I ever had was in Reykjavik, Iceland. The fish was never even flash frozen, and had been in the sea only a few hours before.

In London, even the tiniest fish and chip shops seem to adhere to similar bags of tricks. Fresh or carefully thawed white flesh, (cod, haddock, or pollock) fish patted dry does very well. Batters vary from thick and fluffy to thin and crispy. Many old timers prefer the coating to be thick and greasy. Millennials seem to favor no excess oil and crispy coat. The batter should be cold, beer frothy, and the fish should enter the fryer moments after being battered. The oil should be fresh, heated to about 360F. Frying time is eight minutes give or take thirty seconds more if the fillet is thicker than average. The result, moist fish just cooked through and golden brown batter without burned parts.

Churchill saw fit not to ration fish and chips during WWII.

Fish head curry Among my favorite places to explore and enjoy the visuals, tastes, textures, and aromas of foods with strange-sounding names, are the food courts of Singapore. And fish head curry, gulai kepala ikan, shares the blue ribbon with chili crab. The fish is a red snapper, ikan merah. Each head weighs roughly a pound, about half of which is edible. The curry sauce is Indian in the style of the southern state of Kerala. Even though émigrés from Kerala in southwestern India were the first to make fish head curry in Singapore and Malaysia, one cook from Kochi in Kerala insisted that no such dish existed in his homeland. He said that Singaporean chefs created it to appeal to Chinese customers who liked fish heads, particularly in clay pots and soups. Fresh snapper heads washed free of blood to keep them from becoming bitter, are cooked in soupy curry made from curry leaves, cumin, tamarind, hot chili peppers, lemongrass, coconut milk, and vegetables. The sweet milk and sour tamarind balance each other nicely with the edge going to the tamarind. Most Singaporeans eat it with rice, but the Indian subculture adds peppery papadams and chutney-like pickles along with rice, and ethnic Chinese substitute sweet buns to soak up the sauce.

Meanwhile in China from Shanghai to Hunan to Hong Kong, people adore fish heads because of the magnificent sweet tender cheeks, prized eyeballs given to the most revered elders, tastiest cartilage and tendon in the animal kingdom, and a lower jaw of larger fish that kids like to chomp like drumsticks. Cooks remove the brains, gills and vessels and then use cleaved chunks of fish heads in clay pot casserole dishes, in peppery main dishes, and in milky white soups.

Shā guō yú tóu, fish head clay pot is a standard menu item at one of my favorite Chinese Restaurants in the San Francisco Bay Area, Shanghai Taste Delight Restaurant in Mountain View. Typically this kind of clay pot includes bean curd, shallots, black mushrooms, and ginger in a spicy and slightly sweet light-colored sauce garnished with garlic sprouts and sesame oil.

Duò jiāo zhēng yú tóu is a classic Hunanese tongue burner that dates all the way back to the early Qing Dynasty in the 17th century. Salted and sautéed fish head is covered half in red and half in green diced hot chili peppers and is steamed.

Originally from the town in which Chairman Mao was born, double pepper fish head continues to be a favorite in many Hunan restaurants worldwide.

In a seafood restaurant that must have accommodated two hundred people in Hong Kong, I tasted white creamy fish head soup, hee tao tung, for the first time. The flavor was as rich as the finest New England bisque, hearty, velvety, and not gamey. The slow simmering seemed to have emulsified the fish meat, gelatin, and fat into unctuous perfection. Gentle overtones of ginger, scallion, and rice wine melded perfectly. This particular rendition included just enough lightly cooked baby bok choy, slippery translucent noodles, and cilantro leaf garnish to create contrasting texture and color. I have since had it with tofu cubes instead of noodles, and with either canned Sichuan preserved vegetables or Napa cabbage rather than bok choy.

Back in Singapore, Teochew (Chiu chow) style fish head steamboat is similar to Hong Kong fish head soup.

Hunan steamed fish heads with salted chilies, jiao yutou in Mandarin, may be made with fish fillets or whole fish, but the classic use only fish heads. If you are dining in Changsha, Hunan's capital, or in an authentic

Hunanese restaurant elsewhere, you might be put off by the appearance of both the fish heads, and the topping of myriad red chili pepper pieces that all but hide the heads under a vividly colored coat. The red peppers are pickled and less incendiary than the usual varieties. The heat in the dish is still challenging to the uninitiated, but less likely to cause discomfort for veterans.

The cauldron of bubbling stew arrived at our table in the wholesale fish market in Seoul. It was gorgeous even with the six fish heads afloat on the saffron and chili pepper flecked surface.

"You are on your own Bubba. Those are fish heads. I dare you to eat them." My wife wrinkled her forehead, smiled with the lower half of her face, and leaned back, to distance herself farther from the food.

"Dare accepted with pleasure," I responded. "Fish cheeks are a delicacy all over Asia and I'll be delighted to have them all to myself." Challenged, she leaned forward and deftly lifted a prized morsel from a fish head with very long thin silver Korean chopsticks and popped it in her mouth.

In short order we were jousting like children for the remaining fish heads. We sucked the incredibly sweet flesh off the entire heads.

Fish skin Crispy, lightly battered, deep fried fish skin reigns as an addictive snack all over coastal South China that delights lovers of kettle style potato chips. In Taiwan, cooks love to top noodle dishes, soups, and stews with something crispy. Fried fish skin may be the most frequent choice. The scaled and fried skin loses its crispness quickly sitting out in the humidity of South China and Taiwan. Unless it is about to grace a plate, it should go into an airtight container. A cellophane bag of skin chips from most markets fits the bill. Dace, eel, grey mullet, and sole are all used as common skin doners.

Flying fox soup In Micronesia, flying fox soup supposedly possesses restorative physical and sexual power that gives comfort to aging men. The flying fox, the common fruit bat of Southeast Asia, may be seen crashing into bushes for unceremonious landings or grabbing at branches, as large as a house cat and just as furry. Its face does look like a fox. On some islands, children keep them as pets. On Saipan, bats, fur and all, are washed and boiled in a broth seasoned with salt, ginger, and onion. The bat is lifted out of the broth. The furry skin is removed. The thick layer of fat is scraped off the underside of the chest skin and returned to the broth with deboned meat. It is thickened with coconut cream and served hot, topped with sliced garlic, chive or scallion. It is often served to honor special guests. I'm told it tastes better than it sounds.

Foul madamas Few foods satisfy as much as a hearty breakfast prepared for you. Foul, ful, as in foul madamas is pronounced fool. The foul is a stew of fava beans similar to Boston baked beans without the molasses. The beans are usually heated with olive oil, lemon, and salt, and dressed with the diner's choice of diced onion, tomato, Aleppo red pepper, chopped parsley, or yogurt. In Egypt, foul venders hit the streets just after sunrise. They push their carts through neighborhoods and ring their telltale bells. People pour out of their homes with large cups or bowls in hand to purchase a ladleful for breakfast. The. Versions we had in Syria and Egypt were the same.

Four happy meatballs elevate the Shandong version of Canton's lion's head meatballs, with bolder flavors, better texture and richer colors. Juicy pork with the added crunch of minced water chestnuts deserves credit. A darker red/ brown color emanates from chili powder and catsup (actually a native sauce rather than a condiment in Shandong). The spheres may be glazed and sprinkled with sesame seeds in one of many presentations. They depart from the pale, mild, southern version as much as spicy, garlicky Italian meatballs differ from pale soft Swedish meatballs. Meatballs served in fours appear all over China, particularly during the New Year celebration. Avoid the confusion caused by English menu offerings of four happiness pork balls. They, too, are a northern dish, but utilize ground pork mixed with mashed yams, eggs and cornstarch fried in a wok and resemble fritters, nothing like steamed meatballs.

French onion soup In the late 1960s, I met Paris face-to-face for the first time. Jet lag be damned.

French onion soup

I plunged into the narrow aisles of the most exciting market I had ever seen as the pre-dawn sky began to show a little light. The original Les Halles teemed with butchers in red spackled aprons hacking away at sides of animal; carts of mushrooms, leeks and onions unloading; seafood on ice still wriggling; upscale revelers dressed to the nines, pausing on their way home after a long night; and a few other wide eyed, slack jawed tourists. An old woman sitting on a cushioned chair in the space where two aisles crossed served ceramic cups of French onion soup.

"Moi aussi, s'il vous plait." Holy merde. I was in love. The rich beef broth, caramelized morass of onions, melted Comté, splash of Cognac, and toasted crusty wedge of a peasant loaf, and a spiral of heavenly aromatic vapor rising above it – I wanted to sing.

If you can't find Comté where you live, Swiss Gruyere is a reasonable substitute. Mushroom broth can replace beef broth for an OK vegetarian substitute. Dry sherry can replace Cognac.

Fried potatoes Belgian style OK, so you think there is nothing wrong with American fries at your average fast food stop. But there is a difference between "nothing wrong" and "the best."

First, you need old starchy potatoes cut with or without the scrubbed skin to any size or shape that you desire. Then you have to agree to fry them twice. Not a problem if the cook fries them for about five minutes in batches that are not so large that the oil cools or the potatoes stick to each other. Average temperature for first swim in the oil is 290 to 320 F. What happens to the fries is that they cook through, soften and only color a little.

At this point, the cook can reheat the oil and fry for the second time at 340 to 360 F for another five minutes or so until the potatoes are golden brown or he/she can wait for a few hours and do the second fry at the most convenient time to serve them hot and crisp. The only caveat is that the pot or fryer never be covered or they will get limp and soggy.

If you have the desire to wow your diners, try double frying thin squares or rectangles of potatoes of uniform size. I use a mandolin and set the blade for only about an eighth of an inch thick. The second trip into hotter oil will cause them to puff out into crisp golden hollow pillows.

Frikadeller Fried minced pork meatballs commonly served with boiled potatoes and red cabbage are as popular as any dish in Denmark. Some cooks mix beef with the pork. I prefer the juicier all pork. Breadcrumbs, grated onions, egg, garlic, half and half, and minced sage leaves may all mix together and go into a buttered skillet as meatballs to caramelize on the outside. They are usually a litter flatter than spherical, resembling little thick sliders. One cook suggested mixing cream with seltzer instead of half and half for lighter texture.

Frittata connotes an egg-based Italian dish. In many ways, it mirrors an open-topped omelet, crustless quiche, or Persian kuku. All three enhance with additional ingredients such as cheeses, meats, pasta, potatoes, fruits, and vegetables. The Italian word frittata derives from friggere and roughly means "fried". Historically, the lineage seems to be from Asia to Persia, to Spain where kuku became Spanish tortilla, then to North Africa as just a potato omelet, then to Italy where it became a many-splendored frittata, and finally to France as a perfect omelet, and/or crusted quiche resplendent of mushrooms, spinach, pork lardons, seafood, and/or aged soft cheese; then to the U.K. where the cheese became cheddar, the lardons are bacon, and where peas make their mushy debut with brussel sprouts, leeks, asparagus and salmon; and across the Atlantic as quiche with or without a crust, greeted by ham and pepper jack cheese. It was probably the less motivated Brits and/or Americans that left off the crust on occasion.

Frittata

A Frittata is most often a breakfast item in the United States but can be eaten for any meal, either hot or cold.

I once had a late night meal in Rome of quiche that included capicola, ricotta cheese , and arugula. We had been to a concert. I don't remember the program, the performers, or the company that night. We ate in a trattoria with a bar. I was too tired to indulge. You can guess how the crusted egg pie served at room temperature at midnight impressed me. It was 45 years ago.

Where was I?

Fu This incredibly common Chinese word has more than a dozen meanings, but the only one, which is edible is actually the Japanese word, not the Chinese word, for wheat gluten. In Japan, solid raw wheat gluten, nama fu, mixes with glutinous rice to form a dull gray block. From the block, chefs cut and color all sorts of edible decoration from autumn leaves to flowers to small animals.

It is also transformed into a sweet by coating pieces with confection, and stuffing them with tasty red adzuki bean and sugar paste, and steaming them. Although many of this group of manjū yummies are covered with other starches rather than gluten, I couldn't resist including the gluten variety because of its name, fu manjū. Not related to the mustache.

G

Gallo pinto If any one dish were to typify Costa Rican cuisine, it would be gallo pinto (pronounced GAH-yoe-PEEN-toe). The literal translation is "painted or spotted rooster," referring to the color, black and white with red and green flecks. The dish combines precooked black or brown beans with precooked rice. In a little oil, dices of green onion and sweet red pepper cook for a couple of minutes. Add to the rice, local English sauce, Salsa Lizano, cilantro, and the beans, then mix it all and reheat. The beans are usually mildly garlic flavored from their original preparation. If not, you may wish to add a little garlic to the onion and red pepper dice.

A mound of gallo pinto is the basis for most Tico breakfasts. It comes with eggs, fried or scrambled, tortillas or toast and, frequently, meat, cheese or cooked plantain and sour cream. Less often, but commonly, gallo pinto is the starch at lunch as well. If not, separate small scoops of rice and beans replace it, providing the leftovers for the next batch of gallo pinto. On occasion, gallo pinto is a side dish at the evening meal as well.

Garbure A thick soup or stew with many ingredients, garbure was and remains standard peasant fare in Gascony in the southwest of France. Basic ingredients seem to be smoked meaty ham hock or shank; many vegetables including beans, carrots, peas, celery root, turnip, potatoes and cabbage; stale bread and cubes of cheese. It has the reputation of being a receptacle for rounds of multiple leftovers, becoming more complex and savory each time it is expanded and reheated, the perfect resting place for comforting food. When the solid ingredients finally exit the pot, the residual juices may be mixed with red wine and drunk from the bowl. That custom, called chabrot, is on the wane.

Gâteau fondant au chocolat Molten chocolate cake, moelleux au chocolat, or lava cake originated in France, supposedly created by Jean-Georges Vongerichten. The rich outer cake encases molten thick chocolate pudding-like liquid that escapes when the diner pokes into it.

When it became the rage among chocolate cakes in the 60s and 70s in North America, it seemed native to this side of the Atlantic. It is a simple cake constructed from ordinary ingredients: butter, chocolate, eggs, and sugar. The trick to its creation is the precise baking heat and time. A little too long in the oven and it becomes a brownie, quite a nice one in fact. Under-baked it is a mess of chocolate syrup and raw batter.

The size of the baking dish matters. Most bakers seem to prefer six inch ramekins for ease of removing individual size servings and consistent texture. Consider the ease of preparing this recipe. Spray the ramekins with non-stick mist, chop and melt high quality semi-sweet chocolate in butter. Sequentially mix in all-purpose flour, confectionary sugar, a little salt, tempered whisked eggs and extra yolks, and bake in a pre-heated oven at 425F until the sides attain cake consistency and the top is still soft. Ovens vary, but the average baking time is 13 minutes. After the ramekins cool for a minute or two, cover them with a plate and gently invert them. Voila. The individual portion is ready to eat. Bakers vary their presentations, from simple minimalistic powdered sugar to fresh raspberries and vanilla ice cream. Amounts of ingredients vary with the number of ramekins. Rough rule of thumb, six ramekins, six ounces of chocolate. Half cup each of sugar and butter, quarter cup of flour, and two eggs plus two more yolks. A pinch of salt. From start to finish, this best chocolate dessert ever takes less than an hour.

My second favorite chocolate cake?

Baked by ten-year-old Lily and seven-year-old Jack Karpman.
What a team of grandkids!

Gazpacho Is this the world's most famous cold soup? This tomato-based Andalusian soup can surprise those who aren't expecting it be cold , but in the searing heat of a Seville summer, they will welcome it. Its principal ingredients, aside from tomato, are sweet peppers, garlic, bread to thicken, and lots of olive oil.

Gnocchi Making gnocchi can be an event. It's a great way to get the entire family in on the fun. Set up the kitchen and give everyone a job, whether it's mashing potatoes, measuring flour, or rolling the dough. Freeze a batch or two for quick weeknight meals, and pair with a different kind of sauce each time. And for a lighter dumpling, use ricotta instead of potato. They may be baked, fried, or boiled. To serve, add herbs, tomato sauce, veggies, spice mixes, or even serve them on toothpicks as canapés

Goulash. Hungarian Goulash is a hearty, paprika-flavored soup/stew with cubes of seared beef, parsnips, carrots, and potatoes. Goulash, Gulyás, Hungarian goulash, American style, is a rich, thick savory stew of meat and vegetables flavored with generous amounts of Hungarian paprika, usually served over broad buttered egg noodles and topped with a dollop of sour cream. In Hungary and its neighboring countries, gulyás is a lot thinner and more like soup.

The history of the dish goes back to the 9th century when Magyar tribesmen boiled meat in flavored water until it was bone dry, packed the pieces into the boiled stomach of the animal and stitched it closed. Thus preserved, the meat was removed later and re-hydrated in boiling water to make gulyás.

Gluten duck People in China love to eat duck. Not to be left behind, vegetarian Buddhists have created an incredible mock meat cuisine including tasty, texturally correct, and visually appealing faux duck. Sheets of wheat gluten marinate in soy, MSG, five spice, oil, sugar and ginger. The sheets adhere and resemble the pattern of layered strands of actual meat "with the grain". The surface caramelizes dark brown like lacquered real duck, and the skin is dimpled to look as though it had feathers that were plucked. The flavor rocks if you drain the liquid off, pat the pieces dry, and stir fry them with your own choice of seasoning. When I entertained a vegetarian friend, I served the fried pieces atop cellophane noodles dressed in a little rice vinegar; slivered cucumbers and shallots; leaves of fresh cilantro, basil and mint; plus hoisin sauce, and sriracha sauce on the side. She asked about taking home the leftovers, but after her seconds and my thirds, there weren't any. Using similar techniques, chefs use protein rich gluten to fashion facsimiles for abalone, beef, chicken, fish, lamb, and pork to comfort vegetarians.

Granita mandorlo Not your 4th of July cardboard cones of plain shaved ice lathered with iridescent blue and white sugar syrup. All over Italy and Sicily, granitas approach perfection with a variety of natural tasting flavors, not overly sweetened. Almond, mandorlo, is the best in my humble opinion. Agree?

Gravlax is Danish fresh raw salmon fillets cured with salt, sugar, pepper, and fresh dill weed weighed down in the fridge for on average 48 hours. Thin slices served on buttered Danish rye bread with a sweet Scandinavian mustard sauce strike a marvelous balance of tastes and textures.

Green papaya salad I do like the refreshing feel and texture of chilled coleslaw, or Japanese cucumber salad called sunomono, as a side dish in summer. In Thailand, Laos, and Cambodia, it can be quite warm even in winter. Green papaya salad, som tum, refreshes at many, if not most, meals. For a cross section of the populations, a larger than appetizer serving is the single main dish at lunch. Peeled and shredded spaghetti-like strands of nearly tasteless unripe papaya serves the textural base of the salad. The dressing is the key. Individual elements in the dressing are unappealing, particularly to lots of Westerners. Blended together, they are amazing. Consider slightly funky dried shrimp alone. Not my choice, but it adds texture when mixed. Asian fermented fish sauce alone? Not bad if you like anchovies. Blended, it adds saltiness and the essence of depth, umami. Hot Thai red eye chili peppers, called the Thai equivalent linguistically of rat shit chilies by locals. Used sparingly, they add the perfect source or heat. Tart lime juice. Minced garlic. Gooey gray palm sugar disappears in the blend and offsets the fish sauce and lime juice. Believe me or not, the blended mixture yields a perfect dressing that adheres to the crisp papaya matchsticks. Two other standard vegetable components of the salad are tomatoes, quartered cherry tomatoes work best, and fresh long beans, bruised a little to absorb more dressing, cut into inch and a half logs. Where is the crunch? Top with roasted peanuts.

If you care about artistic presentation, add an edible blossom, or a sprig of mint or Thai basil to the top.

Grits, polenta, and pap are ground corn cooked in liquid until creamy. The grind is a little finer for polenta. Grits are the coarser grind of white corn. Polenta may be yellower from yellow kernels. Cornmeal boiled in chicken stock or water until creamy, becomes polenta, what some call Italian grits. It can be kept simple, topped with freshly grated Parmesan, and served alongside meat, or as a main topped with your favorite tomato sauce instead of pasta.

Grits come packaged as an instant or regular type. The so called stone ground regular variety is the most popular in America's southland. A 4:1 mix of about a quart of water to a cup of grits stirred relentlessly for a minute, then simmered covered for a half hour does the trick. The last minute addition of about four tablespoons of butter, a sprinkle of freshly ground black pepper, and a twenty second stir creates the perfect side dish, or the platform for Savannah's best shrimp and gits. Foreign? Well sort of.

In Puglia, polenta/grits with local shrimp had the added Italian distinction of garlic, capers, basil, and local caciocavallo cheese. As comforting as shrimp and grits? Dead heat.

But there is more. In Havana, we had harina con congrejo, meat from boiled blue crabs, and cornmeal stew, polenta Cuban style. The creamy corn porridge played platform for the crab, sofrito of red and green bell peppers, white onion, garlic, and a little oil, splashed with hot chili pepper liquid and lime juice. It was a great, very different polenta dish that clearly is a homemade comforter in Cuba.

Pap is an Afrikaans word for porridge. Made from ground corn, it comes smooth and soft, slap pap; dry and crumbly, phutu pap: or a thick, style pap. Like polenta and grits, pap is a basic inexpensive belly filler throughout southern Africa. We had it served from a three legged pot over an open fire in a game park in Botswana. It accompanied barbecued meat. We were told that pap also serves as a hot breakfast cereal and as a sauce for cooked vegetable dishes that often contain pumpkin leaves.

Thick pap is also the starch that accompanies seswaa, Botswana's national dish, a goat meat stew, cooked for hours, removed from its bones and shredded. The stew often also includes pumpkin leaves and other greens.

Goat meat tastes like lamb or mutton. Both become gamey if the butchered animal is old.

Mamaliga stone ground grits Romanian style make great buttered morning porridge.

H

Haak Just another name for the essential comfort food side dish, southern-style collard greens. Dozens of countries and regions worldwide have their own names and recipes, but only in Kashmir do the greens, haak, appear in one form or another at every meal. I remember reading a recipe for haak and white rice as a main vegetarian course described by Madhur Jaffrey, whom I greatly respect. The combination of asafoetida, mustard oil, dry red chili peppers, and fresh green ones in the recipe distinguishes the dish from my standby southern style greens with hog back or smoked pork neck. The cooked greens look similar made both ways, but the Kashmiri version wins for flavor. My own fusion of the two is to add the chili peppers to the southern-style recipe or to add a little liquid smoke to the Kashmiri vegetarian version. Small fresh leaves are preferred for this dish. Broth made from the whole, larger, older leaves attached to stems is called haak rus. Leftover white rice adds body to it. Haak-e-aanchaar is the pickled version of fermented haak roots, multiple spices, and ginger root served as a condiment with hearty winter dishes.

Haggis I could try to make a case that haggis is comforting, but I won't bother. I like savory barley dishes, choose organ meats intentionally to honor my roots, respect Scottish national pride, and love that the first waterproof containers in which liquids were heated after fire was tamed in prehistoric times, were animal stomachs, not ceramic vessels. Still, the reality remains that most of the world would laugh if I called it comforting. But, consider Burns Suppers.

My friend hails from Scotland. She and her husband split their time between homes in the U.K. and Costa Rica. She corrected and authenticated the menu and had me spell whisky without the "e". She explained that with an "e" it's Irish."

She added that Athol Brose is popular – a mixture of oatmeal, whisky, and honey with the cheese course. She also insists the King of the Haggis-makers is MacSween, which is now available all over the world (except in the US). Having had some bad haggis in my time, I now wouldn't eat anything else.

"Burns nights are very traditional and formal, though some traditions are being watered down. My husband has been in several of these, because he is imposing in a kilt and likes to help with the chore of imbibing the processional whisky.

'Scotsmen are rather chauvinistic so only men take part in the procession. In fact, I believe there are still many Burns Suppers, which are men only! The Burns Supper is not a very long affair because everyone is eager to progress to listening to Burns poetry. Tam O'Shanter is often recited – a wonderful, funny long poem, which warns about the evils of drink!"

Here is her husband's contribution: "The greatest night of the year for Scots is here. The dark chill and haar (sea mist) of an early highland night is kept at bay by the shutters and rich drapes over the windows. The flickering red glow of the dining room fire and candles reveals the men, for it is usually only men, sitting ruddy faced with pre-prandial whisky. Dressed in their highland finery of tartan kilts and silver buttoned dark jackets, they speak in low tones around the dining table, one ear cocked. The table is dressed in white linen and set with polished silver. Beneath the table, each man has his sgien dhu, or short dagger, tucked into one of his long woolen socks.

'The tall double doors of the room are flung open. All look expectantly towards them. The doorman formally announces The Haggis.

'Accompanied by the skirl of the pipes the solemn procession marches in, kilts and sporrans swinging to the raucous tune. For centuries, the rousing notes led wild highlanders into battle and terrified their enemies. This night, they raise the shoulders and step of the stalwart sword bearer, marching proudly behind the piper, who is dressed in his finest at the head of the procession. The naked dirk or short sword, born upright, gleams. The sword bearer is followed by the haggis bearer carrying that hot, rich and bulging item on a silver trencher for the occasion. He is followed by the man carrying the quaich, or ritual silver drinking cup. Behind him walks another important man. He carries the aged malt whisky, an essential of the event.

'At the head of the table the procession stops. The others make way for the haggis bearer. The person chosen to speak the words of the immortal poet gives the address to the enraptured audience. The poem is accompanied by actions, as he cuts open the haggis. Its tightly stuffed and delicious contents spill forth. The gathering toasts the haggis. The whisky is poured into the quaich and each member of the procession follows the speaker in drinking from it. The piper is last and drinks deeply, for by tradition, he holds the hopefully empty cup upturned over his head. I have never seen a drop spilt yet!

'The dinner is served and the feasting begins."

Confession: When we visited Edinburgh, I ordered haggis, tatties n' peep out of a sense of duty as a food explorer despite a little trepidation, knowing the ingredients. I loved it and had it at least every other day while we wandered Scotland's lakes and castles.

Ingredients: intact sheep stomach soaked in salted water, dried and filled with any combination of tender boiled cubes of sheep liver, tongue, lung and heart, oatmeal, toasted oats or barley, onions, fat, and herbs. Because of the sheep lung, authentic Scottish haggis has been banned in the United States since 1971 by the US Department of Agriculture (USDA).

Preparation: Fill the stomach about half to two-thirds with the other ingredients moistened with the broth from boiling the offal, sew closed, pierce in a few places to allow steam to escape and simmer in water or broth for about three hours.

Hainan jifan An iconic dish of Singapore, it actually originated in Hainan. Called Hainan jifan, it combines free range chicken from Wenchang, Hainan, with rice cooked in chicken fat and chicken broth. A whole chicken actually poaches in water that neither boils nor even visibly simmers. There is enough heat to lightly poach the meat and to perfuse the liquid with chicken flavor and fat from partially rendered skin and fat deposits. Rice cooked in the same liquid, fortified with ginger, garlic, and screw pine leaves, emerges as the flavorful, slightly oily, star of the meal. Its origins were during the Japanese occupation, when poverty necessitated stretching the flavor of a chicken into several cups of rice. Unique to this recipe, the poached chicken goes into an ice bath as it comes out of the pot. The texture of the skin becomes almost gelatinous. The bird then air dries and comes to table at room temperature with cucumbers that cooked in the broth alongside the chicken, and a dipping sauce of diced chili peppers, ginger, garlic and soy sauce. It is nearly as popular in Malaysia as it is in Singapore.

Hakarl has to be one of the most repulsive smelling foods anywhere that locals love, and from which they derive comfort.

Sharks are ancient in design. Most species have extremely primitive urinary systems. It is for that reason that the majority of them are thought to be inedible. The ammonia (urine) taste and smell of the flesh is extremely off-putting. Mako sharks, leopard sharks, and some types of sand sharks have more advanced kidney function, and can be eaten with ease and pleasure. They do need to be bled promptly when caught, and most are soaked with at least a few changes of fresh water before cooking.

Greenland sharks and sleeping sharks have primitive kidney function. When they came ashore in Iceland, they were traditionally decapitated, gutted, and buried in a pit of sand for six to nine weeks depending on the time of year, to squeeze the blood and body liquids out of them. Atop the sand, gravel and rocks helped weigh down the sand and the sharks, and augmented the squeeze. The sharks fermented. The euphemism remains that the process cures the flesh. In recent years, plastic squeezing machines have begun to replace the sand pits. After they are cured, the sharks are cut into strips and hung out in the sun for many months. The brown crust that covers the strips remains until they are ready to eat. Months after they were hung out to dry, the strips lose the brown crust when a buyer arrives on scene. The fishmonger cuts decrusted strips into smaller chunks. The buyer reduces the chunks into bite-size pieces, skewers with toothpicks, and offers to unsuspecting tourists who are instructed to hold their nose with one hand and use the other hand to move toothpick to mouth. They need a third had to cover their mouth when they almost immediately gag.

Is It Jook Yet?

Like so many acquired tastes, fermentation is the culprit. Only with hakarl, is the vomicatious (made up euphemism) offender from fermentation exacerbated by eau d'urine. Beware the adage, it tastes so much better than it smells. When ripe, it tastes like… Oh, I forgot. I refused to taste it.

Haleem Haleem a type of pasty stew popular in the Middle East, Central Asia, and the Indian subcontinent, varies from place to place. Ingredients include these: grain, wheat, or barley; meat, minced beef, goat, sheep, lamb, or chicken; lentils more often than rice; and regional spice mixes. It simmers in cauldrons for up to eight hours in Yemen, for export all around the Muslim world as part of the post-fast Ramadan iftar feast fare. Historically, it was first described in Baghdad in the 10th century, and followed Arab incursions to the far reaches of the empire.

Handkäse mit Musik Hand-rolled soft cheese from the Frankfurt area of Germany comes on a slice of hearty bread topped first with plenty of raw onions, then the cheese. The Musik refers to the flatulence that follows. It can be ordered without Musik and the onions are omitted.

Haxe Giant bone-in shanks of lamb, pork, or eal have been hearty economic comfort foods in Austria and Germany for more than a century.

Haxe

The hock or knuckle is the end of the leg bone above the ankle and below the ham. The meat is tough and interlaces with tendons, connective tissue, and fat. The haxe marinates for days and then roasts until tender enough to succumb to hungry carnivores. Mixed root vegetables fortify the sauce that comes with the haxe on a large plate. Bavarian menus list the pork knuckle as Schweinhaxn. Look for potato dumplings and red cabbage to fill the paltry space left by the hock. Farther north in Germany, the menu may call it Eisbein. In Austria, the name changes to Stötzn. The Viennese version adds a taste of Poland and/or Hungary to the roast with a pre-boil of broth laden with garlic and caraway seeds, and plating with horseradish and chili peppers.

Himmel und Erde In Germany, this "heaven (or sky) and earth" dish is actually mashed potato and applesauce, paired with black (blood) sausage and grilled onions, a very satisfying basic combo, particularly for locals.

Hoe Not what you may think. In Korea, hoe is the suffix appended to words for fish, beef, or liver when they are sliced and served raw with a dipping sauce. Saengseon hoe is the fish and/or seafood version similar to Japanese sashimi. It is the hoe I know best. It may also be dipped in wasabi sauce, but the most popular dip for sliced raw fish is gochujang, a sweet and spicy bold sauce made with garlic, ginger, chili pepper purée and toasted sesame seeds. The sauced raw fish hoe is typically wrapped in screw pine leaves and eaten with one's fingers.

Hoppin' John When a large contingent of Sephardic Jews from North Africa settled in Georgia in the 1730's, they brought with them the tradition of eating black-eyed peas on the new year as symbol of and a wish for prosperity. Their Christian neighbors began to eat black-eyed peas on the New Year as well. Some added a dime to the pot to enhance the likelihood of prosperity. They added greens to represent folding money and up the ante. Unlike their Jewish neighbors, they used ham hocks, bacon, hog jowl, fat back or smoked pork in the pot. In West Africa and in the South, rice was a frequent addition. Southern rice and black-eyed peas is called Hoppin' John. Better than a penny for your thoughts, was a dime in pea pot for prosperity.

Huevos rotos, broken eggs, name this winter belly filler and warmer all over Spain. A pile of French fries topped with eggs over easy, and paper-thin slices of serrano ham can appear at breakfast or lunch. When the diner breaks the firm egg whites, the yolk needs to be runny. Could Canadian poutine be a descendant?

Hunan hot and spicy shrimp These iconic large shrimp are coated with a generic batter of egg whites, rice wine, mung bean starch, sugar, salt, and white pepper, fried in a wok, and sauced with hot chili oil, oyster sauce, ketchup, and soy sauce. They are topped with chopped scallion and served with white rice. It is a tasty dish for those whose taste buds don't die from the hot chili oil and can still appreciate the taste of the large shrimp.

I

Iftar comfort feast 1.6 billion Muslims celebrate the holy month of Ramadan. They fast from sunrise to sunset, but the entire family comes together in the early evening for a relaxed slow feast that rewards them for roza, the daytime fast. Iftar, the feast after fast, traditionally adheres to the belief that that Prophet Mohammad ate three dates when he broke his roza, along with either fruit juice, milk, or water. Beyond that, menus vary by location and tradition. Women spend hours preparing enough taste treats to cover a large family table with elegance and festivity. Restraint reaps rewards. Curries, kabobs, pilafs, porridges, soups, stews, followed by decadent desserts describe the dividends. Be they shakshuka eggs in spicy sauce in Tunisia, stuffed grape leaves in Turkey, samosas in India, sambusas in Yemen, shrimp curry in Indonesia, meat and eggs in Nigeria, upsidedown in Jordan, vegetable pakoras in Pakistan, jalebis in Iran, or haleem in Central Asia, becomes secondary to comfort that comes from beliefs, family, and breaking the fast.

Intestinal fortitude In China, Japan and Korea, health aficionados consume beef intestine for more stamina, better complexion, to treat anemia, and to warm up bodies that tend to be too cool according to the yin and yang of ayurvedic medicine. Add to my list of intestine favorites, marinated and deep-fried Filipino isaw manok, along with Chef Slim's Divisadero fried chitlins, Gandma's kishka, and Greek kokoretsi. I can hear some of you mumbling to yourselves, not on your life. I'll never eat intestines. Well, if you have ever eaten sausage with natural casing, you have eaten animal small bowel. And many hot dogs, cold cuts and sausages contain diced intestine, particularly andouillettes, in nearly every bistro in Paris. Buck up. It hasn't killed you yet and, admit it, you loved much of what you ate. Some gutsy food explorers seek out the extremes.

More than a decade ago, Robert Sietsema, the restaurant critic for The Village Voice, went to dinner with a group of bold foodies for an organ meat feast at Northeast Taste Chinese Food in Flushing, Queens. The name that seems to have gotten the most attention was "crispy colorectal." According to Sietsema, it turned out to have a "licoricey spice that masked the skunky taste — proving that anise and anus go surprisingly well together."

Involtini di pesce spada My wife and two friends independently proclaimed that the best fish dish they have ever eaten was fresh swordfish prepared in the local style in Sicily. Joan's favorite was at a pleasant restaurant in Trapani called Da Peppe. She begrudgingly offered me one small taste and then devoured every last morsel. She usually shares generously.

Involtini di Pesce Spada on the menu, means rolled up swordfish. This may well be the hallmark seafood dish of Sicily. The swordfish fillets are about four ounces each, roughly two inches wide, and five or six inches long. They are carefully and gently pounded between sheets of wax paper to a thickness of a quarter to half an inch. Each fillet is topped with a breadcrumb, grated pecorino cheese, onion, and a caper and olive mixture about the same thickness as the fillet. They are rolled up, secured with a toothpick, delicately floured, lightly browned in olive oil, and sautéed gently for another fifteen minutes or so over a marinara or sweet and sour sauce, or brushed with olive oil and baked on a bed of bay leaves without sauce. Some recipes replace the capers and olives with plumped currants and pine nuts. Each pair is inseparable, but all four ingredients are not usually combined. There are many variations and they are all worth trying. My favorite was spread with the currant and pine nut mixture served on a bed of marinara sauce in a little seaside town near Agrigento.

Swordfish up to fifteen feet long are the kings of the fish markets. Paper-thin fillets are bathed in lemon juice for twenty to thirty minutes and eaten uncooked like carpaccio or over pasta with basil and diced tomato. Pieces of swordfish are also grilled, brushed with a little olive oil and sprinkled with herbs; deep fried; cubed and tossed with tomatoes, mozzarella, and mint over pasta; and even baked in a pie with both raisins and pine nuts, and capers and olives, called impanata di pesce spada, after the Spanish empanada.

At the Trapani restaurant, with a little reluctance, the chef described the recipe for swordfish de Peppe in the following way: The fish fillet was laid on a bed of thinly sliced potatoes in an oven proof oiled ceramic dish and baked under foil in vinegar, salt, pepper, and a little sugar, and topped with sliced sweet onions only long enough to soften the potato. When the foil was removed, it was topped with breadcrumbs and lightly browned under a broiler, dressed with a little parsley and served with lemon wedges. Sorry I can't be more specific.

Personally, I would begin with the potato slices baking uncovered in seasoned vinegar for about ten or fifteen minutes. Then I would layer the fillets and cover with foil so the potatoes were soft and the fish barely cooked through.

J

Jacket potatoes. In the states, a potato jacket is the baked crisp skin of the potato. In England a jacket potato is a baked potato stuffed with a laundry list of ingredient combinations. Among the additions are bacon bits, butter, baked beans, cheese, chicken, chili con carne, chives, cold cuts, chutney, diced tomatoes, feta, gravy, ground meat, ham, olives, onions, ragu, roasted peppers, sausage, scallions, sour cream, tomato sauce, tuna, and turkey. The choices of herbs and spices are many.

Starchy large potatoes work best, e.g. Russets (US) or King Edward potatoes (UK).

In the UK, the potatoes are often wrapped to be baked in aluminium foil. Some Americans also use it but spell the foil, aluminum. Most of us prefer a little oil and a dash of salt on the outside of the skin. Don't forget to pierce the skin with a fork to assure that it doesn't explode.

Baked Stuffed Potato

Decades ago, I had a baked stuffed potato in Istanbul called kumpir. It was sliced nearly through down the middle. The underside intact, it opened like a book. The inside was covered with melted butter and kasar, a Gruyère like sheep cheese. It was very nice.

While on the subject of Gruyère, we shared a fondue in Switzerland that came with a baked potato to slather with melted cheese. The pairing of raclette and baked potato also appeared on a bistro menu in Paris.

Jalebis This Indian age-old spiral sweet hails from western Asia, possibly Persia where its name is zolbiya. I watched a woman pipe yellowish batter from a squeeze bottle with an old unrelated mustard label on it, over a skillet of hot oil on a grate over coals.

We were in her small town on the edge of the Thar Desert in western India attending a town meeting to decide on how the town council would vote to spend federal funds offsetting the cost of a long draught. Most towns spent their subsidy digging the town well deeper. This town had an unusually deep well, so they voted to improve the road to the cemetery.

She piped her batter in expanding concentric circles, fried them crisp, dipped them in sweetened glaze, and rested them on a wire rack. Our guide translated all my questions. The color came from saffron. The flour was a mixture of chick pea flour and ordinary cake flour. It was fermented with a liquid bacterial starter. After the town meeting, the guide and I bought three each and enjoyed the crunch and sweet flavor usually reserved for kids a fraction of our ages. She asked if we wanted a glass of milk with our treats. We declined.

Jalebis

Jamaican stew peas is the name of this dish, but it might better be called kidney bean, pig tail, salt beef, and coconut milk stew. It is a thick creamy stew with loads of flavor. In a restaurant in Ocho Rios, a few hundred yards from the waterfalls, I learned little because a dozen or so ingredients were simply tossed into a pressure cooker. And then ladled into bowls

A Jamaican friend in Brooklyn walked me through the real deal from scratch. For starters, he soaked dry kidney beans overnight in water, seasoned with thyme, garlic, onion, and peppercorns. He butchered a whole eight-inch-long pig tail into half-inch logs after trimming off about half the fat from a thick strip down the underside length of the tail. He had a piece of salt beef from the local Jamaican grocery store and cut it into cubes about the same length as the tail logs. The beef looked like flank steak, but he wasn't sure of the cut. He simmered the two kinds of meat together in water through two changes of the steaming liquid to lessen the salt load and soften the meat without rendering off all the fat. He simultaneously cooked the beans in enough water to cover until they were tender. He added the drained meats into the bean broth and beans, added an entire can of coconut milk, a whole scotch bonnet pepper, a few tablespoons each of diced garlic, scallions, some all-purpose yellow seasoning granules, about half cup each of diced red and green bell peppers, dried thyme leaves crumbled, about a teaspoon of freshly ground black pepper, and a few pinches of salt. He added just enough water to cover the top the beans and meats, covered the pot and simmered the stew for about half-an-hour with thin corn flour and water dumplings added, about the size of a child's finger.

What a unique combination. The gray-brown muddy looking stew tasted so much better than it looked. Despite the challenge from the Scotch bonnet heat, we each ate two large full bowls.

Jellied eel My companion and I were in East London on our way to a Chinese market to buy some dried herbs and spices when we happened upon a "Pie and Mash" shop. In he darted. I followed. Not for pie or mash, but for cold jellied eel. I had enjoyed eel since childhood, fried or smoked, and loved both versions for their firm white richness, moistness, and flavor. No tiny bones. Jellied was a new experience, and it was yummy. It seems that stewed eels in a green gelatinous aspic/sauce with mashed potatoes or cold jellied eels are standard comfort fare in most shops advertising pies and mash. The sauce seasoning includes white wine, vinegar, onion, bay leaf, and parsley.

Jerky On the lovely walk down the hill from Macau's Senado Square to the base of the stairs up to the ruins of St. Paul's Church, venders tempt tourists with a panoply of taste treats and souvenirs. The must-try items along the descent are the jerky samples. Pork and beef jerky made with sweet glazes, salt, spice, heat, and multiple flavor combinations, sit in stacked sheets about the size of printer paper. Inviting attendants armed with scissors cut the sheets into smaller squares for sale by weight, and cut pinky finger shaped strips for free samples. Definitely worth a try. The jerky is less chewy than most, high quality, and a great opportunity to try flavors unavailable in most of the world. Don't be embarrassed to try more than a few.

Jianbing is its name and it is a great breakfast on the run. The largest jianbing are in Beijing. More like an Egg McMuffin, jianbing is a circular pancake made from yeasty cruller dough with a scrambled egg and hoisin sauce inside. The simplest little bings are bao bing, the kind you see with Peking duck and mu shu pork rolled up with scallions and sweet bean sauce or hoisin sauce.

Egg coated crepes, jianbing, may be breakfast street food number one in Beijing, Tianjin, Jinan, Shanghai and many other Chinese cities where street vendors ply workers with breakfast to go on the way to work. A crepe on a round drum or skillet receives a layer of beaten egg. The crepe flips, gets painted with bean sauce or a facsimile and either diced scallion, cilantro, or both. The egged crepe folds into a paper pouch before exiting into a mouth on the move. In different locales, lettuce, bacon or other additions hop aboard. The eggy northern Chinese crepe has recently taken New York by storm. Jian Bing Man on west 23rd, and The Flying Pig Jian Bing on Lexington Avenue are both hot spots. You can find them in a few places around San Francisco, the East Bay and the Peninsula, but some of the best and most consistent can be found at a pop-up called Tai Chi Jianbing, where Cheng Hu is making organic versions of the street food he grew up with.

Xian bing are large round stuffed pastries often called pies. They are Beijing favorites and, appropriately, a highly acclaimed and very affordable xian bing can be enjoyed at Beijing Pie House in Monterey Park, California.

Jook, juk, congee is so common anywhere Chinese ex-pats live, that most of us have seen and tasted it. Indeed, it may be the most common breakfast food in the world. It also makes it to the table for occasional lunches and late night suppers. Jook is fairly thick rice gruel cooked in water or chicken broth slowly for hours. I prefer it made with broth. The diner usually gets to choose from a handful of different additions. My choice most often has been "thousand-year-old-eggs" and pork bits. The bowl usually arrives with a drizzle of sesame oil, a few scallion slices and a few peanuts on top. About half the time I ordered a stick of fried bread to tear into pieces and add to the jook. Something about that morning ritual must have stirred memories or feelings of security and comfort from deep within my subconscious. The texture is soothing. There is no other way I know to explain the level of peaceful satisfaction I felt each time I ate my jook. Even to this day, I always order a bowl of jook whenever Joan and I have dim sum. Now, however, I like to share it with her.

Unlike most of their Asian neighbors, Koreans cook with milk and milk products. Tarak juk is rice porridge cooked with milk.

In Bangkok I ate chao vit, a fabulous marriage of jook and roast duck.

The alternate name congee probably is the Anglicized version of the Tamil word from India, kanji, which means boiling as water for rice.

Jumbuck Stew In Australia, jumbuck is slang for sheep or lamb. A stew of lamb chop meat really fits my bill of comfort on a plate. Consider seasonings of curry powder, Worcestershire sauce, tomato sauce, vinegar, brown sugar, onion, ginger, and either beef or lamb stock in stew. What about Vegetables? Pumpkin and carrots suffice. Thickened with a roux, and served with a side of roasted herbed potatoes. Yes, please.

Jumbuck stew

K

Kadhi is an Indian comfort soup made with yogurt, chick pea flour, ghee or oil, lime juice, and spices, served over rice. Too simple to be from India? Well it isn't as simple as it sounds at first. Count the herbs and spices. Asafoetida, bay leaves, black mustard seeds, black peppercorns, cloves, chili peppers, chili powder, cumin seeds, fenugreek, ginger, salt, and turmeric. The magic of this soup is that it blends creamy simplicity with layered nuanced tangy flavor. If you are hesitant to buy, store, and use asafoetida, add garlic and onion instead.

Kapana With Fat Cakes Namibia is a fabulous destination from the capital city of Windhoek, across the ancient Namib desert past oryx, zebras, and ostrich, to Walvis Bay and the ocean. We looked around a few open markets in Windhoek to load the car with snacks and drinks before crossing the desert. I was tempted to try Nimibia's favorite, kapana, grilled cubes of beef and fat, dipped in red pepper powder and salt, then basted with bile.

The bitter aftertaste of bile lurked in a memory of baby goat stew with bones and bile from the Ilocos region of the Philippines and neem leaves from western India. Despite my so called cast iron stomach, the bitterness bothered me for a few hours both times. I passed.

Locals love the bitterness and heat. Fat cakes look like popovers, added to the kapana order to soak up juices. Instead, I opted for a hot dog as plump as a fat sausage, served on a roll, basted in butter and topped with grilled onions. Not bad. Number two street food behind kapana, I was told.

Karniyarik In a small restaurant in Konya, the pot-bellied owner/waiter/chef with a bristle, bramble, black moustache touted a dish that "makes you feel good." He took my order for eggplant halves stuffed with chopped lamb, pepper, garlic and onion. I asked what the Turkish word karniyarik actually meant. He smiled exposing his gapped pearly whites and said, "Watch this." He took in a deep breath, closed his mouth and strained his muscles. A large vertical bulge showed through his shirt and strained the buttons. "It means split open belly, like I got from my hernia." Good thing that I am not squeamish. Great dish.

Kare-kare unites two of my favorites, peanut butter and strange animal parts.

Kare kare

This sweet stew from the Philippines brings to the pot a strange array of bedfellows – oxtail, calves and pigs feet, tough cuts of beef, ham hocks, beef tripe, and/or organ meats.Vegetables most often added include the heart shaped red flower that hangs at the bottom of banana bunches sliced after the outer petals are removed, bok choy, green beans, and eggplant. Quite an eclectic group. The red color comes from annatto paste. The star, the sauce, is made from chunky peanut butter. Ground rice or rice flour thickens the stew. The other flavors derive from garlic, onion, fermented shrimp paste, salt, and pepper. Despite marginally likable shrimp paste and funny meat parts, most Westerners like the finished product, even kids.

Karfiolleves A bilingual guide showed me an enclosed rectangular apartment complex in Obuda in Budapest, with a synagogue that survived the holocaust hidden under one of its walls. A sobering site. The weather suddenly turned cold, and dark. A chilling rain was headed our way.

"It's a little early for lunch but I know a small café nearby that makes great hot soup. If you are OK with a bit of a wait, we can sit at the counter and watch Rada cook."

"Sounds like just the kind of break my empty stomach and tired feet would appreciate to lighten the darkness inside and out."

We were the first patrons in the eatery. Rada was dicing herbs and chopping vegetables. She and Raakel, exchanged pleasantries. Rada smiled and pointed us into seats next to her cutting board and line of pots and pans.

"I ordered the most comforting vegetarian hot soup in this part of Hungary, for people like me, who won't mix milk and meat and won't eat non-Kosher ingredients. I'm sure you will like it."

"What's in it?"

"Watch and be surprised."

Rada poured some oil in a pot. In went diced onions followed by minced garlic. She turned the mix dark red with lots of paprika. After a few minutes, peeled and sliced carrots and turnips, pieces of green peppers sans ribs and seeds, and chopped celery followed. Vegetable soup paprikash? Then came the so-called surprise. Florets and thinly sliced stems of what must have been two large heads of cauliflower surpassed the volume of everything else in the pot. She added what appeared to be half water and half clear broth to cover and turned up the heat. She made a roux with oil and flour and set it aside. She then whipped up a batter of eggs, water, flour, and salt that looked like pancake batter with too much liquid in it. She left us for about fifteen minutes to prepare loaves of bread for their foray in a wall oven behind a partition.

On her return, she added sour cream to the cooled roux, ladled a little of the broth from the big pot into it and stirred the mixture to temper it. The cream and roux thickened the soup in the pot without separating. She took two generous servings out of the big pot, into a smaller pot over a flame, and pushed some of the batter through the larger holes of a cheese grater. In minutes little dumplings floated to the top. She served us spicy, dark red, vegetarian velvety creamed cauliflower and vegetable soup with dumplings, garnished with a few chopped parsley leaves.

Absolutely the most comforting paprika-spiced cauliflower soup I could have imagined.

Karpfen is German for carp. Until the last two centuries, Jews were called by their trade, not by a family name. Goldschmidt smithed gold. Schneider was a tailor. Our family, the Karpman clan lived along the Dneiper River and its tributaries and probably fished for, cleaned, or sold carp. Because of the golden color of the scales, karpfen dishes were extraordinarily popular from Belarus to Japan as an omen for prosperity.

Kasha I did find a local coffee shop in Moscow that served "satisfying American breakfasts," but I opted for a non-American favorite that I hadn't had for 60 years, *kasha* with browned onions and mushrooms. My dad always ate it cold with milk. I preferred it hot. Buckwheat groats overcooked are mediocre mush at best. Tossed in beaten raw eggs, toasted in a dry skillet, and then steamed in broth until barely cooked through, the individual grains retain a little crunch, remain separate and exude a nutty smoky flavor that I adore. That's how Mom and Grandma made kasha.

Katsu donburi commonly contracts to Katsudon. Tonkatsu is the Japanese word for pork cutlet. Donburi is a rice bowl. Katsu is a homophone for the verb to succeed, to be victorious. Superstitious students often eat katsudon, a rice bowl of sliced deep fried pork cutlet coated with panko crumbs; cooked onions; beaten eggs simmered in mirin, soy sauce, and dashi; and a dipping sauce, the night before the grueling national placement exams.

The thick, tangy, rich dipping sauce is Japanese-style BBQ sauce for fried meats that adds sweet and salty flavor. The main ingredients are Worcestershire sauce, soy sauce, sugar and other seasonings.

Of the different donburi rice bowls, the katsu version is far and away the most popular, hearty, and traditional in Japan. Revered single item katsudon restaurants fill early by well-dressed business folk in central Tokyo.

Khichdi I wonder if dal bhat is among the most widely consumed soups in the world. Consider the combined populations of India, Pakistan, Bangladesh, Nepal, and Tibet, where it is eaten virtually daily.

It is clearly one of the oldest soups. Seculus I Nicator, the king of Greece, marched into India during the third century BCE to retake the Indus Valley in the Seleucid–Mauryan War. His writings noted that rice with pulses was very popular among people of the Indian subcontinent. Among the dal bhat family of rice and lentil soup or stew, khichdi is the godfather of the family. Over the millennia, the combination hasn't changed much. When mung beans replace the lentils, it is called dal kichri. When the substitute is pearl millet, it becomes dal bajra.

All of the cousins welcome warming spice additions on cold nights. Chili peppers, garlic, ginger, and turmeric enter the single pot preparation. Conversely, sides of cooling yogurt or raita appear most often during hot weather. Other flavorings include curry leaves, cumin seeds, and bay leaves heated in ghee. Papadoms often accompany the khichdi.

The government of India proposed that khichdi be anointed the national dish. Opponents argued that it was far too mundane and would lessen India's international prestige. The yeas beat the nays.

When babies in India graduate from liquids to solids, khichdi leads the way.

Kiaulės ausis are Lithuanian pig ears. One unusually warm day in Vilnius, we walked many miles up and down tiny alleys and through parks. In a Russian Orthodox Church we listened to a heavenly choir practice. But towards afternoon's end, I was dragging and whining. We stumbled into a neighborhood bar and ordered cold beers. The place was jammed with young office workers snacking and drinking a cold draft on their way home from work when sunset and the evening meal were still several hours away that far north. We squeezed into the last two seats, surrounded by happy people snacking on either fried strips of pig's ears or fingers of rye bread fried in garlic and butter and served with delicious nutty caraway cheese and marinated olives. You guessed it. I ordered the ears, Joan the bread and cheese. We each had a mug of yeasty local beer. The ears were a medley of textures, crispy on the outer edge, chewy from the cartilage and nearly jelly-like in between. The flavor was basically that of any fried bit with a hint of bacon. Over the subsequent days in Vilnius and Riga, we saw an impressive array of pig offal fried parts as beer snacks, usually including similarly prepared ears. In one restaurant, whole boiled ears were served with horseradish, beet salad, and boiled potatoes.

Fergus Henderson, the Godfather of nose to tail offal cuisine, serves up his famous split pea soup made with smoked pig's ears in his London restaurant, St. John.

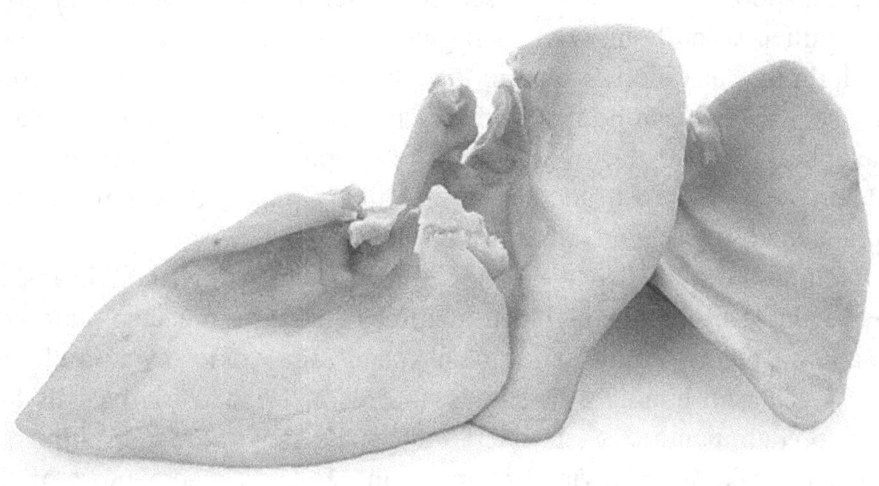

Pig Ears

Kishka Kishke is a Slavic word for intestine. Eastern European kishka is pig intestine filled with pig's blood and barley or oats. The Jewish version starts with cow's intestine, laboriously cleaned, cut into foot long tubes, stuffed loosely and sewn shut at the ends. The stuffing is bread or matzo crumbs and/or wheat flour, moistened with rendered fat, usually chicken fat, and seasoned with browned onions, salt, pepper, and paprika. The sausage-shaped tubes are then boiled for five or ten minutes before baking, roasting, or stewing. Out of the boil, their color ranges from pale grey to fall-foliage orange, depending on the amount of paprika inside. Roasting turns them mahogany. The chewy, yet crispy coat tastes like thicker browned turkey skin. Napped in rich brown gravy-yum.

I doubt that the reality of taste and texture of cow duodenum filled with monochromatic stuffing and roasted, can match the pleasurable memories and associated feelings I have for kishka.

Why does kishka matter? Because of what it represents. My father came to America as a boy of five from the Pale, an area south of the Baltic and north of the Black Sea that was home to the majority of Jews in Europe from the mid 1800's until the Holocaust. Kishka was only one of many Jewish peasant foods that kept the wolf of starvation at bay during the harsh winters. The ingredients were as dirt-cheap as his family was dirt-poor. It took hours to scrape and clean the inside-out intestine in a milieu when housewives struggled for more hours than there was daylight to wash clothes by hand, cook and bake, sew and mend coats and socks and clean houses with needy kids under foot. Kishka was a metaphor for hardship overcome. The simple substance sat front and center on the Sabbath and on other holiday plates. It was more than appreciated. It was a medal of pride.

If one were to map the major cities in which Jewish-style kishka was a staple in the late eighteen hundreds and early nineteen hundreds, Warsaw, Cracow, Vilnius, Kiev, Minsk, and Riga would stand out. It was also a staple in hundreds of shtetls, those small ghetto farm towns that were predominantly Jewish. The Pale was the area of Poland, Lithuania. Romania, Ukraine, Latvia, Bohemia, and Belarus where most of the world's Jews lived after expulsion eastward from Germany and Austria and westward from Russia. The kishka map tells the story of persecution and pogroms. It also reflects the imposed poverty of harsh discriminatory laws. The Jews of the Pale were called Ashkenazi (adjective) or Ashkenazim (plural noun). Denied the rights of owning land, of attending universities or becoming faculty, of owning businesses, or of engaging in finance, they became middlemen, tutors, teachers, musicians, bookkeepers, peddlers, and tenant farmers. Since Jews were segregated into ghettos in cities and shtetls in the countryside, their cuisine rarely reflected the national predilections of the food that Christians ate. Ashkenazi meals remained similar despite the diaspora and kishka reflected the history, segregation, religious dietary restrictions and poverty.

The Polish non-Jewish version, kiszka, is pork casings stuffed with pig's blood and starch. The German grützwurst, also called kaszanka or kiszka, like its Polish namesake, is another non-Kosher variant with pork blood and offal stuffing in porcine intestine. Silesia has alternately been part of Germany, Poland, and Czechoslovakia. Historically Silesians made their krupńok out of porcine casing stuffed with buckwheat, barley or rice, black pepper, marjoram, and onion. A food detective could surely discern the nationality and/or religion of a cook by her/his kishka.

When the Holocaust resulted in the murder of half the Jewish population in the world, the post World War II kishka map changed. No more Jewish-style kishka in any of the aforementioned cities. I have visited most of them and have yet to find a decent Ashkenazi restaurant with stuffed cow's intestine on the menu. In Kazimierz, the old Jewish ghetto in Kracow where Helena Rubinstein lived and parts of Schindler's List were filmed, there is a cluster of "traditional Jewish restaurants." None of them offer kishka. When I found one that served helzl, stuffed skin from a poultry neck, I ordered it, expecting traditional Ashkenazi stuffing. Disappointed by non-traditional ingredients, I asked the waiter about kishka. He was only aware of the Polish kind and pronounced, "It is made with pig's blood. We wouldn't serve it here." They did however have pork roast on the menu.

Simply mention the word kishka to an Ashkenazi Jew seventy or more years old and he or she is likely to whisper a nostalgic sigh, smile, and cast a glance skyward. The eyes follow memories of the food, grandma, and mama, family holidays, survival, and pure gustatory pleasure. The images soar above like phantasms in a Chagall painting.

There appears to be an Algerian dish called Mebbaur closely related to kishka. It is made up of calf derma stuffed with lamb served atop a bed of baby chickpeas drenched in a rich brown gravy .

Kishimen Guys who kish the girlsh a lot? Not much of a pun, even for me, but the name tickled my inner child's curiosity. It felt like part of a game and, circuitously, it is.

On one of our trips to Japan, Joan and I flew into Nagoya to explore Kyushu, Sakurajima, and the Samurai homes and gardens in Chiron. Before boarding the train south, we ate at a local noodle house. Nearly every dish on the menu contained the local favorite noodle, kishimen. White like udon, it is broader, flatter, and the edges are a little ruffled. Most fellow noodle slurpers ate kishimen in what looked and smelled like a soy sauce based soup. I opted for a plate of them in curry gravy. A fellow traveler was bilingual. I asked him about the name. He said it meant "go stone noodles" as in the smooth black or white stones used to play the Chinese board game of Go. Japanese can read Chinese pictographic writing even though the pronunciation is totally different, so he was able to offer the translation of the Chinese characters. He didn't know why the name was chosen, nor what it might represent. But he added that either hot or cold, dishes made with kishimen noodles are calming and satisfying. It is somewhat similar to Italian tagliatelle. I find all three, kishimen, tagliatelle, and udon soothing and satisfying , but I know of no Chinese noodle similar to kishimen.

Kokoda, pronounced *koh-kon-da,* is a Fijian take on the raw fish dish, ceviche. Kokoda is made with fresh fish soaked in lemon or lime juice, which 'cooks' the fish. Spring onions, red onion, chilies, sweet peppers, and tomatoes are regular additions, with the combination then soaked in coconut milk for a refreshing local fish dish. Kokoda is usually served as a starter and can come delivered in a coconut shell, bamboo, or even a pineapple.

Kolo mee In Kuching, Sarawak, we ate char siu (roast pork) over Chinese egg noodles for breakfast. Locals ate the same, called kolo mee, for breakfast, lunch, or dinner.

Koshari As India debated whether humble rice and lentils, khichdi, was worthy of designation as the national dish, Egypt followed a similar path, albeit without controversy. A kihchdi look alike, koshari, became Egypt's national dish. To the rice and lentil mix, koshari adds noodles, garlic, vinegar, chick peas, spicy (clove and chili peppers) tomato sauce, and a topping of fried onion.

Koshari

Falafel may be an add on. It usually remains a vegetarian dish. An exception may be combining it with schwarma.

Koshari, also spelled koshary or kushari, appears on virtually every Egyptian table, at home or in restaurants. Originally from Persia during or before the Middle Ages, it became popular in many parts of the Arab world. Name changes with location include salatet ruzz wa adas in North Africa, mjadarah in Palestine, and mudardara in Syria.

The dish is considered so humble, an Arab cook will generally not offer it to a guest unless the guest requests it.

A common street sound emanates from a spoon clanging the bottom of a metal bowl in Cairo. It is the koshari man, calling diners to his cart. Restaurants that feature koshari, typically serve it with a carbonated non-alcoholic drink, and a dessert of rice pudding, ruzz bil-laban .

Kratom leaves The leaves of this member of the coffee tree family have been chewed, brewed into tea, or swallowed as a powder for decades in Southeast Asia. In low doses, they are a mild stimulant. In high doses, they sedate, reduce pain and, at times, produce a euphoric high that comforts teenagers. Unfortunately, studies have not been done to assess safety, addictive potential, use in pregnancy, or interaction with active pharmaceuticals. It may become a useful agent in treating opiate withdrawal. It is not illegal, but the FDA has not yet weighed in on its safety. Teens suffering from side effects are starting to show up in hospital emergency departments. Proponents in Thailand think it is safe in moderate doses used less often than daily and not addicting

Kreplach Kreplach have been labeled the Jewish versions of Chinese wontons or Italian tortellini. Similarly, they are filled pasta packets, boiled, and usually served in hot chicken soup or broth. There is no commonality beyond that. The wrapper is thicker than wontons, the size larger than tortellini, the shape triangular, and the filling, Slavic rather than Asian or Mediterranean. Traditionally they are filled with ground or minced beef and, less often, with mashed potatoes. Mom bought cow's heart and lung for pennies, ground them, added onions, salt, pepper, an egg or two to bind, and a dusting of flour to make the filling. She boiled them in chicken broth.

On other occasions, she made the meat-free version with sweet cheese inside. Boiled or fried, we ate them with a topping of sour cream.

Mom usually made kreplach when she made her standard offal stew, since so many of the ingredients were common to both. We ate the kreplach in chicken soup the day they were prepared. She braised chunks of heart, lung, and spleen in rendered fat, added onions, garlic, potato quarters, carrots, and celery and simmered the lot in a quart of water until all the components were tender. Into the refrigerator (we graduated from the icebox when I was a toddler) it went overnight. Mom removed the layer of hardened white fat from the surface and heated and thickened the stew with a dark roux before serving. She sent me across the street with a bowl of her stew for Natasha from Ukraine. Her husband Nikolai was away in Canada visiting his sick mother. Natasha couldn't drive, so Dad took her shopping until her husband returned two weeks later. She asked Dad and he told her that we did not keep kosher, that we ate pork. She reciprocated by sending over a metal bowl of Ukrainian salchison, a stew of pig ears, feet, liver, kidneys, stomach, heart, tongue, and blood loaded with garlic and onion. Susan was away at summer camp. The three of us ate it over two days and liked it. As we finished off the last bit of it, Mom oinked. Dad and I, amid raucous laughter, made it a trio pig noises.

In later, more affluent times, she stuffed the triangles with similarly seasoned ground beef and mushrooms. For Mom's and Dad's fiftieth wedding anniversary, I made kreplach for a party honoring them. The menu included brisket simmered for hours in carrots, onions, celery, parsnip, and fennel. I used part of the brisket, barely chopped in a blender with wild mushrooms and a little port, to fill kreplach. Yes they were sumptuous, but the overriding ingredient was nostalgia.

The wrapper dough consisted of two cups of flour, two eggs, a tablespoon of water and half teaspoon of salt, well kneaded until smooth. Rolled out to a thickness about twice that of a wonton wrapper, the sheets were cut into three inch squares, filled with a teaspoon of the meat mixture, and folded over to form a triangle.

Italian cooks brought the two widest tips together to make the same belly button shape of tortellini. The edges were pressed together with the tines of a fork and sealed with a little water. Mom boiled kreplach in salted water for about twenty minutes, drained them in a colander and reheated them in chicken broth before serving. She always garnished with chopped parsley.

Dad liked the cold leftover kreplach with sour cream, a meat and milk mixture he would have eschewed had he cared about kosher laws. He characterized his religion as "proselytizing atheist," despite his orthodox upbringing. Yet he waxed eloquent about the grandeur of high-holiday tradition, culture, and cuisine. It was emblematic of the journeys from near starvation to happy family banquets, from insular shtetl dogma to cosmopolitan higher education, from paranoid isolationism to ecumenical humanism.

Kreplach preparation is a labor intensive task, but never too difficult to make for Rosh Hashana, the Jewish New Year, or for the somber celebration meal at the end of Yom Kippur's 24-hour fast. The formerly indispensable regal additions to holiday chicken soup have all but disappeared from the culture. A few decades ago, I was served hamburger in store-bought won ton skins in chicken soup at a Purim dinner in Budapest. The cook proudly misrepresented her packets as kreplach.

Kuching When we went to the capital of Sarawak on the island of Borneo, we were determined to learn why it was the city of cats and even had a cat museum. We discovered what many already knew, that the city was named not after a feline, but an edible fruit, mata kucing. It is first cousin to a lychee and a member of the same soapberry family. We know the fruit as longan. In Mandarin, lóng yǎn literally means eye of the dragon. The pale fruit the size of a small plum has nearly translucent yellow flesh inside its thin coat surrounding a jet black round central pit. It really does look like an eyeball. So the fruit can be referred to as cat's eye fruit as well as mata kucing. It is sweeter and less watery than lychee, but also comes in cans with syrup and becomes part of East Asian soups and puddings. The addition adds a mellow sweet component. The cat museum was only marginally interesting.

Kummerspeck Literally, Kummer is grief and Speck is bacon. Since everything goes better with bacon, even bacon, does this fascinating word imply that grief also goes better with bacon? No. Grief, sadness, loss, emotional pain of any sort seldom spares appetite in its complexity of visceral manifestations. Many lose the desire to eat anything, but others eat everything in what pop psychologists' term a desire to bury all feelings under a distended stomach. Such grief responders who attempt to find comfort in food, gain weight, which the German language artfully describes as Kummerspeck.

L

Lancashire hot pot As Joan discovered twice, you absolutely must not order Turkish coffee in a Greek restaurant. I wonder if the same holds true of not ordering Irish stew in a British pub. When we had Irish stew at home during our leaner years, Mom simmered mutton neck, onions, carrots and potatoes in a covered pot for several hours. At times, she added barley to make it thicker and more filling, as she also did with canned mushroom soup. When the meat became fork tender, we ate it with crusty bread to mop up the bottom of the bowl. Her choice of thyme, salt, pepper, and parsley kept it simple. The flavors were more than adequate. It was most comforting on a winter's eve.

Lancastershire hot pots

When I began making my own, I roasted lamb bones with onions, carrots and celery until they were dark brown and boiled the lot to make lamb broth. Mutton became harder to find so I switched to lamb necks and sometimes added kidneys. The stew often went into a slow oven when I had errands to run.

When I went looking for proper London pub food, a friend insisted that I try Lancashire Hot Pot. The name was new to me and sounded intriguing. The cook ladled me a bowl from a large covered pot in the oven. Surprise! It was classic Irish stew made with lamb necks, onions, carrots, and potatoes and seasoned with thyme, parsley, salt, and pepper. I asked my friend if it were typical of Lancashire Hot Pot and he nodded. "Sometimes cooks add kidneys or barley."

Lasagna in Italy taught me once again that less could be much better than more. Less cheese, less sauce, more flavor. More satisfying.

The American version too often buries everything under inches of commercial rubbery mozzarella. Underneath, sheets of pre-cooked pasta dry out during baking and curl along the edges.

Between layers of pasta, enough ground hamburger meat to fill a Big Mac tastes only of salt and oregano. The tomato sauce soaks everything and fills a shallow pool under the lasagna. The portion size is about twice the volume of a self-respecting pasta course in Italy. Ricotta fills the interstices, but I have seen it replaced by ordinary cottage cheese, particularly in vegetarian versions, as some mistaken attempt at better health.

The only two American variations on the lasagna theme are meatless vegetarian with vegetables between layers, and Tex-Mex, where tortillas replace the pasta, the dominant flavor is jalapeño, and the cheese is salty fresh Mexican. The Tex-Mex dish is not bad, but not hardly lasagna.

Many American cooks treat lasagna as a receptacle for leftovers. Italian cooks cringe at the thought.

By comparison, Italian lasagna varies by region. The pasta is fresh, paper thin, tender, and delicate. The light sauce uniquely complements the other ingredients. Meat varies by region, but is high end. The mozzarella is carefully thinly sliced fresh buffalo balls that add texture without suffocating the delicacy beneath it. The edges are straight and clean, the underside moist but not swimming in a pool of anything, and the portion does not preclude a subsequent meat or fish course.

Creamy béchamel often alternates space between layers, transforming the texture and richness of the whole dish. That is particularly true of the lasagna of Emilia-Romagna in the sophisticated trend-setting north, with its meaty Bolognese sauce between one pair of layers, and the béchamel between another pair. Surprise. Green lasagna made by adding spinach to the dough, is common in traditional Emilia-Romagna. Green pastas are otherwise uncommon in Italy.

The other end of spectrum from Genoa, Liguria, is lasagna that is tomato free and is either very lightly baked or not baked at all. Piccage, as it is called, layers hot thin lasagna sheets with freshly made pesto.

Perhaps the richest variety is from Marches. No paucity of flavor, fat, and calories when they combine most or even all of these ingredients: chicken livers, cream, Marsala, mozzarella, sweetbreads, truffles, and veal ragout.

Less refined but maybe even more hardy is the Neapolitan version eaten during carnival time, layered generously with local pork sausage, tiny fried meatballs, fresh mozzarella, ricotta and hard-boiled eggs, and Neapolitan ragu, thinner but just as flavorful as Bolognese ragu.

In Langhe, Piemonte, lasagna al sangue is indeed bloody lasagna. One ingredient, unique to this area, is fresh pig's blood.

Lasagna da formel is a sweet buttery dessert dish served warm. In it are apples, figs, golden raisins, poppy seeds, and walnuts. You can find it in eastern Veneto. Sounds more Polish than Italian.

There are at least half a dozen more regional variations.

Le cigar volente Flying cigar is a slang expression for flying saucer in France. Many decades ago, with friend, fellow cardiologist, and student and author of viticulture, Robert Blumberg M.D., I helped create a food and wine event for the San Francisco Heart Association. Of the handful of fine boutique wineries that supported us most was Bonny Doon and its delightful and talented owner, Randall Grahm, nicknamed "the Rhône Ranger" as he sought to grow the perfect pinot noir in California's Santa Cruz Mountains. To my palate, he succeeded.

When the famous wine-producing town of Châteauneuf-du-Pape (new castle of the pope) in Côte de Rhône passed a local ordinance prohibiting flying cigars from landing in its vineyards, Grahm responded by naming his very nice red table wine "Le Cigar Volente". He also had a restaurant by the same name in Santa Cruz for 25 years that closed at the end of 2012. The annual Heart Association event, "Celebrate with Heart", is still going strong.

Innovative acclaimed Australian vintner, Charles Melton created a blend in the1980s that has become a lasting favorite. He dubbed his mix of Shiraz, Grenache, and Mataro grapes "9 Popes". Neuf can mean new or nine in older dialects. His 2010 vintage was off the charts.

Lijiang egg soup We are in the foothills of the Himalayas in southwestern China in Lijiang, home to the enchanting indigenous Naxi people. Only once are our language skills and pantomimes inadequate. We wander into a charming traditional restaurant in which the small staff speaks Dongba, a dialect I can't begin to grasp, and they don't comprehend my minimalist Mandarin. A group of about a dozen diners are on the way out as we enter. The remnants of a lavish banquet are being cleared from the table. All the dishes I recognize are available only for banquets. After a frustrating few minutes of charades, the waitress leads me into the kitchen and gives me a small bowl and a pair of chopsticks. The chef takes me from pot to pot and ladles samples from each into my bowl for me to taste. I nod approvingly at my two favorites. Before exiting the kitchen he has me taste a spoonful of aromatic mushroom vegetable soup. "Tang hao shi," the soup is delicious, I utter. This bit of Mandarin he understands and beams. He then booms out his only word of English, **EGG**, as he holds a brown chicken egg between his thumb and forefinger. "Egg," I repeat and he laughs with unbridled pleasure. He sends my two choices to the table in gargantuan quantities. We eat well beyond satiety to please the nodding staff. We have passed the point of comfort but don't want to offend. Then comes an entire tureen of steaming mushroom vegetable soup with what appears to be a ten-egg omelet floating on top. Oh, the pain.

We walk twice around the market to diminish the bloat before heading back to our room. As we pass the poultry section, my wife points to a full wicker basket. EGG, she booms. We howl with laughter and embrace, bloated belly to bloated belly. Tears roll down our cheeks.

Lovers' hotpot North American barbecue mavens can taste a dish and know where the chef learned his trade. Similarly, you can taste hot-pots all over China and know from which regional cuisine they emanate. Seafood – Canton. Mutton – Mongolia. Hot and numbing – Sichuan. Fire hot and not numbing with garlic overtones – Hunan.

The most popular chicken dish in Hunan province, dong anzi chicken, was so hot the one time I ate it, that my taste buds numbed so much, I never really tasted the chicken. I love hot spicy foods be they Indian, Korean, Mexican, Thai, Emirati, or Peruvian, but many dishes in Hunan exceed my comfort limit and mask my ability to taste some wonderful ingredients like eel, turtle, tender lamb, fragrant mushrooms, shallots, and chestnuts. One saving grace is that Hunan "love hot pot" usually comes in a divided dish – only half of which is incendiary. The hot side is supposedly for males, the less painful side for females. Crossovers are not a problem for foreigners.

Yuānyāng huǒguō is the menu name of the hot pot found in restaurants all over Yunnan. Many represent standard Chongqing or Sichuan style, while others feature Yunnan ham, goose broth, mutton, or beef. The prize, however, should go the mushroom hotpots served in specialty restaurants some of which are only open during winter months.

If you visit the hanging monastery up near the border with Inner Mongolia, try Datong hotpots that are like other hotpots in principle but not design. They are traditionally ornate, tin-lined copper pots that arrive individual or group size. The spicy broth simmers the impressive array of thinly sliced meats and veggies that the diner adds. Mutton is the dominant meat.

Bahang chicken hotpot stews cut up pieces of a rooster in sour soup, bahang in Zhuang language. Local fermented rice vinegar adds both sour tones and many additional layers of nuance beyond those of most other vinegars.

Lumpfish Lump, lump, what lump? Do you remember the hunchback played by Marty Feldman and his hysterically funny line in Young

Frankenstein "Hump, hump, what hump?" Well the lump on the underside of lumpfish is actually paired and fused pelvic fins that have evolved into an adhesive sucking appendage, not just a lump. Another name for the fish is lumpsucker.

One of my favorite hors d'oeuvres is anything but typical comfort food because of the price. The only thing in Iceland that didn't seem overpriced a few decades ago was the lumpfish caviar. It is quite popular in Scandinavia and has become an acceptable more affordable substitute for sturgeon roe. The little glob of a fish remarkably travels huge distances to spawn in a body that is anything but sleek. When I serve tiny bowls of finely diced sweet onion, egg yolks, egg whites, and toast points with caviar, my preference is to pile on enough caviar so the add-ons don't mask the marvelous flavor of the caviar itself. Comfort food? Yes, when the precious eggs are more affordable.

Lu pulu I knew first hand that Hawaiians and Koreans still eat and seem to enjoy canned Spam, but in Tonga, the locally popular comforting dish of canned New Zealand corned beef steamed in a taro leaf packet really surprises me. When taro leaves are scarce, large leaves of spinach substitute. The corned beef on a bed of half a dozen taro leaves receives a topping of diced onion and tomato and is then moved onto a foil bed placed in a shallow pool of coconut milk. Some cooks also surround it with mayonnaise. The foil is sealed and baked. If taro rather than spinach is used, the baking has to last for at least a few hours. Wow! Not my favorite fusion ingredients, but Tongans love their lu pulu.

Lung, liver, and spleen sandwiches Palermo in Sicily is high among my favorite offal meccas. A street side cooking crew across from the docks in Palermo, near the famous Vucciria market, cooks for a horde of hungry workers at lunch time lifting fatty slabs of mixed organ meats from caldrons of shiny dark cooking juices and serving them on fresh baguettes with a wedge of lemon and a shake of salt. A block away, a vendor serves milza, thin strips of bovine spleen deep-fried and served with a slice of cheese on a hard roll. It is greasier and tastier than the stewed spleen my mother served us in childhood. The Yiddish word for it was similar, miltz.

Street vendors fry lamb innards over smoky charcoal fires in neighboring town squares. A dish that tastes far better than it looks is one of my favorites.

Capozelle is half a lamb's head, rubbed with garlic, oregano, salt, and olive oil and roasted in an oven with the flat side down on a pan. The presence of an eye and rows of teeth are the features that drive away the visually challenged. Those of us who are stout of heart and stomach savor the flavor of the masseter muscles of the cheek, rendered tender by hours of cooking, as the premier cut of lamb along with the tenderloin, and appreciate the flavor of the brains that remain moist and tasty because of the infusion of juices and flavors that bathe them during cooking.

I truly love taste and texture akin to impoverished childhood memories. Praised be the concept of nose-to-tail. Apologies as alwas to vegan readers.

M

Maccu The most common cheap belly fillers in Sicily during and after World War II were similar combinations of beans, pasta, rice, and bread served in soups and stews. Maccu (or Macco), a very old peasant standby comfort food for centuries was one of those belly fillers. It is a purée or mash of fava beans, seasoned with onion and/or garlic sautéed in olive oil and wild fennel seeds, cooked in meat or chicken broth or salted water. The soup has a distinctive flavor similar to a rich anise scented roasted chestnut purée. It was traditionally made from dried fava beans, which probably have a shelf life of decades. They look and feel like solid oak lima beans with darker acorn colored husks. They have to be soaked overnight and peeled before they are mashed and used for soup. Leftover pasta, rice, or stale bread cubes were often added, as well as chicory or other greens. Maccu disappeared essentially entirely from restaurants and even from homes as a modicum of prosperity returned in the fifties and sixties. It seems that everyone wanted to forget the hard hungry bygone days. Memories of pain and death overrode the history of comfort. With the passage of time, nostalgia for the dish has risen to the fore. Maccu is reemerging as an old standard, as authentic, Sicilian cuisine has had a resurgence in fine eateries.

Maksalaatikko What's in your Christmas pudding? Does it matter as long as it is tasty and comforting? In Finland, if it's maksalaatikko, your pudding is made of ground liver, along with rice, raisins, honey, and eggs, served with lingonberry jam, loved by adults and despised by school kids when they find it in their lunch boxes. Some ingredients elicit universal responses. The pudding is fine. Liver can be awful when overcooked, bone dry, and metallic. Properly prepared or concealed in yummy pudding it is OK.

When I first heard the suffix of word spoken, I thought the speaker knew I lived in Costa Rica, Tico land, and was offering to make us a Costa Rican salad.

Mandu Dumplings are a common appetizer or side dish in most Asian restaurants, but the Korean version is called jjin mandu and is usually filled with a meat mixture (pork and beef though some versions feature shrimp), onions, cabbage, carrots, mung bean noodles, or other complementary ingredients. They can be steamed, boiled, or fried; and are usually served with a variety of sweet, spicy, and savory sauces for dipping. The result is super soft, juicy pillows of flavor.

Afghani mandu or mantu in Kabul, are steamed dumplings filled with chopped mutton, garlic, and onion and topped with yogurt-vegetable dressing or green parsley and pepper dipping sauce. Near our former home in San Rafael, California, Joan and I often ate at Bamyan, an Afghani restaurant. My favorite dish was mandu, a plate of simmered dumplings filled with spicy ground lamb and topped with yogurt.

One afternoon in Seoul, we were caught in a cloudburst. We ducked into a dumpling café and ordered tea and a steamer basket of very similar dumplings. Their menu name was mantoo. Why are the disparate nations of Afghanistan and Korea wed by the mandu or mantu connection? It took me many months, but I had to find out. Whether eaten with fingers, forks, or chopsticks, mandu are bite-sized, dough-wrapped packets of seasoned ground meat. They are simmered in Kabul and served with yogurt and vegetables, and steamed in a basket in Seoul and served with a spicy dipping sauce. Around the globe, savory meats wrapped in a panoply of doughs are baked into little pies, fried into fritters, boiled or steamed into dumplings, and rolled into blintzes to the specifications of local palates. Consider wontons, empanadas, fritters, *crêpes*, filo triangles, and ravioli as variations on the same marvelous theme. The ingredients are so similar, and the morsels are so deliciously different. The origin of the word mandu seems to be mantou, an old term from the lamb and mutton eating regions of northern China. In ancient times it was the name for a packet of meat stuffed into a casing of sheep intestine somewhat akin to sausage or kishka. If we look for similar names, mandoo, mantu, or manti, we find them in the kitchens of Central Asia, Eastern Europe,

North Africa, and the Middle East. There seems to be a pattern. The meat-filled dumplings with similar sounding names survive to this day in many of the major cities along both the northern and southern arms of the ancient Silk Road that connected China and Eastern Europe.

From Northeast China, Korea received religion, ceramics, ink paintings, and delicious dumplings. Dumplings from China called mantu are even mentioned in the Koran. In Ankara, the same dumplings were called by their Silk Route name, manti, and when they migrated south, down the Arabian Peninsula and across North Africa, they were mandu. Superimpose the waves of conquest by Mongols, Islamic armies, the Ottoman Turks, and the mandu connection reached from Siberia to southern India, and from the Sea of Japan to the Atlantic.

The old word has new meanings, which can cause confusion. In Northern China, mantou is now the name of steamed wheat flour yeast buns sans filling. In Malaysia, mandu is a sweet or chocolate filled pastry rolled into a pinwheel pattern unrelated to our mandu. And Kathmandu has nothing to do with meat or dough. Kath means wood and mandu means temple. Thus the capitol city of Nepal is named after an ancient temple believed to have been hewn from a single giant tree. A rarely used word in our own language, manducate, means to chew. It comes from a Latin root and is probably unrelated to our mandu.

Eastern European and Central Asian borek (burek, bourek, boorak, boreg) share the same thin dough as Turkish manti. Similar, but a little thicker is the wrapper for Russian and Polish pirogi. Thinner dough brought us filo in every conceivable shape filled with everything from lamb to nuts.

The worldwide mandu family tree contains all of the cousins from countries contained in alphabetical order below, and many more that some of you surely can add.

The French elevate the art of preparing simple stuffed purses, pockets, and pies to typical culinary heights with the incorporation of bone marrow, brains, sweetbreads, tongues, and liver from several species. Although better known for his novels, Alexander Dumas wrote this description in his "Dictionary of Cuisine" 150 years ago, about the most extravagant of all mandus: "Heliogabalus, that emperor who came from Syria and entered Rome on a chariot drawn by naked women, had a historian just to describe his meals. He never had a meal that cost less than sixty gold marks (about $25,000). He had pies made of the tongues of peacocks, nightingales, crows, and parrots." Not quite four and twenty blackbirds.

One blissful evening in St. Petersburg we ate an early dinner at an Uzbeki restaurant near our apartment. Nineteen people sat at table festooned with flowers. Two additional seats remained empty. It was a twenty-first birthday celebration for Annitshka. Local custom dictated that the gathering be of the same number of guests as years. We were invited by the host to replace the two no-shows. What a delight. Two of the other guests spoke a little English and kept us involved as celebrants. The menu included the largest of all giant meat-filled dumplings. Called manti, they were served in chicken broth. We passed on the vodka but did join in a champagne toast. Before dessert came we had to excuse ourselves to get to the opera before the curtain rose on Aida at the Mariinsky Theater. The entire gathering bestowed cheek kisses on us as we thanked them for a memorable event and rushed out the door. How large is the mandu connection? Behold this nearly everlasting list:

1) Afghani mandu or mantu. In Kabul, steamed dumplings are filled with chopped mutton or lamb, garlic, and onion and topped with yogurt-vegetable dressing or green parsley and pepper dipping sauce.

Baked bichak. These baked triangles can be filled with berries and preserves, farmer's cheese, and egg yolk or the same savory ground mutton or lamb, garlic, and chopped onions combination as the steamed dumpling.

2) African chopone-choptwo. These sub-Saharan open-ended baked tubes are filled with a mixture of shredded mutton, onions, green and red peppers.

Curry meat triangles. Fried pastry triangles are filled with diced mutton or beef, onion, and curry powder.

3) Algerian samas. These are essentially the same filo filled cigars or triangles that the Moroccans call brewats and Sephardic Jews call betzels. They are ground lamb omelets flavored with cilantro and parsley leaves, garlic, and onion.

Marik. These are a cross between a *crêpe* and a pancake. The filling is a mixture of browned ground meat and onions, seasoned with cumin and nutmeg, and mixed with yogurt. A spoonful is placed in the middle of the thin pancake, which has been lightly browned on only one side. The bottom is folded up and the sides are folded over like a baby's blanket, cooked side in. The outside is then buttered and baked until crisp. They are sometimes served with a garlicky fresh salsa of tomato, onion, and cilantro.

4) Armenian lehmejun. Despite protests from Greek and Italian "authorities," these may be the original pizza pies. Flat circles of yeast dough are baked with a topping of ground lamb or beef, chopped tomatoes, parsley, garlic, and onion, seasoned with allspice and red and black pepper.

5) Austrian Fleish Palatschinken. Austria, France, and Hungary all claim original creation of pancakes. In fact, they seem to have come from ancient Egypt. Roman legions brought them to Rumania. They didn't explode onto the tables of the rest of Europe until the seventeenth century. They are filled with browned beef or pork, flavored with garlic, onion and/or caraway seeds.

6) Bosnian filo meat pies. Baked triangular flag-folded buttered sheets of filo encase finely ground lamb and chopped onion mixture and are seasoned with allspice and lemon juice.

7) Brazilian empadas. These baked pies may contain chicken, peas, olives, garlic, potatoes, hot peppers, chopped parsley, and onion. In Portuguese, the diminutive is empadinhas.

8) Central and South American empanadas. These baked or fried pies of beef, may also contain raisins, chopped olives, and hard-boiled egg. Instead of beef, empanadas sometimes substitute pork, chicken, rabbit, lamb, duck, goose, or even fish. There may be a vegetable component of spinach, broccoli, chard, corn, pepper, or potato, as well. The dough often contains lard and may be flavored and colored with oil made with achiote, curry, or paprika. When they are made bite-sized for hors d'oeuvres, they are called empanaditas or empandillas. In Costa Rica, Joan's and my favorites are cornmeal empanadas filled with savory beef and deep-fried.

Pasteles. These are pies made of pastry dough or yeast dough, either of which may be seasoned with curry oil or powder. The tops may be covered, latticed, or open. They also have a variety of fillings. Some popular combinations are ham and cheese, fish and chard, and meat and corn. The small ones are pastelitos.

9) Chilean caldudas. The name is derived from caldo, broth. The empanada most favored in Chile is filled with remarkably soft and moist cubed or ground beef that is boiled in broth until nearly all the broth has evaporated or been absorbed by the meat. Olives, raisins, onions and hard-boiled eggs are included. Oregano and red pepper add zest. The pastry dough contains a little vinegar. An egg wash is painted on before baking to glaze the fist-sized pastry.

10) Chinese wontons. The filling is a blended coarse paste of pork, shrimp, egg white, ginger, green onion, radish, soy, sugar, and rice wine. They are boiled and added to soup, or deep fried and eaten as finger food.

Shiu mei. The literal translation is "cook and sell." These bite sized steamed dumplings have an open top that may be decorated with a single green pea or small carrot shaving. The filling is ground fatty pork usually combined with ground chicken or shrimp, diced water chestnuts, ginger, and green onion.

Dumplings. After shiu mei, har gow (shrimp and egg filled), and fan gor (pork and mushroom filled) are the two most common of several dozen different Canton style dim sum dumplings. Others contain chicken, ground fish, chopped garlic chives, beef, crab, scallops, cabbage, mushrooms, tofu, wood ears, spinach, and water chestnuts

Spring roll. Simple dough made from flour, water, egg, and salt is rolled thin and wrapped, closed on the ends, around a combination of ground pork, shrimp, ham strips, chicken, black mushrooms, carrot sticks, green onions, water chestnuts, cilantro, celery, and bean sprouts.

Peking duck. Dried duck is lacquered with brown sugar-saltwater, glazed with maltose, and air-dried again before roasting. Small thin pancakes are brushed with a little sesame oil. They are painted with hoisin sauce. Thinly sliced pieces of duck skin and slivered green onion are sandwiched into the centerfold of each pancake and eaten.

Curry turnovers. Flaky lard pastries in the shape of hand sized half circles are filled with browned curry beef, pork, or chicken.

Mu shu pork. Thin pancakes are wrapped around stir-fried pork strips, bamboo shoots, bean sprouts, mushrooms, wood ear, scallions, and ginger. Hoisin sauce is spread in a thin coat inside the pancake.

Steamed and baked baos. Slightly sweetened dough balls are filled with barbecued pork, ginger, and onions; chicken and hardboiled egg; or shrimp and vegetables.

Xinjiang style pancakes. Slices of roast lamb are wrapped in corn or wheat flour pancakes.

Lop cheong bao. Sweet sausages wrapped in a blanket of the sweet white dough used in bao recipes are steamed. The result is a fluffy white cylinder, with a nubbin of sausage sticking out of each end. My two favorite brands of lopcheong come from Vancouver, British Columbia and Alajuela, Costa Rica. I was surprised by the latter.

Kwo tieh, guo tier. These are pot stickers. They are filled with ground pork, green onion, ginger, and cabbage. The round wrapper is filled, folded and crimped along the free edge. The rounded side is flattened a little, and it is browns in oil on a griddle or in a wok. Broth or water drizzles over the top. It cooks covered. The rest of the dumpling is thereby steamed to completion. A traditional dipping sauce contains combinations of black vinegar or rice vinegar, soy sauce, sesame or red pepper oil, shredded ginger, and rice wine.

11) Cornish pasties. These coal miners' baked meat pies from Cornwall, England, baked from pie crust dough filled with pork, beef or both, diced potatoes, sliced onions, and a choice or combination of turnips, carrots, or rutabagas. Folktales claim that the miners carried them in their pockets for lunch or snacks.

12) Czech knedlicky polevky. These liver dumplings are virtually identical to the jatrove below. It seems that all over former Bohemia and Moravia, no meal is complete without dumplings and gravy.

Morkove and jatrove. Boiled dumplings made from eggs, cream, and breadcrumbs derive their flavor from rosemary. The former are mixed with chopped bone marrow, the latter with chopped chicken, or calf liver. Very similar dumplings can be found in Austria and Germany.

Houskove knedlicky. Very similar to the previous breadcrumb dumpling, they are made with more bread and less meat, and simmered in the shape of hot dogs. This particular mixture combines crisp crumbled bacon, chopped onion, and parsley. The rolls are sliced and served with gravy or pan juices from roasts.

13) Ethiopian injera. It used to be a pancake made from fermented millet flour. Now it is often made with self-rising flour, water, and club soda. Small pieces are torn off and used to lift food from the bowls of stews such as doro wat, the chicken stew made with hard boiled eggs and onions, or from spicy lamb stew, or from mounds of beef tartare, which are mixed with diced sweet and hot peppers, chopped onion, and curry-like spices.

14) Filipino empanaditas. These baked pastry turnovers come filled with ground pork and chicken, sweet pickle relish, garlic, onions, tomatoes, and diced hard boiled eggs.

Fritong pinsec. These simulate fried Chinese wontons, with comparable filling. They differ in their triangular shape.

Lumpia. These small spring rolls are most commonly fried Shanghai style and dipped in a sweetened soy and pepper sauce. Fresh lumpia are prepared when thin rounds of dough are barely cooked on greased cookie sheets, removed while pliable, and placed on individual lettuce leaves, filled, folded, and eaten. The filling for either kind remain the same, but ingredients vary from island to island, and house to house. It usually contains chopped cooked pork and shrimp, and any combination of cabbage, potatoes, yams, garbanzos, hearts of palm, water chestnuts, green beans, carrots, and onions. Lumpia are often served with a dipping sauce made from thickened chicken broth seasoned with sugar, garlic, soy sauce, and fish sauce.

15) Finnish kalakukko. Fish baked in pastry.

Vendace. Pork and fish baked in rye dough. With Saint Petersburg so close to Helsinki, Russian dumplings are also ubiquitous.

16) French crêpes au jamon or à la saucisse. These crêpes fill with ham or sausage.

Bouchee de ris de veau, or de foie gras, or de langue. These walnut sized cups of puff pastry may be filled with bits of sweetbreads, goose liver, beef tongue, smoked salmon, lobster, or any other delicacy.

Croûtes au foie gras. These hollowed out bread croustades or cubes may be filled with any one of dozens of meat treats, then buttered and baked to a golden brown This particular one is filled with puree of goose liver, with an aspic topping of reduced port or sherry. Expensive. Fab.

17) French Canadian meat pie. Pork, veal, and mashed potato pie flavored with cinnamon, oregano, sage, and thyme baked in a pie.

18) German sausage roll. These are as they sound.

Fleish Knodel. German dumplings employ flour, potatoes, yeast dough, breadcrumbs, or bread cubes as the starch base. They generally add into soup or stew. Beef, pork, or veal are sometimes ground, seasoned, browned, and added to the dough before boiling. The yeast dough variety are usually browned in butter rather than boiled.

19) Greek trigona kotopita. These filo triangles are filled with chicken pieces baked with herbs, grated cheese, and sometimes, sliced onion.

Kreatopitakia. This is the diminutive form of kreatopita, the large filo pie served to usher in Lent. It is filled with cubed lamb, and a combination chosen from small potatoes, carrots, onions, eggplant, rice, toast points, feta cheese, tomatoes, and hard-boiled eggs. The seasonings include any mix of oregano, cinnamon, nutmeg, thyme, allspice, garlic, mint, and parsley.

Burekia. This is another name for bite sized filo pies, filled with leftover combinations from the larger varieties.

20) Hungarian Hortbagyi palicsintak. Veal cubes and chopped onion are cooked in lard, and then thickened with sour cream. The mixture is wrapped in pancakes, and drizzled with a mixture of pan juices and sour cream, laced with paprika.

Bokolgny palicsintak. These pancakes are filled with ground cooked veal and chicken mixed with a thick sauce made from sour cream, flour, and beef broth, made orange by liberal amounts of paprika. The rolled, filled pancakes crisp and brown in butter, and receive a topping with the same sauce used on the inside.

Ham paliscintak. Pancakes spread with a layer of minced ham, egg yolks, and sour cream, fold into squares, dip consecutively in egg, flour, egg, and bread-crumbs, then brown in butter in a frying pan.

Majgomboc. Small dumplings of chopped chicken or calf's liver, onion, and parsley mixed with dough, boil in broth.

21) Indian samosas. These fried or baked pastry crescents or triangles are filled with a variety of potatoes, beans, lentils, vegetables, and occasionally, mutton or goat. The meat is ground, mixed with chopped onion and seasoned with the usual panoply of Indian spices and fresh ginger.

22) Indonesian martabak. A fried egg roll-like morsel fills with peppery ground beef, diced carrot, fried onion, and garlic flakes, and green onion, plus curry powder in Java.

Risolles solo. Originally a Dutch meat crêpe, it is seasoned to Indonesian spiciness, dipped in egg white, rolled in bread crumbs, and pan fried in butter until brown.

23) Iraqi boorak or booraq. Some are seasoned with cumin, cardamom, and cinnamon; others with allspice and pepper. The basic ingredient is ground lamb or beef. They are crimped into triangles or rolled like large egg rolls, then baked or fried.

Koobe. These dome shaped meat filled dumplings originate from the Kurdish region of northwest Iraq, and neighboring Syria, and Turkey. Burghul, the cracked wheat used throughout the Middle East, best known to us as the grain in tabooli, fills all sorts of ground lamb meatballs or loaves, mixed into the dough, adding additional texture and taste to these dumplings. To the ground meat or chicken, chopped onions, diced celery, tomato paste, and uncooked rice may be added. Seasonings vary from simple salt and pepper, to allspice, clove, red pepper, and garlic.

24) Italian meat tortellini, ravioli, cannelloni, and calzone. These little twisted dumplings, square pasta packets, stuffed pasta tubes, and baked half-moon pies are so common in Italian- American cooking that further description is unnecessary.

25) Japanese gyoza. They look like and are cooked like Chinese pot stickers. The filling is usually made from ground pork, shredded cabbage, a hint of ginger, and minced garlic chive. They can be dipped in a thin sauce of soy, and sweet sake (mirin), or served in soup. Although they can be steamed or boiled, they are most often browned on the flat bottom away from the fluted edge, then doused in broth in the skillet or on the griddle and covered to steam through the upper portion.

26) Jewish kreplach. These boiled dumplings, originally filled with chopped organ meats such as cow's lung, spleen, liver, and heart, arrive floating in soup. Because of Kosher prohibition against mixing meat and dairy products, they were seldom served with sour cream, or browned in butter as were their first cousins, Uzbekistani dushpera, Russian pelmeny, and Polish pierogi.

Meat blintzes. Blintzes, filled crêpes with tucked-in ends, like egg rolls, typically brown in chicken fat or oil, but occasionally bake in the oven. They are usually filled with cottage and/or farmer's cheese mixed with egg, alone, or in combination with berries or jams. These non-meat varieties brown in butter and top with sour cream The meat filled variety contain the same combinations of meats as knishes (see below), or simple ground beef. My grandmother used to brown them in rendered chicken fat and omit milk from the crêpe batter.

Knishes. Long before they appeared in deli cases, the size and consistency of baseballs, and were nuked to death in a microwave, they were baked bite-sized meat-filled jewels passed on trays with drinks before dinner at weddings and bar mitzvahs. The meat was typically ground beef, calves' liver, or chicken liver, often flavored with black pepper and ground onion. Usually the dough was simple pastry dough. Sometimes, however, the meat was encased in a mixture of mashed potato and oil, then dipped in flour, egg wash, and flour again before browning in a skillet, like a fritter.

26) Jordanian and Lebanese sambusak. These meat-filled fried triangles filled with ground lamb and onion, taste of allspice, salt, and red pepper.

Sheesh boraq. These thimble shaped dumplings filled with ground lamb, cilantro or flat leaf parsley, and pine nuts, flavored with cinnamon and garlic, brown under the broiler, then finish in a pot of barely simmering yogurt, butter, beaten eggs, garlic, and mint. Served in a shallow bowl sitting in the sauce, an entire platter of them in Aleppo in northern Syria, disappeared. Joan and I devoured every last one.

27) Korean mandu. Separated egg whites used along with pure white flour in the dough give it a silvery sheen, when they are steamed. The yolks are added to the variable combinations of beef, ginger, garlic, green onions, Chinese garlic chives, bean sprouts, tofu, sesame seeds, sesame oil, and kimchi. They may be dipped in vinegar, sesame oil, and soy sauce. Served in chicken broth, they are called manduguk. Like Chinese pot stickers or Japanese gyoza, they can be fried on one side then covered and steamed in a little broth or water. Those are called goon mandu.

28) Latvian piragi. These bite sized baked meat pastries, look and taste a lot like the Jewish knishes described above. The difference is that these are traditionally made from ground pork browned in bacon drippings.

29) Libyan bestil. These are similar to the potato-fritter style of Jewish knish. The Libyan variety more typically taste of cinnamon and citrus, and may be browned in butter.

30) Mexican tacos. No explanation necessary.

Nachitoches. Baked beef, pork, and onion pies

31) Moroccan brewat, briouat, or bariwat. These fried or baked filo rolls are filled with a ground lamb, parsley, cilantro, and scrambled eggs, seasoned with cinnamon, cumin, and turmeric.

Pastels. These are similar to the above, but a thicker dough than filo is used.

Burek. These are another variety of filo pie, larger than brewats and pastels, and smaller than bastilla. In these, the ground lamb mixes with cinnamon, allspice, garlic, and pine nuts, then bakes.

Bastilla, b'steeya, pasteeya, basteela, b'stilla. The signature dish of Moroccan cuisine is this large filo pigeon pie made by alternating layers of beaten eggs simmered in chicken broth until curd-like, toasted almonds, and cinnamon-sugar, and boned, skinned pigeon or chicken. The filo leaves are buttered. The baked pie is dusted with confectionery sugar.

Khobz bishemar. Rectangular packets of dough filled with beef fat, red peppers, cumin, onion, parsley, pan fried in butter.

32) Polish nalesniki. These pancakes are folded over spicy diced mushrooms, meat, or both.

Meat pierogi. The staple Polish dumpling, filled with dozens of different ingredients from mushrooms, to farmers cheese with raw egg, to cabbage, to potato, to sauerkraut, to savory ground meat, sometimes in combination, delite millions of Poles. Caraway seeds or dill seeds add the types of flavoring that make them so typically Slavic.

33) Portuguese empadas. The dough combines flour, cornmeal, and lard. The meat filling may be pork, mutton, beef, or spicy sausage. Unfortunately, it is more likely to be the ever present bacalhau, reconstituted dried codfish, delicious in all its hundreds of forms to native Portuguese and to those few foreigners who have undergone genetic alteration.

34) Russian pelmeni. Boiled dumplings filled with seasoned minced pork or beef, serve up in soup or with sour cream, or appear fried and topped with melted butter.

Pirozhki. These deep fried ovals about the size of a potato filled with ground meat and chopped hard boiled eggs, with or without mushrooms and cabbage, sometimes pair with hot sweet mustard.

Bliny. We are most familiar with these delicate buckwheat yeast pancakes when they are folded with a dab of sour cream and caviar on top, sometimes with pinches of hard-boiled egg forced through a sieve and finely diced chive. Bliny may also be spread with butter and folded over smoked white fish or paper-thin smoked meat.

35) Samarkand dushpera. These pasta tubes stuffed with spicy ground meat were native to ancient Persia.

36) Saudi and Emirati sambusak. Typical of Middle Eastern fried meat triangles, they also contain chopped hard cooked egg whites, pine nuts, leeks, and cumin.

37) Siberian mutton manty. Boiled chopped mutton dumplings in piping hot soup, counter Siberian freezing temperatures. Dry manti with cracked pepper sprinkled on top appear less often.

38) Singaporean and Malaysian popiah. These modified pancake rolls of Chinese origin are among the most popular snack food in the hawker stalls and markets. Complex to assemble, the pancakes are first spread with a thick dark sauce that tastes like hoisin sauce spiced up with red pepper. Then a large lettuce leaf is laid flat and topped with variable combinations of thin match sticks of yam bean (jicima), bean sprouts, strips of fried tofu, long slices of lop cheong (Chinese sweet sausage), or bland hot dog-like sausages, shrimp, crab meat, green onions, cabbage and peanuts. The pancakes roll up around the filling, sliced in half on an angle, exposing the various inner layers.

39) Slovenian beloikranjsko cvrtje. Fried pancake dough filled with seasoned mixture of pork, garlic, and parsley remains easier to eat than to spell.

Pumpkin manty. Steamed diced pumpkin and meat dumplings come served with sour cream or melted butter.

40) Syrian sfiha. Small Syrian or Lebanese pizzas are topped with a little tomato sauce, garlic, and onion flavored diced lamb or beef, and a liberal sprinkling of Aleppo pepper. Try it with the addition of pomegranate seeds, sfihat ruman.

Sambusik. These are fried meat filled triangles seasoned with sweet and hot Aleppo red pepper, fle fle halibi.

Fatayar bi laham. These small baked triangles often contain a soft cheese made from yogurt, in addition to the finely chopped lamb or beef, onion, garlic, red pepper, and allspice.

41) Turkish malsooka. Larger than filo triangles, these pan-sized pies of buttered filo sheets encase chopped eggs, lamb or veal, onion, beans, fresh cilantro leaves, and tomato, all bound together with beaten raw eggs and baked to a crispy golden brown.

Brik a l'oeuf. Perhaps the most common street food in the old medina in Tunis, this tasty snack challenges cook and diner to prepare and eat. A mixture of cooked chopped onion, garlic, pepper, cilantro, and lamb or beef or canned tuna, is layered onto a filo square. A well made in the middle, receives a fresh egg, cracked and dropped into it. The edges gently appose without breaking the yolk and the filo triangle lowers into hot oil. When the outside is fried to a golden brown, the egg white is cooked but the yolk remains runny. The trick is to eat it while the outside is still piping hot without dripping egg yolk down your shirt or blouse.

42) Turkish talas borek. These baked pastry rectangles fill with browned lamb, raisins, and pistachio nuts.

Cig borek. The pastry is pan-fried in butter or browned on a griddle, stuffed with ground veal, diced tomatoes, and green chili peppers.

Baklava boregi. Baked filo triangles filled with ground lamb or veal, add flavor with any combination of chili peppers, raisins, pistachios, parsley, dill weed, and tomatoes.

Manti a la tartare. Dumplings filled with seasoned ground veal and basil are steamed, topped with a garlic yogurt sauce, melted butter, and paprika.

Baked manti. They are similar to manti a la tartare, but dumplings bake until brown before boiling, then accept the same topping as manti a la tartar.

Tavluku borek. Pastry or filo triangles or rectangles filled with savory chicken pieces.

43) Ukrainian varenyky. In Kiev, dumpling dough is often more than the usual flour, egg, salt and water mixture. Buckwheat flour, mashed potatoes or cream cheese can be added. As with Jewish blintzes, the most common filling is a cottage cheese and egg mix. Less common, but not rare, are seasoned ground beef or pork and onion filling, potato, cabbage, mushroom or any combination of them. Like Russian pelmeni, and Polish pierogi, they are boiled, then added to soup; drained and topped with sour cream: or browned in butter. Pyrohy are traditional varenyky in all the farm towns scattered across central Canada, inhabited for a century or more by descendants of the Ukrainian steppes.

44) Uzbekistan manti. These baseball sized dumplings have a twisted top like a large Hershey's Chocolate Kiss. The meat filling is the generic ground beef and ground lamb, chopped onion mixture without distinctive seasoning. They are served with sour cream. The Mongolian version is similar but smaller.

Samoosa. If an extra egg and some baking powder are added to the manti dough, and it is baked in a tandoori clay oven, manti becomes samoosa.

45) Vietnamese cha gio. These little spring rolls are filled with ground pork and shrimp or crabmeat, mung bean clear noodles, green onions, and julienned carrot or white radish. The wrappers seem thinner, crispier when fried, and less absorbent of oil than either the Chinese or Filipino varieties. They are wrapped in lettuce leaves with purple basil, fresh mint, or cilantro leaves, then dipped in a sauce of rice vinegar, sugar, lime juice, and nuoc mam, the ubiquitous fish sauce. Delicious is an understatement.

Banh xeo. Translated, these are "sizzling rice dough." They are crispy crepes made from rice flour and water, folded and filled with pork, shrimp, bean sprouts, green onion, and mushroom.

Goi cuan. The wrapper is a thin hard rice paper disc made soft by quickly soaking it in water. It will remain pliable until in dries out again. It is rolled around a veritable salad of lettuce, mint leaves, garlic chives, bean sprouts, and basil. Under its transparent walls are slices of pork and butterflied shrimp. It is sprinkled with chopped peanuts and dipped in a sauce of vinegar and nuoc mam.

46) Yugoslavian burek. These are similar to the Moroccan variety except without pine nuts, and with generous amounts of paprika in the style of Hungary, which shares a long common border.

Man'oushe za'atar, Lebanese flatbread baked in a very hot oven, usually a tandoor or pizza oven, develops chacteristic air pockets because of the level of heat. Za'atar, a spice mixture of marjoram, oregano, sesame seeds, sumac, and thyme graces the surface. Other spice mixes and toppings appear at times, but za'atar topping is number one. Tasty, versatile, inexpensive, popular, perfect.

Marmite chip sandwich This unusual sandwich consists of sliced buttered bread that is coated in Marmite spread and sandwiched together with crispy potato chips. Though the thick, yeast-based Marmite spread is originally British, it is incredibly popular throughout Australia and New Zealand. More comforting for Aussies and Brits than for yours truly.

Matahambre Hambre means "hunger" and mata is a form of the verb "to kill." Breast of veal or flank steak pockets serve as receptacles. They receive stuffing of well-seasoned ground pork or veal mixed with spinach, chopped nuts, and diced carrot, onion, celery, and sweet pepper. The closed packet of meat usually boils then roasts until caramelized on the outside, and cooked to tenderness through and through. When it is eaten, it kills hunger pains, tastes quite nice, and chases the mythical wolf of starvation from the door from Mexico to Uruguay.

Maté The cured and crushed leaves of the Ilex paraguayensis (Paraguayan holly) are steeped in hot water to create a bitter, super-caffeinated tea, claims the title of Argentina's national beverage. Sipped through a silver tube called a bombilla, maté delivers a kick worthy of an enraged llama. The image of the Argentine with his maté cup — a palm-fitting gourd tricked out with silver and gold trim — is a unifying symbol of national identity.

Matzoh balls Called knaidlach in Yiddish, matzo balls epitomize meatless dumplings made from matzo meal, coarse unleavened wheat flour. All the different brands of matzo meal have recipes for knaidlach on the box. The rule of thumb is that if you alter the ratio of meal to liquid, more meal yields heavier, denser dumplings, and more liquid results in lighter, fluffier ones. The usual ratio is for every cup of matzo meal, you need about three large or four smaller eggs, a half cup of liquid, four tablespoons of chicken fat or about three and a half tablespoons of oil, salt, pepper and optional herbs and spices. It sounds simple and it is. Yet a matzo ball never escapes scrutiny and comment. The divide is between dense sinkers in the broth and light floaters, older folks seeming to favor the former, younger the latter.

Although most cooks lightly beat the eggs with a fork, some separate the whites from the yolks, beat the whites until stiff and gently fold in the yolks. The same cooks, who strive to incorporate more air into a lighter matzo ball, will use carbonated water for the liquid. Others settle for tap water or chicken broth. Chicken fat is often replaced by a lighter, less saturated vegetable oil in more modern health conscious kitchens. Substituting oil for chicken fat will also make the knaidlach lighter, but some of the richness will be gone.

Reva, a matzo ball maven from Poland, insists that only kosher salt imparts the proper flavor. The danger is that the large crystals may not disseminate evenly in the batter. She therefore uses warmed broth salted with kosher salt as her liquid of choice in making the batter. Many cooks add chopped green onion and/or parsley for flavor and a little color. My cousin Kari adds nutmeg. Reva seasons with ground ginger. I add a little ground caraway seed. Alas, what was so simple has become as much nuance as substance.

The wet ingredients and seasonings mix in a bowl into which the matzo meal is slowly added and stirred. The batter needs to be refrigerated for at least an hour, covered in plastic wrap. Wet or oiled hands then shape walnut-sized rounds and drop them into a large pot of boiling water, salted with about a teaspoon per quart. Cover and simmer for about half an hour. They will triple or quadruple in size. Remove to a platter and cover with a tea towel or more plastic wrap. Reheat when ready to serve and add to the soup. Each cup of matzo meal should yield a dozen to a dozen and a half knaidlach. We never used baking powder during Passover to make them fluffy, because it was verboten. We did add about two teaspoons of baking powder to the batter (one cup of matzo meal portion) during the rest of the year. A few decades ago, special baking powder, approved for Passover by the Rabbinate, arrived in New York.

Oh humility. Must we create everything from scratch? Matzo balls made from a packaged mix, to which Aunt Rose added a little canola oil and a pinch of celery salt, were as delicious as any of our elitist labor-intensive alternatives.

Dad: "This chicken soup is so rich and robust, that even Tanta Chaika's heavy-as-lead matzo balls would float in it."

Meatloaf, mashed potatoes, and gravy No description for meatloaf is necessary. But isn't it American? Loaf of minced meat was mentioned in the Roman cookery collection *Apicius* as early as the 5th century, a thousand years before Columbus reached the western hemisphere. Wikipedia lists 29 different national variations, most of them older than the American. The ancestors of all of our moms' meatloaves were undoubtedly German, Scandinavian, or Belgian. The first cousin must have been the Dutch meatball. The Pennsylvania Dutch, as you know, were not Dutch, but Deutsch, German. They came to Pennsylvania and the mid-Atlantic states with scrapple, a mixture of ground pork and cornmeal. That was the most likely link way back in colonial times. Meatloaf in the contemporary American style did not appear in cookbooks until the late 19th century.

First on Wikipedia's alphabetical list is Austrian Faschierter Braten. It was and is meatloaf wrapped in ham, served with mashed potatoes, and often served with Cumberland sauce. Aha! The comfort trio. The 29th entry is Vietnam. A certain sameness pervades all 29. Many can be eaten hot or cold, as a dinner entree or in a sandwich. At least half a dozen line up hard boiled eggs end-to-end inside the meat before cooking so slices have a circle of egg in the middle. Onions are a common addition to the meat. Mushrooms and carrots occasionally join in. Filipino meatloaf alone often includes pineapple and raisins in the meat mix. Pork may either mix with beef or replace it, but beef is the most common meat. Potatoes rank number one as the accompanying starch. Usually mashed and plated alongside but occasionally on top of or below the meat. The covering of ketchup or tomato sauce before baking seems to be rare away from American shores. Some meatloaf recipes call for pan frying, smoking, braising, or even boiling rather than the most common, oven baking.

Migas begins with stale bread recycled. Saving stale bread seems to be an old process, dating back to the Roman empire. We all use stale bread in many different ways.

Consider breadcrumbs, French toast, thickeners for soups and stews, croutons, panzanella salads, stuffing on Thanksgiving, bread pudding, bruschetta, or simply wetting a stale loaf and rejuvenating it in the oven. Let's begin with Spanish Migas. Definitions sound simple, stale crusty dense loaves of peasant bread made soggy with water; fried in a pan with lard, lamb fat, or olive oil; and chorizo, paprika or chili powder, and garlic. In reality, it is far more complex only because so many regions in different countries vary the hows and whys. Historically, migas probably descended from a favorite dish of the Prophet Mohammed, tharid, stale bread softened in meat and/or vegetable broth. Tharid became migas when Arabic rule came to Iberia in the 8th century. Cheap, easy to prepare, tasty, filling. No surprise that migas spread far and wide.

Spanish Migas, Chorizo-Garlic Pan Fried Bread

Migas translates as crumbs. Spinach is a fairly common addition. The dish may be an appetizer, side dish, or a main cheap belly filler appearing solo at breakfast or lunch. Bacon, ham, fish, chicken, or eggs may join the leftover party. The same basic fried bread, garlic, and paprika may undergo transformation from savory to sweet with the addition of chocolate, cinnamon, fruits, nuts, sugar, and/or vanilla.

In Andalusia in the south of Spain, cooks often use chorizo and bacon together, and add olive oil to fry them in. Tapas bars in Andalucia may serve sardine migas.

If you find grapes and other fruits in your migas, you are probably in the Aragon region of southern Spain.

In Extremadura, the greens in migas are alfalfa or spinach and the meat may be from pork ribs.

In southeastern Spain, migas uses North African couscous, using flour and water, rather than stale bread, and fish often replaces meat.

In Aragon and la Mancha, migas combines, moistened stale bread with eggs, onions, garlic, regular sausage, morcilla blood sausage, and grapes.

Move over to Portugal and the bread may be stale corn bread. Any leftover meat may replace chorizo or linguiça. If a green is used, you guessed it, kale is more common than spinach. Other additions may include beans, rice, tomatoes, and asparagus. Portuguese cooks tend to prefer bacon fat over lard or olive oil.

Remember Açorda Alentejana from earlier in the book? Portugal's southern region of Alentejo stretches along the Spanish border to the Atlantic. This rustic farmhouse dish is dirt cheap, recycles stale homemade hard wheat bread, and is simple to make. The cook drops enough slices or pieces from stale crusty peasant loaves into the boiling water to thicken the liquid into a hearty nearly stew-like consistency. Cilantro, olive oil, salt and pepper follow. The cook breaks raw eggs over the pot and they poach. On occasion, potatoes replace the bread.

West of the Atlantic, migas is not the same. Mexican and Tex-Mex migas differ in these ways from Iberian classics:

Mexican migas uses fried corn tortilla strips rather than bread. The rescued tortilla pieces fry with eggs whole or scrambled. If we were to substitute salsa for the eggs, we would have another popular Mexican dish, chilaquiles.

In Mexico City, migas changes again, to garlic soup thickened with stale bread plus pork shanks, ham bones, epazote (a local herb), oregano, and dried chili peppers. A raw egg is usually added to each plate when served, stirred into the liquid to cook.

North of the border, primarily in Austin Texas, a platter called migas include fried tortilla strips, scrambled eggs, refried beans, pico de gallo chopped salad, jalapeños, cheese, tomatoes, avocado slices, and cilantro. The mixture may also end up in a taco shell.

Millet and kombu Millet was my father's comforting grain.

When Japanese cooks prepare white rice for sushi making, they add a piece of fleshy kelp to the rice cooker, which they have scored or punctured to release its essence. The purpose of the added kombu is to bring a savory depth of additional flavor called umami. The seaweed piece gets tossed once the rice is done. A health conscious friend in San Francisco added kombu to her brown rice.

My dad loved millet since his childhood in Belarus. Most millet now goes into birdseed in North America. When I found a very old Japanese recipe for millet, sure enough kombu went into the boil. Millet has become rare in Japan as a result of post war prosperity. It was considered the grain of poverty.

Both the local health food stores and Korean markets in San Francisco provided millet and kombu. I made the pair for Dad. He had never heard of umami, but insisted that it was "the best millet I have ever eaten in all my ninety years."

Teff, the smallest form of millet, is ground into flour, used in a thin fermented batter to make injera in Ethiopia. Injera batter poured upon a griddle in a large spiral, blends into a large 24" circular flatbread. Cooked in minutes, the spongy sourdough like bread becomes the plate for the stew, doro wat, and replaces a spoon.

Mofongo. Mofongo, a hemisphere shaped dish of pickled, fried, and then smashed plantains flavored with garlic, salt, and oil in a wooden pilón (mortar and pestle), emerges as a Puerto Rican staple, usually served alongside a hearty stew or broth. In Central America plantain coins, sequentially boiled, smashed, and fried become patacones or tostones.

Mohinga, mohingar Maybe not in North America, but in other parts of our world, street vendors serve up breakfast food. Among my favorites are foul medames in Egypt (mashed fava beans cooked in vegetable oil and flavored mostly with cumin, usually served on the street with bread and pickled vegetables), baozi in Shanghai (small savory filled steamed dumplings), pho in Hanoi (fragrant noodle soup with thin slices of different cuts of meat that cook in the broth as it is served), jook or congee (short grain rice gruel with pork, chicken, fish and/or hundred year old eggs) all over China and everywhere else in Asia where Chinese live, and another Chinese street dish, jian bing guo zi, aka Chinese breakfast burrito. If you see a hawker spreading thin batter on a flat pan like a Brittany crêpe maker, take the time to watch him transform thin pancakes with filling into the final roll that does resemble a burrito.

Mohinga is probably the least known of the morning street delights. Many thousands of bowls of this fish noodle soup are purchased from street vendors in southern Myanmar for breakfast, and lesser numbers sell for lunch and dinner in parks, public squares and all sorts of gatherings. Like pho, it is noodle soup with very tasty aromatic broth. Unlike pho, mohinga broth is cloudy, an opaque gray. Rather than meat, it contains fresh fish, fish paste, garbanzo flour, and toasted broken rice, all seasoned with onions, garlic, lemongrass, dried chili peppers, garlic, ginger, turmeric, and banana tree shoots. The noodles are vermicelli and the bowl is dressed with crisp fried onions, fish sauce, cilantro, lemon juice, and scallions in any combination.

Hawkers carrying pots suspended from both ends of a shoulder pole, ladle soup out of one and noodles out of the other. The dish has risen to new heights in many restaurants that dazzle with an impressive array of additives in small side dishes. Markets now carry dried packets of mohinga broth powder. Just add water.

Mole I learned the song from folk star Logan English. "I wish I was a mole in the ground…" Just about everyone who likes Mexican food knows mole, pronounced MOH-lay, has nothing to do with the furry mouse-like creature that burrows in the ground in Logan's native Kentucky. In Mexico there are entire families of mole sauces containing spices, nuts, and seeds. Perhaps the most famous also contains unsweetened chocolate – mole poblano, a dark rich sauce served on and with chicken and turkey. There are also red and green moles. Perhaps Mexico's most famous sauce, in Costa Rica, this labor intensive multi-ingredient sauce of many herbs and spices, ground seeds, nuts and unsweetened chocolate, exists only in Mexican restaurants.

Muloukia, Mlukiya, Mulukhiyah, Mloukhiya, Molokhia, Molohiya, Mulukhiyya, Malukhiyah, Moroheiya, M'loukhia - They are all accepted spellings for this leaf/vegetable that grows from North Africa to Asia and has a fibrous stem from which burlap is made. Several edible variations grace the tables of many different countries, but in Egypt alone it is so popular than many consider it the national dish along with the mashed fava bean breakfast dish, ful madamas. Egyptians separate the leaves, remove their central spines and boil them to make slightly bitter mucilaginous broth for making soups or stews. In Cairo, it came to the table a lot like chicken gumbo minus bell pepper and celery, but similarly heavily flavored with garlic. Some Louisiana Catholics make a meatless version of gumbo for Lent loaded with leafy greens that looks very similar. Like gumbo, the meat, fish, or fowl in the dish vary all over the lot and from location to location. The waiter laughed when I asked if it contained okra. "Everybody asks the same question. No. It is slimy without okra." Parenthetically, okra, which is called bamyah in Arabic and gnawiyah in most of North Africa, is called m'loukhia in Morocco. M'loukhia is also called jute and Jew's mallow. It is referenced as a pot-herb in the Book of Job.

Mom's comfort food, lobster. My mother lived into her late eighties despite an arm's length list of maladies that made her chronically depressed and anorectic…. except for lobster. Place a pair of one pounders or a single pound and a half specimen(s) of Homarus americanus with drawn butter on a platter in front of her and she would exert more negative pressure than a TV commercial vacuum cleaner as she sucked the meat out of every nook and cranny, all the while smiling. My wife Joan insists that I inherited the same crustacean sucking gene. Guilty. Growing up in New England, we were the seafood variants of Pavlov's dogs, salivating at the mere mention of lobster, clams, oysters, and scallops. Alas, the family migrated south and west. My sister lives in Maine during each summer. And my younger son lived there all year for a few years. So, is the green that I wear from envy? No, it is from hummingbirds and parrots, palm fronds, banana leaves and new growth on the mango tree outside my window. We have our own Tico langostas, clawless, but very nice.

When I first ate spiny, rock, red rock, South African, Floridian, Australian, warm water, lobster tails, clawless lobsters, or crayfish as they are known in the Southern Hemisphere (Palinurus argus), I was disappointed only in comparison to the North Atlantic variety. These were less juicy, less sweet, less tender and devoid of all the tiny hiding places for discovering an extra morsel, which in my youth was more fun than finding the toy in the Cracker Jack box. Two reasons that spiny lobsters may have missed the mark of excellence were that they were inevitably deep frozen and then grilled or broiled when defrosted. How could they compare with the live fresh captives plucked from a saltwater pound in a town with an inscrutable Algonquin name, boiled or steamed just enough to cook thru, bathed in melted butter, and served with fresh picked corn and ice cold watermelon?

To avoid confusion, crayfish in Southern Africa, Australia, and New Zealand are the same genus as our Costa Rican lobsters. Crayfish in the warmer climes of North America are unrelated although they look like miniaturized Maine lobsters. They are freshwater dwellers also called crawfish, crawdads, ecrevisses, or mudbugs. Another species is also called mudbug (or Belmain bug, shovelnose, Moreton bug or Spanish lobster) but it is a saltwater flat nosed crustacean usually called by the more appealing menu name of "slipper lobster" all over the southern Pacific from Chile to Australia.

In Christchurch, New Zealand, I had a pair of large juicy fresh-caught lobster tails steamed and drizzled with Pernod flavored butter. They were delicious. Kiwis extolled the uniqueness of their lobsters from deep icy fjords like Milford Sound on the west coast of the south island. In Rapa Nui, Easter Island, I had my first slipper lobsters prepared under the aegis of a chef from Normandy. Not quite French homard, but quite satisfying with a splash of Calvados (apple brandy).

In Sydney's fish market, fishmongers sold three different crayfish (lobster) varieties. The local New South Wales type, which they chauvinistically described as the sweetest and most delicate, was admittedly a little small. From the deeper and colder waters of Tasmania came the largest, considered the best to South Australian palates. East and south alike disparaged the lobsters from Western Australia as too tough for anything other than sauces and bisques, probably because they arrived frozen solid from a few thousand miles away. In Western Australia's capital, Perth, the local spiny is considered the best and is exported all over the world.

In Cape Town, locals insisted that cold Antarctic currents were the reason that theirs were the best. Namibians preferred their own from the pristine waters of Walvis Bay, a fabulous oasis where the Namib Desert meets the Atlantic Ocean.

Our best in Costa Rica come from the Gulf of Nicoya by way of Puntarenas, and to my tastebuds, they are fine. Mom would have loved them.

Momos Standard Tibetan street food, momos, are steamed dumplings filled with chopped yak meat, cilantro, scallions, ginger, and hot pepper. In Nepal, displaced Tibetans make and sell them substituting beef or lamb for yak. Dipped in soy, hot pepper, and vinegar, they are yet another mantu variation. Boiled, fried, or dropped into soup, these savory dumplings served with hot dipping sauce contain meat, milk curds, and vegetables alone or in combination. Momos are the best-known Tibetan food in the world. They are either round or crescent shaped, the latter more often serve as the fried shape, and find their way onto nearly all Tibetan dinner plates.

Mooncakes. Suzhou moon cakes win acclaim as the most famous. Suzhou shì yuè bing. Mooncake heaven happens every September when everyone gives and receives fancy boxes of them as gifts during the Mid-Autumn Festival. And, oh yes, they eat them too. These shiny ornate cakes, works of art, enclose fabulous combinations of taste and texture. Dense and at times a bit dry because of the recipe, they are so carefully packaged that they are not likely to lose moisture. In Souzhou, Jiangxi Province, only 20 minutes by high-speed train northwest from Shanghai, rougher looking unglazed mooncakes evolved and filled bakeries year-round. They have become omnipresent in Shanghai from open-fronted bake and snack shops that sell them still hot from the oven. The most popular savory ròu yuè bing, flavor ground pork with soy sauce and ginger. The flakey crusts though fabulous and superior, lack the appearance of precision that the Cantonese cousins exhibit.

We were in Shanghai before and during the festival and witnessed lines fifty people long waiting to buy local mooncakes. It is a very important family celebration and train stations and airports were packed with people carrying shopping bags full of decorative boxed mooncakes home to family reunions. Lotus mooncakes with salted egg yolks are only one of many kinds of dense decorative sweet or savory mooncakes. There are none more popular, especially during the Mid-Autumn Festival that celebrates the eighth full moon of every year. Golden orange salted duck egg yolks fill the center of each, surrounded by sweet lotus seed paste, inside the orate dome of each cake. The yolks make them a little drier than other mooncakes, but the balance floats my boat.

Moors and Christians In Cuba, the mixture of red beans and white rice carry the name Moors and Christians, Moros y Cristianos. This standard satisfying belly filler in Havana and beyond, belongs to the family of Cajun dirty rice, and Costa Rican gallo pinto.

Moroccan pigeon pie. See B'steeya.

Moussaka Three's a charm. This three part casserole challenges for the blue ribbon among one dish comfort foods anywhere. Its first cousins line all the coastal cities along the eastern Mediterranean shores from Egypt counterclockwise to Italy. The classic trio in Greece begins with a base of eggplant sautéed tender in olive oil. The middle layer seasons lightly browned ground lamb with allspice, black pepper, cinnamon, diced tomatoes, garlic, onion, and red wine. The top layer adds smooth creamy béchamel or silky egg custard. The béchamel begins as a butter flour roux. Warm milk whisked in keeps it smooth. Tempered egg yolks and grated Parmigiano-Reggiano or Kefalotyri cheese plus a bit of nutmeg complete the sauce. All the parts assembled, go into an oven until heated through and until the top turns golden brown. The wise cook lets the casserole rest for a while to set and cool a little. Otherwise, the hot-out-of-the-oven slices tend to separate. Leftovers reheat easily and don't separate when hot.

The Turkish version is not layered. Thin fried eggplant slices mix with tomato meat sauce seasoned with garlic, green peppers, and onions, usually served at room temperature.

In Arab countries, moussaka is usually served cold.

In Egypt, alternating layers of eggplant and ground boldly spiced beef bathe in tomato sauce in the oven, then they spend a day in the fridge, letting flavors meld. When moussaka comes to the table in Cairo, it may be at room temperature or reheated.

In Aleppo, we had a mezze of tomatoes, eggplant, and chick peas served chilled, also called moussaka. My heart breaks when I remember the beauty of the city, the incredible warmth and hospitality of the people, its place in history, and the marvelous cuisine. Moussaka and Aleppo deconstructed.

In Sofia, the moussaka was very tasty. I was disappointed to discover that it contained no eggplant, but the spicy ground beef base, layered sliced potato, and velvety rich custard topping combined wonderfully.

In Bucharest, it had neither eggplant nor potatoes. The cabbage substitute worked less well.

Mulligatawny soup From the days of the British Raj, this soup emerged as a composite of chicken vegetable rice soup flavored with Indian curry. Soups were not common in South Indian cuisine. The colonial Brits, however, expected a soup course with dinner. In the language of South India's Tamil people the name molegoo tunes means pepper water, mispronounced mulligatawny. To accommodate the occupying masters, native cooks often just added water to their favorite dishes. You are most likely to find this soup on British pub menus. Most often, it is curried chicken/vegetable soup with rice or noodles.

In many parts of the world including the United States, curried chicken soup is called "Senegalese" on menus. In Senegal it is just that – chicken broth with lots of curry powder, plus cayenne pepper, garlic, onion, cilantro, and salt. It usually does not include rice and vegetables, but there may be some mulligatawny overlap.

Munchy box All through the United Kingdom there are hundreds of smallish Indian curry houses and kabob shops, but only in western Scotland will you come across a 12 inch pizza cardboard box full of all of these Indian snacks: chicken tikka, donner kabob pieces, naan, onion rings, pakoras, and samosas. The name: munchy box. They come in different sizes and oft' include lesser combinations.

Mussels grow worldwide in cool to icy waters, but nearly 90% are farmed. Unlike most farmed sea creatures, they improve rather than impair their local environment. Mussels eat plankton, bacteria, and all sorts of waste by filtration, and normally require neither antibiotics, supplemental feed, nor toxic chemicals for health and growth. The water becomes cleaner. They can be raised on bottoms or suspended from rafts of seaweed.

China is among the leading aqua-farmers of mussels. They grow well from the bays of Shandong Province north to the Arctic. The United States plays a relatively minor role.

The blue mussel is favored among species for harvesting wild, for farming, and for eating. They grow in cool to icy water worldwide. Aliases include bay mussels and Prince Edward Island mussels. There are also fresh water edible mussels.

Few tasty affordable edibles require so little effort to prepare. From Montparnasse to Qingdao, cooks steam them in white wine, plain or seasoned liquid, with or without a subsequent sauce bath. When they open, they are done. Excessive cooking makes the texture rubbery. In China, after a thorough washing, they steam just enough to barely open and then toss in a hot wok with sauces that contain any combination of garlic, ginger, chili peppers, black beans, bell peppers, chili peppers, scallions, lettuce, rice wine, white pepper, and chicken broth, often thickened with a little cornstarch. The Belgian version is simply bivalves steamed open in white wine with beer and fries alongside.

Mussels

N

Naan. Soft, pillowy, and marked with gorgeous golden spots, naan, which is baked in a hot tandoori clay oven, is a type of Indian bread that's perfect for dipping, particularly in curries. Ingredients are wheat flour, water or ghee, yeast, starter, and salt. Naan resembles pita. You can choose buttered, plain, or garlic topped flat loaves in most Indian restaurants worldwide.

Natto Fermented soybeans challenge many food adventurers because of smell, taste, texture, and appearance. Have I omitted anything? Even native Japanese subdivide into natto lovers, the majority, and the minority, haters. Once again, food preference seems cultural. The lovers adore it.

Usually offered as a part of an otherwise pleasant composite traditional Japanese breakfasts, natto is the stringy, mucilaginous, salty dull brown glob with small spheres in it that smells a bit like Belgium's best Limburger cheese. It has a sour aftertaste called earthy by some and barnyard by others. Though I am not a fan, I must admit that the taste is better than the smell. Japanese kids seem to prefer cornflakes and milk. It is one of the small dishes that surround rice in the morning. But, please don't let the presence of natto dissuade you from trying a traditional Japanese breakfast. The other components artistically arranged and plated are rolled omelet (tamagoyaki), gomae spinach with sesame sauce, tsukemono pickles, broiled fish, miso soup, an occasional raw egg to mix with the hot rice, and dried toasted seaweed (nori). For those who like natto, they eat it with the rice. The nori often serves as a wrapper for the rice and any of its additions. I have heard that modern householders in Japan most often skip the labor intensive and time-consuming preparation of traditional breakfasts except on weekends or holidays. Popular and quicker are westernized breakfasts of coffee (kohi), orange juice (orenji jusu) and Texas toast spread with fruit jam (tosto to jamo). For those of you with scientific curiosity, the soybeans are fermented by the organism bacilis subtlis natto and the resultant pyrazine is the source of the smell.

New herring A double standard immediately after natto? Guilty as charged. Among my favorite comfort foods are some with aromas that others find offensive. Early summer in Amsterdam and we were walking along a shimmering canal in the company of gulls and coots when Joan asked, "What's your hurry?" Without conscious intent, I had left my usual slow shuffle behind and was striding with purpose up onto a bridge. At its apogee sat a vendor of neuwe harring, new herring. Raw herring sitting in pickle brine gets fattier, larger, and a bit greasy as the summer months pass. In the beginning of the season they are leaner, smaller and delicious. Most passersby stop for a fish on Styrofoam with a bit of diced onion topping. With or without, "met of zonder?" asks the vendor. "Met dank yu" I answer, with onions. Downed in a minute. All smiles. Joan laughs and offers me a breath mint. In addition to brining, the new herring freeze in barrels for a day or more to eliminate possible parasites.

Nihari Bashir was a Pakistani resident in a hospital in Brooklyn in which I took an elective rotation during my fourth year of medical school. Because they were so understaffed, senior students got to act as house physicians. The chance at autonomy and hands-on experience was great, particularly since I knew that Bashir would come in an instant if I had a question or problem. He was fully British trained but needed another year before qualifying for American licensure. One particular Friday night our poor ghetto neighborhood erupted in violence and Bashir and I spent all night and the following morning splinting, casting, sewing and patching up victims. When we finished, exhausted, he offered me a Pakistani lunch at a nearby restaurant, which advertised dishes from both India and Pakistan.

"Come let us have a bowl of nihari with nan. My treat. It is the least I can do. Without you I would have been overwhelmed most of the night. I am sure that they will have nihari. It is considered the national dish of my homeland."

We ate magnificently seasoned beef stew that included cracked marrow bones. with two orders of naan and a cold beer each. The combination of cumin, clove, cardamom, and hot pepper was new to me then and the meat was very tender. And the marrow, I loved it. He grumbled.

"What's wrong?"

"It's supposed to be lamb or goat, not beef, and what makes it special is the bone marrow from cracked shank bones. When there was no marrow at home, we added lamb brains. This stew didn't have enough marrow for me. But what can you expect from an Indian chef who cooks beef?"

Pakistan's national dish is a very slowly cooked stew of lamb or goat bits, garam masala and shanks included to impart the marrow flavor that makes it unique.

Marrow Bones

When I ate marrow dumplings in England, the preponderance of breadcrumbs, cream, egg yolks, parsley and thyme obscured any contribution from the marrow. To me, the flavor of yellow marrow is subtle, but rich, with umami similar to the juice that exudes from the caramelized crust on a roast or essence of mushrooms buttered and grilled. The texture is also buttery but not greasy, as its fat content would lead one to expect. The key for me is that less is more. A little salt on roasted marrow accentuates the flavor. Garlic, thyme, sage, and even delicious browned onion marmalade mask and detract from my pleasure of the marrow flavor. The texture alone can be a desirable additive to soups, stews, and dumplings crafted with a light touch.

Forty years ago, I endeavored to make authentic Russian coulibiac from a recipe in a tattered old cookbook. It called for vesiga, marrow from the spine of a large sturgeon. A friend had just caught one under the Richmond San Rafael Bridge in the San Francisco Bay. He had butchered the fish and discarded the bones, head, skin and tail in preparation for smoking before I could ask for the spinal marrow. I found a Russian market that offered to order me some dried vesiga for many rubles, but when pressed, the storekeeper admitted that the collagenous marrow added so little to the flavor or texture of the salmon stuffing, that his wife omitted it from the recipe. So did I.

Nogozee Early in our relationship, Joan flew to Tbilisi, Georgia, on a medical humanitarian mission to help set up a pediatric heart surgery unit with equipment donated by Kaiser Permanente and Stanford Hospital. The Georgian agency that orchestrated the project threw a party and grand feast in Northern California to celebrate the successful opening of the program in Tbilisi. Georgian feasts are world famous for sacks of wine, roasted lamb served several different ways, eggplant, stuffed cabbage leaves, herbed chicken, lots of pomegranate desserts, and loaves of khachapuri -- sweet pastry filled with mixed farmers' cheese, feta and eggs. Everything was wonderful, but what stuck in my mind were three appetizers made with the same simple sauce, nogozee, finely ground walnuts and garlic in red wine vinegar with chopped cilantro, fresh dill, red chili pepper flakes, and turmeric. The three star ingredients were pickled beets in one, sliced mushrooms in the second, and quartered hard-boiled eggs in the third. As different as they were, the same sauce seemed to marry and accent each one perfectly.

Nothing soup In Częstochowa, Poland, near the site of the Black Madonna, I saw Zupa Nic on a menu. Greta, a German fellow traveler joined me for a few days. I met her in Krakow. She read the German side of the Polish menu and explained. Zupa Nic, nothing soup, is milk and cream flavored with a vanilla bean and has egg yolks and sugar beaten into it. People eat it cold for breakfast or dessert. Mothers love it as vehicle to get kids to eat eggs. "Kids simply love it," she added. I smiled, nodded and started to giggle.

O

Oeufs a la neige combine three standard treats together to make an elegant, gorgeous, yummy dessert. The eggs are simple egg white meringues poached in oblong shapes. They float on top of vanilla scented crème anglaise. Caramelized sugar, dripped over the top, forms a dark brown crunchy net over the diaphanous pure white meringues. It looks like master chef material, but is actually fairly easy to make.

Offalessence So, from whence cometh the word offal? Most etymologists agree that it originated in old England during the fourteenth century and was used to describe those parts of animals that fall off the chopping block or table because they were perceived as having little or no value, and were therefore brushed aside. Before you turn up your nose, remember that offal preparations include such common fine fare as pâté, liver and onions, steak and kidney pie, Thanksgiving giblet stuffing and gravy, pork rind crispy snacks, many hot dogs, most sausages, and some cold cuts. Look to many a fine French restaurant menu. Featured delicacies often include foie gras, tripes à la mode de Caen, and ris de veau aux champignons – yes, liver, stomach, pancreas and thymus gland.

"Opalescence is a type of dichroism seen in highly dispersed systems with little opacity." What this Wikipedia definition describes is a feature of opals, crystals, the sky above and a glass of water with a splash of milk in it, the ability to split a beam of light and have it appear different at variable angles. The material typically appears yellowish-red in transmitted light and blue in the scattered light perpendicular to the transmitted light. So does the sky changes color at sunset. Offalessence is my own word for the metaphoric inherent essential quality of organs, blood, snouts, tails, and guts, which makes them appear totally different depending upon poverty, the skill of the cook, and the attitude of the beholder.

Okro soup warms the innards of many people throughout West Africa. Although goat meat and okra predominate, it often contains a wide variety of meats and seafood including smoked catfish, turkey, lamb, crayfish, and shrimp, and a mix of other veggies including bell peppers, habaneros, jalapeños, onions, spinach, and locust beans. It looks much more like a stew of many colors than a soup. Look for it in Nigerian restaurants.

Omelet The perfect omelet has a French accent. Fresh eggs are not lazily stirred with a fork. A whisk beats them into a solitary froth that shows only a singular yellow color. A little salt and pepper. Enough good quality unsalted butter to prevent sticking, in a frying pan the same size as the intended omelet, that heats evenly. The eggs pour in and the cook stirs/ moves then relentlessly until they solidify into custard, with no brown edges. Soft but not runny. Then comes the artistry, the shake of the wrist that causes the outer edge to turn inward again and again, forming a symmetrical log. Slid onto a warm plate, dusted lightly with finely diced green garnish, and you have it. Perfection.

Orecchiette Puglia, the heel of the boot, is among the least visited and most charming of all of Italy's regions. The people are gentle, breezes warm, architecture awesome, ocean blue, and meals simple, healthy, and the epitome of home style splendor. Antipasto items reflect the best in the farmers' market that morning. From delicious hospitable Lecce to stark historic Matera, women sit in the backs of restaurants or out front at street side tables making orecchiette by hand. Yes, these Italian pasta pieces do look like "little ears". They are most popular in a dish made with broccoli rabe, olive oil and a little garlic and a bit of anchovy for added depth of flavor, orecchiette di cima di rapa. The local wines are excellent.

Be forewarned. Our American habit of ordering antipasto followed by a pasta is overkill in towns like Lecce. Either alone is as much as even a hungry youngster can down comfortably. Buon Appetito.

Osso Buco The Italian translation of the name is minimalistic - "bone with a hole". What we mean by the name is far more complex; a cross cut veal shank slowly simmered until the surrounding meat is tender, plenty of browned juicy marrow in the hollow of the shank, and the white wine simmering liquid awash in tomatoes, carrots, onions and celery. A crusty baguette to sop up the leftover sauce. Ah, nirvana.

Oyster omelet. This hallmark street dish in Taiwan is also fairly common in seaside Fujian. In Kaohsiung, southern Taiwan, oysters show up in vermicelli and on the half shell as well. The key ingredient in the omelet is a sweet potato slurry spooned onto the oysters creating a unique texture combination of firm eggs, custard like slurry, chewy little oysters, and superb taste.

Taiwanese oyster omelet

P

Paella When the Moors occupied Spain, they brought a multitude of new crops with them.

Notable among them was rice cultivation along the eastern Iberian seacoast as early as the 10th century. The presumptive story goes that workers in the rice fields gathered for a communal lunch of mostly foraged ingredients. What emerged often included tomatoes, butter beans, onions, snails, water voles (a semi-aquatic rodent), eels, fish, rabbit, duck, or an occasional chicken. They built fires with dead branches and leaves from orange trees and pines, along with pine cones. They mixed their ingredients with short grain rice in a flat bottom wide pot, and ate directly out of the paella, the name of the pan seemingly derived from the Latin word for pan – patella. They ate with wooden spoons.

By the 15th century, rice was a staple throughout Spain, and paella was the number one regional dish in Valencia. An all seafood version became popular for Lent. By the 19th century, paella had spread beyond Spanish borders, to the world.

What survived to this day is typically a mixture of meats, seafood, and vegetables with crusty interface between the rice and pan called socarrat.

The modern vegetable component often includes sweet red peppers and artichoke hearts, with an array of greens, tomatoes, and beans.

The meats may include beef or pork pieces, poultry, snails, and chorizo.

From the sea, expect shrimp, mussels, cuttlefish, and lobster.

Paprika, saffron, garlic, onion, and rosemary add flavor. Olive oil and either water or broth are the liquids.

The modern pan has handles on both sides and sits on a trivet on the table when presented. Intact presentation is a decided plus. The essence of paella is the rice, all but bursting with the absorbed flavors of the ingredients. The choice of rice is therefore all-important and it must be absorbent, firm when cooked and not so gluten rich that the individual grains stick to each other. The short grain Bomba variety native to southern Spain seems to work best, but requires twice the cooking time of other short grain varieties (30 rather than 15 minutes) and costs more to import. Undercooked rice is hard, overcooked mushy. The goal is plump, tender and juicy. Basmati is too fluffy, Asian too sticky, long grain insufficiently absorbent, and Arborio too creamy.

The seafood has to be very fresh or the entire dish can be tainted by degraded flavor. More often than not, the shellfish presents with shells intact as a token of freshness.

Pan Bagnat Stale bread, the impetus for French toast, bread pudding, bread salad, and bread soups and stews, has another incarnation in Provence. Stale baguettes cut lengthwise, are moisten on the cut surfaces with garlic flavored olive oil. The halves reunite, encasing a filling of salad Niçoise. The sandwich rests under a weight for an hour or more. The oil soaks and softens the bread, and the salad ingredients coalesce into a favorite summer lunch treat under an awning on a palm lined street with an ocean view. Beware the drip of olive oil.

Papa a la Huancaina The central Peruvian city of Huancayo sits at an altitude of a little less than 10,000 feet. It is the capital city of the Junín region. It is linked to the Peruvian capital Lima via the trans-Andean Ferrocarril Central Andino, one of the world's highest train routes. When the route opened, a special cold dish appeared for sale at the stops along the way. Details vary, but recipe for the dish, papa a la Huancaina, stayed the same. Yellow coastal chili peppers, aji amarillo, turn into a smooth sauce with blended queso fresco and condensed milk. It bathes thick slices of boiled yellow potatoes. They rest on lettuce leaves and receive garnishes of black olives, white corn kernels, and hard-boiled egg quarters. Wherever you find a Peruvian restaurant, you will see this refreshing mélange of sweet, briny, sour, and salty smoothness on the menu as a light lunch or appetizer.

Papoutsakia If you like moussaka, you will love these Greek "little shoes." Cooks choose small ripe eggplants, scrape out the flesh, mix it with chopped lamb, feta, seasoned breadcrumbs, and olive oil. The herbs and spices are the same as moussaka. The top layer duplicates the same flavored béchamel. Heated through and golden brown on top, enjoy.

Paprikás Csirke Chicken paprikás (Hungarian spelling) looks, tastes, feels rich and velvety on the tongue. Thanks to Elisabeth Viranyi (RIP) who patiently taught me to turn simple ingredients easily into what appeared to be gourmet splendor. Use about two pounds each of bone in, skin on chicken thighs and white onions sliced lengthwise to serve four hearty diners. In a heavy skillet, brown the chicken thighs skin side down until crisp, in butter with a little added oil so the butter won't burn. Flip them briefly and remove. Replace the chicken with the onions after adding another pat of butter to help scrape all the luscious caramelized bits off the bottom of the pan into the onion mix. Cook them until golden. Add a cup of chicken broth, lay the chicken pieces atop the onions.

Next, add the paprika. Caution: if you add the paprika before the broth and chicken, it may scorch and sour. Hungarian paprika comes sweet or hot. Add enough to color the dish red. Adjust the percentage of the hot kind to match the pleasure of your diners. Cover and simmer for about half an hour until the pieces of chicken threaten to fall off the bone. Stir in sour cream whisked smooth with a tablespoon of flour. The sauce will thicken and turn glossy orange. Sprinkle with finely diced chives or parsley. Serve with dumplings, potatoes, or noodles. I personally prefer broad egg noodles.

Pastel de Choclo. One of the most beloved comfort foods in Chile, pastel de choclo, is a meat and corn casserole dish made of choclo (ground Andean starchy corn kernels), ground beef, roast chicken, onions, black olives, raisins, and hard-boiled eggs covered with a corn dough crust and baked, typically in an earthenware bowl known as a paila. The casserole is topped off with a thick layer of creamed choclo corn. The corn "pudding" layer caramelizes in the oven, and the result is a delicious salty/sweet combination that's reminiscent of British cottage pie baked by angels.

Pastitsio What you get in Greece when you cross Italian lasagna with American mac 'n cheese.

Patatas Bravas. Of the vast array of splendid tapas in Spain, this one represents one of the most popular, the simplest to make, and often the spiciest in a land that often eschews heat. The potatoes are cubed, shallow fried in olive oil, and served napped in sauce. The most common sauce combines olive oil, flour, and a mixture of sweet and hot paprika. The relative amounts of the two determine the level of heat. There are no tomatoes in this red sauce. Less common is garlic mayonnaise, aioli, with a dusting of smoked paprika, or both.

Patjuk Ki Kim was a cardiology fellow in the same program as I. We went to one of a small cluster of Korean restaurants for lunch near our hospital in San Francisco's Japantown on occasion.. He mentored me on this particular red bean and rice porridge. It was December 22nd, the winter solstice, the Korean holiday of dongjitnal. It was customary to eat a large bowl of patjuk on this day, donji-patjuk. Its red color scared away ghosts and evil spirits, and promised a good harvest. Small round rice balls that floated on top symbolized prosperity and new beginnings. All the days to follow the solstice were indeed longer.

With my love of the comforting texture of Chinese jook, I was delighted that patjuk was similar. Slow cooked two parts red bean and one part rice turned velvety in sharp contrast to the firmer rice balls, and a sprinkling of crunchy ground nuts on top. During the rest of the year, patjuk serves well as a smaller bowl side counterpoint to the chili pepper and garlic that characterizes most Korean dishes.

Pearl balls Zhenzhu qiu in Mandarin translates as pearl balls. What could be more comforting for a tot than what my mother called porcupine meatballs? They were seasoned ground beef coated in long grain rice, steamed in a closed casserole in an inch or two of beef broth in the oven.

These Hunanese beauties, called little hedgehogs by some, look a bit similar. They are ground pork balls flavored with finely cut black mushrooms, bits of local salt-cured ham, diced water chestnuts, and tiny dried shrimp. The rice coat is glutinous rice, which becomes translucent after steaming in a bamboo basket. Popular on the New Year and as a banquet course, the fabulous savory spheres usually come to the table on a bed of wilted lettuce in the steamer basket.

Pho is eaten for breakfast by most Vietnamese, particularly in Hanoi, but also can be served for lunch or dinner. It is a meal in a bowl that is nutritious, visually appealing, and wonderfully aromatic. There is considerable variation, but basic pho is made in the following fashion: neck bones, knuckles, and/or ox tails are simmered in large pots of water for several hours with cinnamon, star anise, shallots, garlic, and white pepper. The broth is strained and skimmed of all fat so that no globules are visible on its shiny surface. It is ladled over a large helping of cooked white thin rice noodles. Thin slices of beef brisket, tenderloin, and tendon are traditionally added, but you can request pork, chicken, or seafood instead. The bowl is accompanied by a large plate of fresh bean sprouts, Asian purple basil, cilantro, lime wedges, mint, and thinly sliced dark green chili peppers. (The chili peppers can inflict serious pain unless you are accustomed to Thai, Indian, Mexican, or Korean spice.) The diner adds the amounts that please. Some of us (boorish types), simply invert the plate over the soup.

Picadillo. This Cuban-style hash, routinely features a base of ground beef and tomatoes, but you'll find different renditions of the dish depending on which region you're eating it in. Some prefer it with olives for a salty kick; others enjoy it with raisins for sweetness. Tico picadillo is potato hash with the potato cubes no bigger than peas. In a Costa Rican breakfast eatery that caters to locals, if you want potatoes with your fried eggs, your only option is picadillo de papas.

Pierogi It was my second trip to Poland. I carried a list with me of a number of dishes I hadn't had the opportunity to try the first time. This time I wasn't alone. Joan and I had married and traveled everywhere together. She nearly always gave in to my culinary whims, but not during those four days in Warsaw. We stayed in a marvelous folksy hotel where travelers from around the world gathered in the morning for a round table eclectic interchange that lasted for more than an hour. Half a block away sat a pierogi restaurant that served about a dozen different dishes, all of them pierogi, boiled, fried, sweet, or savory. That is where we had our first lunch. Like the young'un that discovered her first ice cream parlor, Joan politely demanded that we had each of our other three lunches there. I didn't protest. The pierogi were that good. Polish pierogi are often filled with fresh quark, boiled and minced potatoes, and fried onions. The other popular pierogi in Poland are filled with ground meat, mushrooms and cabbage, my favorite, especially when garnished with bacon bits. The sweet pierogi encased wonderful assorted fresh berries topped with sweetened sour cream.

Not only a neighborhood lunch gem, they come in special sizes, shapes, and fillings for every imaginable event or holiday. For Christmas Eve dinner, they are filled with rehydrated dry mushrooms and/or sauerkraut. Sweet pierogi are usually served with sour cream mixed with sugar, and savory pierogi with bacon fat and bacon bits.

Pizza Margharita After a week in Naples, we have been ruined. Simple pizza Margharita has blown away the entire gamut of thick, thin, and medium crusted other pizzas. Particularly the over cheesed, oversauced, and over topped American ones.

Pizza Margherita is made simply with 00 hard grain wheat flour milled extra fine and mixed with salted water and local yeast, premium canned Italian tomatoes, e.g. San Marzano, fresh cow's milk mozzarella cheese used sparingly, fresh basil, salt and extra-virgin olive oil. Its alter ego, pizza marinara, omits the cheese and adds oregano and garlic. The same thin crust isn't brittle like Rome's thin crusted varieties. It is soft and pleasantly chewy. The pies bake quickly in wood burning ovens that are extremely hot.

Both pizzas come to the table about as big as a medium pie in the states with six generous slices. Amazing. A pie that large serves a single Neopolitan and leftovers are few.

Pizza had existed for about fifty years in Naples when Vittorio Emanuele II assumed the title of King of a united Italy. He visited Naples with his wife the queen, Margharita of Savoy, and the most typical and beloved local pizza respectfully garnered her name.

Pommes Anna Nearly sixty years ago, I ate in an unpretentious bistro in Paris so close to the open kitchen that I could watch the show. What fascinated me most was a round copper pot about ten inches across with hinged identical top and bottom pieces that fit together. The cook flipped it over three or four times while we were eating, then opened it up and plated a circular layered pie of thinly sliced peeled potatoes about two inches tall. The layering of overlapping concentric circles of slices gave the appearance of a golden brown flower.

I applauded softly. The cook looked up and smiled. Our waiter mistook my brief applause for a rather rude attention getter and came to the table. "Monsieur?"

I pointed into the kitchen red faced. "Pardonne moi. What is that pot called?"

"La cocotte à pommes Anna."

"So the potatoes are pommes Anna?"

"Oui, oui."

"What's in them?"

"Just potatoes, salt and butter."

Pork Ribs. The crown jewels in the city of Wuxi in East China, are red braised pork ribs, hóngshāo páigǔ. The ribs are akin to St. Louis sternal ribs. In times past, the redness of the meat derived from curing in sodium nitrate. In recent years, nitrates have given way to natural yeast grown on red rice to produce the same color. Red yeast rice can be found all over China, but the product is difficult to identify. It bears no picture or English lettering on the jar. The method is ancient. The preparation is complex. The ribs are salt-cured for hours, blanched, stir-fried in dark soy sauce, star anise, ginger, clove, cinnamon and sugar. Then braised for hours with the addition of Shaoxing wine, the red rice yeast, and some water. The meat becomes tender but not mushy. Extra sugar thickens and caramelizes the braising liquid before serving. If you go to China, do not miss them!

Pork Schnitzel "Yes, we did have our fair share of pork schnitzel all over Germany."

"Wienerschnitzel ?"

"No. Much to our surprise, Wienerschnitzel is only made with veal, by law. It is a geographically protected term in Germany and Austria. And another tidbit, Wienerschnitzel is not even from Wien, Vienna. We ate Schweineschnitzel. The two meats are prepared the same way, but personally, I think that because pork has a little more fat, it makes the schnitzel juicier and a little more flavorful."

"What came with it?"

"We expected red cabbage and cottage potatoes with bacon, but got spaetzle and vineger based potato salad. The schnitzel was bathed in mushroom gravy. "

"We had turkey schnitzel in Israel sauced with hummus and tomato. And in Australia, schnitzel was made from chicken topped with would you believe, cheese and catsup."

Schnitzel shows up on menus all over the world. It is called milanesa in Latin America and is usually thin pounded pork, lightly crumb battered and deep fried with no sauce. In Scandinavia, as expected, it may be dressed in bite sized fish and lemon butter. Swiss schnitzel (note the extra letter c) Schweizerschnitzel, has layered ham and cheese in it.

Poutine Imagine a pile of French fries topped with cheese curds and brown gravy. Strange combination, but not to Eastern Canadians. The fries do get soggy. The broth is usually salty canned beef broth, thickened with cornstarch. The only additional seasoning seems to be a few grinds of fresh black pepper when served. That's all? Yup. Comfort food in Quebec? Yup. Why? Beats me.

Pudding Skip British and Irish black pudding, they are blood sausages eaten for breakfast. Consider instead all of the sweet, velvety treats worldwide including these:

Clootie, crème brûlée, crème caramel, chocolate mousse, Christmas pudding, dulce de leche, figgy pudding, flan, jam roly-poly, panna cotta, plum pudding, spotted dick, suspiro, Sussex pond pudding, treacle sponge pudding, and zabaglione.

Pupusas. They are the national dish of El Salvador. To me they are a cross between pita and Colombian arepas, a thickened pancake to be stuffed with savory ground pork, beans, cheese or any combination of the three. They usually come with cabbage and carrot slaw served on the side or layered in with the filling(s). Some cooks offer a second slaw made spicy with cayenne powder. For those of us who like spicy food, let me suggest the hot slaw inside the pupusa with all three fillings. The Honduran variety is the same.

Q

Qebapa We drove to Kosovo for the day from Skopje. We expected ruins, devastation, and despair after Serbian genocide and demolition. Instead we found friendly people with positive attitudes who treated us like royalty, because we were Americans from the same country as Kosovo's two saviors, Bill Clinton and Madelaine Albright. We drove along wide, tidy, modern Bill Clinton Boulevard to a museum that had walls covered with pictures of the saviors and New York Times stories of the salvation and resurrection of Kosovo.

Time for lunch. The guard at the door directed us to a pleasant café where we could find Kosovan cuisine, per my request. The menu boasted an array of Balkan and Italian comfort dishes. Stuffed peppers, rolled cabbage, kabobs, pork roast, grilled roasts, and lasagna seemed too well known to me. So I asked the waiter for his favorite. He touted qebapa. I ordered it, small grilled skinless sausages made of both lamb and beef; served with onions, sour cream, ajvar, and pita bread. I really enjoyed the dish and thanked the waiter. Pleased, he brought us complimentary rice pudding seasoned with cinnamon and dotted with raisins. After a steaming cup of rich, dark coffee, we bought a jar of ajvar to take home along with memories of a day well spent, full of surprises and good food.

Ajvar, pronounced EYE-var, is a red/orange relish made from roasted, minced, and slow cooked sweet red pepper and eggplant. From Albania to Slovenia cooks serve it as a side dish, or paste it on meats about to go on the grill, on a spit over coals, or into the oven.

Qebapa

R

Raie Au Beurre Noir The interchangeable words for ray and skate are the same in French, raie. So this elegant dish is skate wing in brown butter, French style. The only edible parts of the skate are the wings with their cartilaginous ribs. Some preparations require removal of the ribs, but not this one. The wings are lightly floured and gently sautéed in browned butter fortified with capers and lemon juice, and garnished with parsley. The wings must be fresh caught or they will develop a bit of an ammonia smell. The flavor is delicate and refined, at times falsely sold as lobster.

Ramen

Ramen

The ramen story is fascinating. In 1945, when Japan surrendered, ending WWII, the country suffered its worst rice harvest in more than forty years. Starvation loomed. The US occupied Japan through 1952. Initially, street food vendors and the sale of wheat were both against legal regulations. A black market for ramen made with illegal wheat began to grow. To make it, all the noodle maker needed was wheat flour, salt, and water. The process was well known. Ramen noodles actually came to Japan from China 65 years before, but never became popular in such a rice centric country and cuisine. The Chinese name for hand pulled noodles is la mian. Ramen became the Japanese enunciation of the name despite the fact that the noodles were not hand pulled. Historians suggest that the first ramen eatery opened in Yokahama in 1910. Bowls of noodle soup began with meat or fish broth seasoned with soy sauce or miso, and served with a topping of dried seaweed, roast pork slices, dried powder made from fermented bean sprouts called menma, and diced scallions.

In 1958, Momofuku Ando discovered the addition of the calcium salts of sodium and potassium to wheat flour and water created instant ramen noodles. All over Japan, people added boiling water and flavoring to dried noodles. Ramen became simple, affordable food for the masses. Ramen shops metastasized to all of Japans cities and towns. There are more than 5,000 of them just in Tokyo.

Four years ago, we ate in a Tokyo ramen shop with a Michelin star. There is a Ramen Museum in Yokahama. The full cycle reached completion when we waited in a long line at an upscale mall in Shanghai for an elegantly adorned bowl of ramen. Similar venues all over urban China had become millennial culinary hot spots. So too have San Francisco, Los Angeles, and New York. There are innumerable variations in broth, toppings, and decorative artistic presentations to choose from today, all over the world. And hardly a dorm room anywhere lacks a stash of instant ramen cups.

Rejer are the tiniest of shrimp. In Denmark, in the summer, an open faced white bread sandwich may layer more than a hundred of these little shrimp in a pyramid atop a lettuce leaf on a buttered slice of white bread. They are boiled for only about three minutes in water containing salt, sugar, and a little dill. So simple, but they have to be shelled and deveined, refrigerated, and then eaten. Because of the labor, they are pricey.

Riboletta (ribolitta) adds another popular comforting hearty soup that recycles stale bread like French onion soup, cold Russian tyurya, Silesian wodzionka, papa al Pomodoro, Tuscan acquacotta, and Portuguese açorda Alentejana. The name means reboiled. The reboiled soup is Florentine minestrone, vegetable soup reboiled with stale sourdough bread pieces, enough to thicken it from soup to hearty stew that may even be served on a plate instead of in a bowl.

Roast Suckling Pig In Portugal, in quest of basic down home satisfying suckling pig, we left N1 at the Mealhada sign and wound our way into a cozy old town of field stone walls and houses, aged orchards of gnarled trees, and the equivalent of carbon-dated white haired men with deeply furrowed faces, cured and tanned by eight decades of wind and sun. They directed us to the hotel. We checked in and headed out for dinner. We drove five minutes south on N1 to the line of cloned restaurants with parking lots brimming with cars, trucks, and buses. The one we chose randomly bore no resemblance to the charming old town or the tattered grandeur of the Palace Hotel where were going to spend the night. It was a 1950's textured stucco one-story box done in linoleum, Formica, and blue-white neon. Patrons and servers outshouted each other. Generations of large families of large people crowded around long refectory tables. With rare exception, everyone ate from communal platters of roast suckling pig, fries, and mostly iceberg salad. Beer and wine bottles were crammed into every available space. Chunks of crusty bread balanced precariously on individual plates piled high with meat dripping with fatty juices. The hands, faces, and mustaches of the anointed diners glistened. It was more an event than a meal. As soon as the carnage ended, hordes departed, the rubble mounds were cleared and another family descended. The manager stopped at our table concerned that we had only dented the mounds of food before us. Had the atmosphere been more conducive to lingering, we might have stayed another hour to feast our eyes on the patrons and their enraptured feeding frenzy. They knew unpretentious amazing comfort food.

Rocoto Relleno Like potatoes, Peru has a huge variety of peppers, and rocoto is one of the most popular in Peruvian cooking. Hailing from the southern Andean city of Arequipa, rocoto relleno is a large pepper stuffed with oozing melted cheese and ground beef, served bubbling and hot straight out of the oven. It may look just like a bell pepper, but be warned, it's a whole lot spicier. Those traveling to Arequipa will find rocoto relleno aplenty, but you can also find it in Arequipa-style restaurants in other parts of the country.

Rojoes a Moda do Minho Because Portugal has a never ending affair with pork, rojoes are abundant to keep the spark alive! Chunks of pork loin cooked in the very same pig's lard, and seasoned with garlic and white wine. Served with stewed potatoes, variations of this dish may include roasted chestnuts. It can sometimes be served with a side of "arroz de sarrabulho", which is a loose rice dish that includes little bits of meat and pork blood. I wouldn't judge you if you find it too hardcore. Tasty? Very.

Ropa Vieja Cuban beef stew is known as ropa vieja, which means "old clothes" in Spanish. The name describes the shreds of meat and vegetables in the dish, which resemble colorful strips of rags. Ingredients include flank steak, onion strips, minced garlic, chopped celery, diced tomatoes, green pepper strips, and chick peas. For flavor, to the cooking liquid (water or beef broth), cooks add sherry, cumin, bay leaves, salt, and pepper. The stew may be served with white rice, tortillas, or bread. Cilantro leaves and/or avocados garnish the bowl.

This beef stew is hearty enough to eat on its own but also goes well over rice dishes and soaked up with crusty bread. The beef must be cooked and shredded first. For convenience, you can prepare the beef the day before and refrigerate overnight to save time the next day.

As comforting as any popular stew in Latin America, old clothes is a deliciously seasoned, mildly spiced. It is typically featured in Cuba, Venezuela, and Puerto Rico or in restaurants abroad serving those cuisines.

In Cuba, it may lack olives and tomatoes when they are out of season. This shredded meat may be calf, kid, or lamb. In some South American countries, ropa vieja is a salad of shredded leftover meat and cabbage. There is a Tico version in name only, which is an in-the-home meatless soup made with stale shredded pieces of corn tortillas. Tomato, onion, pepper, garlic, cilantro and salt are sautéed in oil and mixed with the tortilla strips, which have soaked up enough water to moisten throughout. Milk is added and heated to the simmer. Eggs are cracked open and gently added to the hot chowder so that every bowl gets an egg with firm white and soft yolk.

Ropa vieja

S

Fresh **sardines** bear no resemblance to even the best canned Portuguese sardines. Baked and stuffed they are a Sicilian treat. The Italian menu word for stuffed is ripieno or farcito. With fresh sardines, the menu designation for stuffed is a beccaficu, after the beccafico bird that gorges on ripe figs, and is therefore stuffed with a favorite taste treat. Serried a beccaficu is a beautifully presented baked casserole in Palermo with the crispy stuffed sardine fillets rolled and neatly arranged in rows with their tails in the air in a dish bordered with citrus slices and bay leaves. The toasted breadcrumb filling is the usual mixture of olive oil, grated pecorino cheese, plumped raisins or currants, pine nuts, etc. I saw only one version that substituted olives and capers for the raisins and pine nuts. Optional additions to the stuffing are egg, sugar, orange juice, garlic, and mashed or diced anchovy fillets. We even found scrumptious serried a beccaficu prepared in a tabletop toaster oven along the roadway opposite the docks.

In Catania, the same name is used for a very different dish. It begins with headless sardines split longitudinally, backbone removed. Two halves are then marinated in vinegar and sandwiched around a filling of breadcrumbs, grated cheese, and chopped flat leaf parsley. The sandwiches are then dipped in beaten egg, floured, and fried in olive oil until brown and crispy.

Another dish is vinegar-marinated fresh sardine fillets that are fried the same way, except without stuffing. For reasons that I could not uncover it is called "fresh sardines tongue style." Scaled sardines are also grilled over charcoal and painted with a mixture of olive oil, oregano, and lemon juice, a mixture that dates back to the original Greek colonials.

Pasta con Sarde is perhaps the most common menu item in all of Sicily. Folklore has it that the dish goes back to ancient times when a raiding Arab sailing ship sent sailors ashore to bring back food to cook, and they returned with pasta, wild fennel, saffron, sardines, anchovies, raisins, pine nuts, and tomatoes. They boiled the fennel, then used the water to boil the pasta, and made a sauce with all the other ingredients until the anchovies liquefied and the sardines fell apart, then tossed the pasta, fennel, and sauce together. The recipe remains the same with minor variations. Because of its cost, saffron is usually omitted, and canned sardines and salted anchovies are substituted for fresh, particularly in the inexpensive pizzerias. It is sprinkled with toasted breadcrumbs, not grated cheese. This is the custom for all seafood pasta dishes in Sicily.

For the purists who would not eat sardines unless they are fresh from the sea, another version omits the sardines, when fresh ones are not available. It is called pasta con le sarde a mare, which literally describes pasta with the sardines still in the ocean.

Many Sicilian Americans don't like pasta con sarde, because the fennel in Safeway is the Florentine variety farmed in America that bears little resemblance to the wild Sicilian variety and "ruins" the taste of the pasta. Wild fennel from California is much closer to Sicilian, and makes a fine pasta con sarde. We found some wild fennel in a farmers' market in Northern California and recreated the Sicilian flavor. A simpler version of tomato sauce, sardines, and anchovies, tossed with tubular pasta, and topped with bread crumbs is traditionally served on Good Friday in Catania. Anchovies are also added to canned tuna chunks, olive oil, garlic, onion and parsley, and tossed with pasta. As you may have already surmised, anchovies are commonly added to other fish dishes as a flavor enhancer and salted, not canned types are used preferentially (the salt is rinsed off first). In a tomato sauce that features anchovies, they are added to capers and olives, roasted red peppers, garlic, and chopped parsley and basil, and tossed with pasta and sprinkled with bread.

Sardinhas assadas A platter of freshly grilled sardines is typical comfort food in Portugal.

194

Malagueño espeto consists of six fresh medium sized fresh sardines on a cane skewer, lightly brushed with olive oil and sea salt before being set before the flames.

Sauerkraut and Pickles Fresh sauerkraut and pickles, just out of their brining barrels, rise to a level unknown by their jarred or canned supermarket namesakes. Choice locales on any trip itinerary include markets of substance. The largest market in all of Europe is Riga, Latvia's Central Market, housed in five zeppelin hangers. Food galore. Tiny eateries squeezed into narrow aisles, bargain clothing, and accessories. Well worth all or most of a leisure day. In the vegetable zeppelin, merchants encourage visitors to sample nearly everything. Don't pass the fresh sauerkraut, crunchy, tasty, flecked with added bits of red and green garden treats. Also worth tasting are the panoply of other herbaceous, spice-laden, pickled veggies, e.g. carrots, cauliflower, cucumbers, garlic, green beans, tomatoes, mushrooms, and squash. Ready to cleanse your over stimulated palate?

Perhaps a piece of bread. Rupjmaize, beloved Latvian dense rye dark rye bread, hardly gives your taste buds respite. There is a Latvian tradition wed to this bread that is unique anywhere, as far as I can tell. Drop a loaf on the floor even in this heavily trod market, pick it up immediately. Give a tender kiss, and put it back in its place. Love. When served with meals, rupjmaize typically pairs with herbed butter. Too much to skip.

Even at bars, strips of this bread appear, fried, and paired with garlic dipping sauce.

Sausage rolls. Think of these Aussie favorites as the larger, heartier, and more sophisticated version of pigs-in-a-blanket.

Sarma One of the dishes we saw in Skopjie that surprised me was a variation on meat and rice filled cabbage rolls with the leaves of the cabbage soured by fermentation. The filling included onion, garlic, mint, and paprika. The rolls baked on a bed of tomatoes, bacon, and sauerkraut. Tangy, unusual, but nice. Purported to be the number one comfort food in Macedonia.

Sausage and Peppers is more an Italian-American dish than Italian. Using generic sweet or hot Italian sausage, red and green bell peppers, and onions in a skillet, and serving it as a solo dish or on an Italian baguette in a restaurant or at a street fair is so common in New York, San Francisco, North Boston, or Eastern New Jersey, little changes from place to place. In Italy, the sausage changes distinctly among a dozen different regions. Short fat peppery sausages served with broccoli rabe are standard in Naples. Salciccia matta from the mountains of Emelia contains a medley of offal. Northern Italian lucaina is an ancient sausage that melds wild fennel hot chili peppers and anise in natural intestinal casing. From Lazo and Abruzzio, comes mazzafegato, yes liver sausage, made with lungs, heart, liver, and cheeks of a pig. Other regions mix beef with pork or added cabbage or rice. The variations not found in the west welcome food explorers.

Seafood On A Stick greets grazers wharf-side along Mediterranean shores, in night markets in China and Taiwan, and in seaports and large fish markets everywhere.

Skewered Italian cuttlefish

Nearly all use only the freshest ingredients and take great care to avoid overcooking. If your only exposure has been American amusement park and county fair food, prepare yourself for a far more satisfying experience abroad without thick pancake batter or grease.

Shakshuka is a stew of eggs poached in spicy sauce of tomatoes, peppers, and onions, flavored with cumin, garlic, and paprika/cayenne powder. Shakshuka is an Arabic word connoting a chaotic haphazard mixture. It probably originated in the Ottoman Empire and migrated throughout Asia Minor, the Middle East, and North Africa. We have had it in Egypt, Tunisia, Morocco, and Israel; and a very similar dishes in Italy called eggs in purgatory. I like huevos rancheros for a wake-up breakfast in Latin America. When we are on the other side of the world, shakshuka substitutes admirably. Easy to make in a single oven-proof pan, inexpensive ingredients, and a great way to add a kick start with a jolt of spice to breakfast. If they want to get a little fancy, cooks add spinach, chives, olives, and/or brussel sprouts. Typical presentations include toppings of cheese, often feta, chopped parsley and/or cilantro, and bread on the side according to location, e.g. flat bread in Lebanon, challah in Israel, and pita in Turkey. If you miss breakfast, have it for lunch.

Shepherd's Pie. English deep dish or casserole of savory ground lamb, topped with mashed potatoes and baked. An American who uses the name shepherd's pie for any similar dish with a different meat, e.g. beef or pork, will be instantly chastised if there is a Brit in his/her company.

"Lamb! Not beef or pork! If it doesn't have lamb in it, it is cottage pie!"

Sisig came to the table on a piping hot black metal tray inserted into a wooden carrier like the sizzling rice dishes one sees in Northern China. Little spicy chunks of caramelized meat danced on the griddle. They turned out to be diced bits of pig's head including chewy ears and snout, tender cheeks, tongue, and soft creamy brains, all of which had been boiled in tart pineapple juice and marinated in hot pepper, vinegar, and lemon juice before cooking on the sizzler. My friend's cousin's husband from Luzon taught her how to make it. I loved it, but never have been able to find it made the same way on a Filipino menu anywhere since.

Sizzling Rice Have you ever eaten sizzling rice soup or smoking platters of spicy sizzling rice dishes in an American Chinese restaurant?

Personally, I love the aroma of garlic, caramelized meats, onion, and fragrant toasted spices, and the crispness imparted to the rice. To my surprise, these dishes are rare in all of China outside of Hong Kong, Kowloon, and Guangzhou. In Hong Kong, upscale restaurants seem to avoid sizzling metal platters as well. They are considered an affront to the gentility of fine dining. The other strange feature of sizzling dishes in China is that the ingredients and hot spices are not typically Cantonese. They reflect the styles of Shandong, Hunan, and Sichuan where I have seldom seen a sizzling dish on a menu. My favorite place for sizzle has been a restaurant in Causeway Bay, Hong Kong with the unlikely name – Cleveland. It is noisy, very smoky, always crowded, reasonably priced, and scrumptious. I did have sizzling rice with sweet and sour tomato sauce and white shrimp poured over it once in Guangzhou at an upscale restaurant. The waiter added that it has been called "the best dish under heaven."

Smoked Bacon Irish Boil Having enjoyed corned beef and cabbage on multiple occasions, and on nearly every St. Patrick's Day, I tried to order the true dish in Ireland at a friendly pub in Dublin. The waiter laughed. "You'll have to go back to America for that. It's an American dish. We make it with bacon."

"With thin strips of fried bacon?"

"No sir. To us, all of the cured pig meat, except the legs, is called bacon. We use everything from loin to shoulder. I have it on today's menu, made with smoked shoulder. The cut is about as thick as my thumb."

I had a great boiled dinner with potatoes, carrots, cabbage and pork shoulder that resembled a ham steak with a round bone slice in it.

Snow peas, he lan dou The Mandarin name translates as Holland pea, because the original seeds were thought to have come from Holland. There is conflicting evidence, however, that snow peas have been in China for centuries before any Dutch East India Company ships ever arrived. The wonderful bright green pod with its immature tiny peas is a dream ingredient since in can be eaten raw, blanched, steamed, simmered briefly in soup or stir-fry until the outside blisters, and still remain pleasantly crunchy. Not only versatile, snow peas are available everywhere and they require little time or attention to prepare perfectly. The outer string is removed and pod washed first. After blanching, a quick dip in ice water assures preservation color and crispness. It pairs very well with the white meat of velvet chicken, with thin slices of tender beef in a stir-fry, with shrimp, and with lop cheong (sweet Chinese sausage). Ginger, garlic, oyster sauce, soy sauce, and sesame oil are all typical flavor enhancers for snow peas, alone or in combination. I know of no other Chinese vegetable that has found its way into the frozen food section of virtually every supermarket in the West.

Spaghetti alla carbonara. Originally from the region of Lazio (which is around Rome), this decadent spaghetti is a creamy mix of crispy bacon, velvety olive oil, fatty egg yolk, and nutty Parmesan cheese.

Spaghetti alla carbonara

Split Pea Soup with Caramelized Onions This classic comfort soup with an Indian twist uses yellow split peas, added depth of flavor from resplendent browned onions, and the lovely addition of flavors from the sub-continent. The additions of garam masala, turmeric, ginger, and garlic to milk, yogurt, and chopped mint leaves creates balanced texture, taste, and flavor. Carrots and potatoes add substance. A squeeze of lemon juice provides the right amount of acid. Indian cooks would never add bacon bits, but you could. I do.

Stamppot – Perfect Netherlands comfort food. Kale and mashed potatoes, topped with smoky sausages, marries well.

Steak and Oyster Pie is a sumptuous variant of the Pub icon, steak and kidney pie. On a writing assignment in County Cork, I had it first at a local cooking school, and again as often as I found it on a menu. Flaky top crust, tasty beef cubes, rich gravy, and melt-in-your-mouth briny oysters. Yes.

Stegt Flæsk Voted in 2014 as Denmark's national dish, is quintessentially Danish. It's basically fried pork belly served with potatoes and parsley sauce. The pork is similar to thick slices of bacon, something that Danes love. Just like stegt flæsk, many of Denmark's traditional dishes include pork, potatoes, and special sauce.

Stinking Bishop describes an offensive smelling English cheese that is so uniquely flavored, that it is a must for cheese explorers. It is bitter without a doubt, but it is also creamy and loaded with mushroom umami. It has nothing to do with clerics and their hygiene. It is named after a type of pear that is, of course, fermented in alcohol. I suggest that you try a tiny bit, if you are so inclined. If you like it, you can always eat more.

Stinky Tofu and other smelly stuff Stinky tofu smells like its fermenting liquid. The brine varies from region to region but usually starts with soured milk and fermented meats, shrimp, and vegetables. It sits in large open earthen jars to putrefy for months. The smell tells all in night markets and roadside stalls from Sichuan to Hong Kong to Taiwan. Boiled, baked, grilled, or fried it can be black, red from chili powder, or golden brown and crusty out of the fryer. Lots of spices and a dousing with pleasant chili sauce lessen the trauma of first taste. The lighter colored versions tend to be less acrid. If you are a renter and bring it home, prepare to be evicted. To find some, follow your nose. Obviously an acquired taste, millions of Chinese love it. After smelling it in seven cities in succession over the span of a month, my wife and I found that the aroma became more readily identifiable and tolerable, but no less malodorous.

Chinese garlic chives sautéed are delicious, and compare favorably with faddy ramp, but raw they can smell unpleasant. Fresh yellow chives, grown like white asparagus in the dark, abound in produce markets in South China, and may be the worst offenders. All of the chive varieties including flower chives impart a garbage-can odor that offends many Westerners with heightened senses of smell, but go unnoticed to many others. Not a problem cooked.

Shrimp paste and powder have inviting names, but both are made from tiny shrimp that are fermented, dried, and ground. Their taste takes time to acquire. So too do fish sauces, fermented black beans, and even some stronger soy sauces have the volatile aromatic amines that cause Western visitors to wrinkle their noses and turn away.

Many canned or packaged preserved vegetables in western and northern provinces have an unpleasant smell.

But oh, the great aromas of roasting duck, of star anise, of sesame oil, of garlic, and ginger, or of dozens of sizzling rice dishes with their heavenly clouds of aromatic steam rising when they are served. Add to the list hundreds of stir-fry combinations that liberate nose teasers when they meet the hot wok, the way that Indian spices expel their magic in hot skillet.

Stracciatella On an unusually cold, wet day in Rome, we warmed ourselves with a soup for lunch that epitomized simplicity. We sat at the counter of a mini café. The chalkboard listed stracciatella alla Romana as an option. We ordered it. The waiter/cook told us that it would only take a few minutes to make. We watched. He poured chicken stock into a pot over high heat, diced some parsley, broke two eggs into a bowl, added the parsley, some ground Parmesan, a teaspoon of flour, mixed it vigorously, lowered the boiling stock to a simmer, and drizzled the egg mixture into it, while stirring continuously. The soup looked like a mess at first. The broth was cloudy, and the eggs looked like the small rags that fit the meaning of the word stracciatella. Within two minutes, the egg strands finished poaching, the broth cleared, and lovely aromatic mist ascended from the simmering surface. He adjusted for taste with salt and pepper, and ladled out our bowls full. Warmed, relaxed, comforted, we thanked him.

Sunday Ragu Mrs. Politano taught us how to make what she called Sunday gravy. We both started with quality Italian canned tomatoes, tomato paste, torn basil leaves, and chopped garlic. What she did differently was add three kinds of meat to the sauce from the outset, stewing it slowly until tender. Her choice of meats were veal cubes that she browned in a pan first, fennel seed laden spicy sausage, and pork spare ribs. Two hours of simmering later, with occasional splashes of water and wine to maintain liquidity, she removed the rib bones. Two choices. She either left the meat in the gravy, or removed it to serve with pasta doused in the gravy, sprinkled with Parmesan. For the first choice, she cut the meat into bite size pieces and returned it the gravy. For the second choice, she left the sausages and pieces of rib meat whole, and served them plated aside vegetables or salad.

Spicy ragu on spaghetti

T

Taiwan Hamburger, *gua bao*. It sounds boring, but actually it is a class A treat, and it has an additional, far more enticing name, "tiger bites pig." A light airy rectangular steamed bun, folded in the middle across its short axis makes this shape: >. Red braised pork, pickled mustard greens, and ground peanuts combine to fill the bun with great flavor, texture, color, and contrast. Originally from Fuzhou, this treat became iconic after it crossed the Straits of Formosa. During the half century of occupation, Japanese adopted the Taiwan treat, and it had yet a third iteration in Japan as a hirata bun. Look for the crowd of hungry students in the square adjacent to the university in Taipei and you will find great Taiwan hamburgers. I found my first in the Shilin night market. Outstanding.

Taiwanese Fried Chicken from popcorn chicken to plate-sized schnitzels is amazing. The chicken is first seasoned with rice wine, five spice, soy, garlic, scallion, and sugar, then coated with a mix of sweet potato and rice flour. The coat becomes very crunchy and the flavor exceeds anything we have stateside. From bits on a stick in night markets to thin crunchy steaks covering an entire platter in restaurants, you won't be disappointed.

Tamales Tamale making is a seasonal family affair and art form. Labor intensive, multiple generations of family cooks assemble pork, vegetables and herb fillings in rectangular packets of freshly made corn meal, wrap them in folded plantain leaves, and tie them decoratively with reeds or twine. They are traditionally given to neighbors at Christmas. In our Costa Rican neighborhood, exchanging Christmas gifts is easy and unpretentious. Everyone gives packets of their family's tamales to each other. No one feels less-than or left out.

They are steamed or simmered before eating. In Colombia and Venezuela, they are called hallacas and may contain raisins or olive pieces. In Mexico, they are wrapped in dry corn husks.

Taramosalata I met a young woman in a New York City Greek market on Ninth Avenue. We were both 17. She was a black-haired stunner. She was buying taramosalata, a light pink blend of codfish roe and what seemed to be light cream cheese or yogurt. I promptly ordered a small container of the same. I had never even tasted it but I already loved what it could do. At the checkout counter she smiled and asked "You like Greek food? You're not Greek, are you?"

Five minutes later we were having strong coffee and baklava a few doors away from the market. She lived in Queens with her parents and brother. She gave me her phone number. I had a crush on Kassiopeia Papadantanakis. We talked on the phone often and went to the Metropolitan Museum of Art together one afternoon. She invited me to visit her home on Christmas Day. It was an open house for family and friends. She proudly showed me the kormos, a Greek version of bûche de Noël, which she had made. The bark was not just chocolate frosting ridged with a fork. It looked like the intricate, deeply grooved bark of a cork tree. At that moment, her parents came into our space for introductions. When I badly mispronounced their last name twice, she blushed, got a bit teary-eyed and asked me to leave.

"How could you not know how to pronounce my name after all these months?"

I tried to apologize by phone but she wouldn't talk to me. She had promised to bake me a New Year's cake called vassilopita, but that never happened. I would have loved to forget that cake experience once and for all, but it seemed like the oldest, most embarrassing memories had the deepest roots. Nonetheless, this "fish roe salad" artfully dressed with a small pool of Greek olive oil on top, a squeeze of lemon, a pinch or paprika for color, and pita points for utensils remains my most comforting meze.

Tarator Cold Bulgarian yogurt and cucumber soup is easy to make. Beat Bulgarian yogurt until liquid. Add garlic, dill, walnuts, salt, and pepper. Lactobacillus bulgaricus does its magic. Tarator sauce is a Middle Eastern sauce that is perfect for meats, vegetables, and seafood. It's even better on pita sandwiches like shawarma. Beware that Lebanese tarator is made with tahini, not yogurt.

Tea Leaf Salad Myanmar cooks make this salad with fermented sour tea leaves tossed with cabbage, fried garlic, and toasted peanuts. Unique flavor. Nice texture.

Tortilla. The humble Spanish omelet can be made with chorizo, peppers and onions, among other ingredients, but purists will tell you it should only contain potatoes and eggs.

The potatoes are diced and lightly fried before being added to the egg mixture and fried on a high heat; the trickiest part is when you have to flip the pan over to turn the tortilla. If you get it right, someone should shout Olé!; get it wrong and you'll have gooey half-cooked tortilla everywhere.

Turkey Carcass Soup Waste not, want not. If energy costs skyrocket, it may be more wasteful to salvage the post-Thanksgiving turkey carcass in a soup that must simmer for three hours, than to toss it. In the meantime, consider salvaging the remaining meat morsels, breaking up the bones, covering them with a few quarts of water seasoned with garlic, onion, salt, pepper, thyme, cumin, and a few drops of liquid smoke. Add pearl barley in the last half-hour or more until it is tender. Add a cup of cream or half and half, and a half cup of dry sherry and simmer. If you had typical green beans or corn kernels left over from Thanksgiving dinner, add them along with the turkey morsels for the last few minutes to heat through. You can also thicken the soup with a few tablespoons of leftover stuffing. Sprinkle with parsley and serve. It warms me all over to feel the holiday joy from a bowl of leftover tasty nostalgia. OK, you are right. It is American.

Tua Tuas These asymmetric bivalve clams live exclusively on both the north and south islands of New Zealand. Juicier than other kinds of clams, their taste is pleasant. On the half shell, steamed, boiled, or made into fritters, Kiwis enjoy digging them out of beach sand and eating them. They scoot under the sand quickly, a challenge to catch.

U

Uncooked Abroad Seared ahi tuna, raw in the center, is now a staple on menus of upscale restaurants all over the world. Crusted in coarsely ground black pepper and sauced with wasabi cream or Japanese ponzu (soy, ginger and citrus), it is wonderful. Tuna carpaccio is more common these days than the traditional beef variety. Steak tartare, sushi, sashimi, oysters, and clams on the half shell, caviar, and prosciutto are raw taste treats most of us devour without second thought. Many soft and blue veined cheeses are made from non-pasteurized milk. What about eating raw meat, soft cheese, and seafood beyond the confines of North and Central America?

The conflict arises between our call-of-the-wild desire for new culinary adventures and muted voices of moderation preaching health and safety. In the Abenaki language of the Arctic coastal Inuits, the word Eskimo means those people who eat raw meat and fish flesh. How unfortunate that such a descriptive word has developed derogatory overtones and has become politically incorrect.

If you want sound advice, all the travel medicine books strongly suggest that you peel all your fruit, eat only cooked vegetables, drink bottled water, and consume meat and seafood that is cooked thoroughly and served piping hot. Yes, I stray from that wisdom, but only in step with local mavens.

In China, everyone seems to eat only cooked or pickled vegetables, peeled fruit, and cooked meat and seafood. Joan and I did the same. In Vietnam and Thailand, nearly every meal comes with uncooked lettuce, mint, basil, bean sprouts, and cilantro. Thin slices of raw beef, pork and seafood are added to soups on the way out of the kitchen, or by the diner at the table. Hanoi and Bangkok have to be among the cheapest and best dining cities anywhere. We ate everything. In Korea, seafood restaurants keep octopi in aquariums. When a diner orders fresh octopus salad, the chef severs tentacles and serves them still wriggling. I popped a wriggler into my mouth on a dare from Joan. She howled with laughter as the food fought back. It grabbed my mustache. The predominant flavors were the sesame oil and chili peppers in the dipping sauce. Alone it tasted like vintage rubber band.

Japan is not only the home of sushi and sashimi, as we know it, it is home to fugu, basashi, and chicken sashimi. Fugu is a species of blowfish with a gall bladder filled with neurotoxin. Fugu chefs are licensed only after years of training in performing blowfish cholecystectomies without spilling a drop of deadly bile. Thin raw fillets are presented as works of art, often looking like cranes in flight. The cost is usually enough to produce the disease, wallet malaise. The delicate flavor and occasional lip tingle seem hardly worth the risk and price.

Tips on eating sushi and sashimi in Japan: salt water fish are less likely than freshwater species to contain parasites. Most are flash frozen, then thawed, killing nearly all pathogens. Freshness is of the essence and is virtually never a problem in Japan.

Is It Jook Yet?

Kumamoto is a lovely city in the center of Kyushu Island in Southern Japan. It is most famous for its grand old castle, strolling gardens, and basashi, raw horsemeat sashimi. The thin slices of meat are tender, and whatever flavor they may have is masked by the dipping sauce. The hard white fat looks like radish pieces. Don't be fooled.

Raw chicken sashimi is also common in parts of Kyushu and special handling supposedly renders it salmonella-free and safe for consumption. It is surprisingly tender and tasty. I am not aware of raw chicken sashimi existing anywhere else in the world.

In Syria, Jordan, and Lebanon, ground lamb seasoned with allspice, salt, and pepper, and mixed with bulgur wheat and raw onion, becomes kibbeh nayeh, raw tartar balls. Served on lettuce leaves or flatbread with a drizzle of olive oil. It should be pink with no brown edges. If not, ask for the spheres to be baked.

In Iceland, I had reindeer carpaccio that was superb – robust flavored dark tender meat. Some hunters go well beyond my outer limits and eat the raw liver of the game they kill. If ever given that option, I suggest that you remember that liver is an excretory organ for eliminating all sorts of toxins from the body and decline the invitation. Particularly dangerous uncooked are the livers and meats of carnivores.

One of my favorite sushi choices is seaweed-wrapped rice topped with flying fish roe and the raw yolk of a quail egg. Another is raw sea urchin roe.

If you indulge with advice from local diners, will "He was what he ate - R.I.P." be etched your headstone? Not likely unless you are particularly vulnerable. Pregnant women, cancer patients receiving chemotherapy, HIV positive folks, and people on chronic steroids need to be extra cautious and conservative. I am blessed with an exemplary immune system and love the adventure. Joan thinks I'm crazy.

No, this is not an invitation for you to cast your vote.

Uni. Joan and I met in a Japanese restaurant outside of Disneyland. The physician and governor-to-be of Oregon was supposed to meet a small group of us for dinner the evening before giving the keynote speech to the California Medical Association House of Delegates the next day.

I was eating *uni.* I love the pasty golden reproductive innards of sea urchins. Uni is subtle and creamy and as rich to my palate as a fine sauterne. I apparently mmmm'd loud enough to be heard.

"Must be wonderful," she smiled across the table. "What is it?' I couldn't offer her a taste. I mmmm'd with the final morsel in my mouth. She declined when I offered to order another plate of uni. She laughed without judgment or derision as I heaped adjective upon hyperbole in a futile attempt to convey the taste verbally, with flailing hand motions. "You really are passionate about the food you love, aren't you?"

"Yes," I responded softly and less flamboyantly. I could feel the redness on my cheeks.

Our guest had missed his plane and I had already exceeded the time limit that my poor butt-less bottom could survive the hard seats. Other cheeks – similar redness. The check came. I left payment and began to excuse myself when she, Joan Hall, rose too, and begged off further forbearance because of a 6 AM meeting. We walked and talked and felt like instant old friends. After nearly an hour we kissed a soft sweet good night that was all tenderness.

I'm not old enough to be her father, not quite. Because of what I perceived to be a two-decade gap, I didn't pursue her despite her charm, wit, and very appealing looks; not until a mutual friend confided (lied) that she was much, much older than she appeared. We lived a hundred miles apart, so it took a while.

For our first "date" she came to my home in San Francisco. I took her to my house of culinary worship, Amelio's. She was impressed but not yet overwhelmed. The staff made us feel very special with grace and dignity that was restored the moment my four weeks in the kitchen ended. When she met my son Matt for the first time, he said "Wow! Dad must have really wanted to impress you by taking you to Amelio's. He took me there to celebrate my twenty-first birthday."

Upside down. From Damascus we flew to Amman, Jordan. The small jet had no first class seating so we ended up sitting with a young man who was part of the royal family. Naturally, the conversation got around to food. He invited us to join him for "the best raw ground lamb *kibbeh* in the world" four days later, but we had scheduled a guided tour of the countryside two days hence on our way to Petra. He asked if we had tried muglaba, a Jordanian dish called upside down. We hadn't. We went into the pristine little restaurant that sat ten people at most, the proprietress asked how we knew of her eatery. Joan showed her the card of our airplane companion and she nearly fainted with delight and apprehension. She bowed like a traditional Japanese, assuming falsely that we were somehow connected to royalty.

We ordered upside down. It took about half an hour, but what came to the table astounded us. She had layered browned roasted lamb slices, fried eggplant, and diced cooked carrots and onions in a round pan. Raw rice and saffron went on top. She added hot broth, simmered the pot covered until all the liquid disappeared, inverted the layered rice cake on a decorated serving platter, and sprinkled toasted almond slices on top. The spices seemed to vary from layer to layer. They probably included garlic, cinnamon, red pepper, allspice, cumin, turmeric, lemon juice, and nutmeg. The combined colors, textures, layers of flavor and acid balance made it one of my all-time favorite rice dishes. The drum-shaped serving could have comfortably fed four. My impoverished-youth gene emerged. I tried to finish it but came up a little short. To walk off my postprandial bloat, we walked to and through two small museums.

Uthappam is a Southern Indian fluffy vegetarian pancake made without eggs or milk products. The light texture comes from ground rice and black lentils, seasoned with fenugreek, and allowed to ferment at room temperature for several hours. Potatoes, cabbage, red and green chili peppers, and peas top the batter, adding color and texture variation. The large round pancake cooks in ghee on one side only on a large metal pan. It is served with dosa, a bread equivalent that looks like a roll of wrapping paper from which diners tear away sheets, cooling raita with cucumbers, and curried vegetables. The impressive multicolor pocked pancake is often the centerpiece of the meal.

V

Vegetarian Buddhist Food in Asia Lentils, split peas or dried beans, and rice cmbined is the most common vegetarian dish in the world. A typical meal on the Asian subcontinent usually pairs this mixture with a yogurt salad, a vegetable curry, and a side dish of pickle or chutney. The spices in typical brown lentil gravy in the monastery that day were cumin, coriander, turmeric, a local wild herb called jimbu, mustard seed oil, salt, hot red pepper, and a pinch of asafoetida.

At the other end of the vegetarian continuum, we visited a mecca in Seoul, a daring adventure in new tastes and textures in charming environs, less threatening than a down comforter, with an English menu containing a New York Times restaurant review, we went to the small street in an area called Insadong. There are three or four small alleys arising at right angles from this street of galleries, antique and curio shops. At the end of one of the alleys, past a restaurant with a peacock and a Polish hen in its front garden is Sanch'on, a famous Buddhist vegetarian restaurant that has made its way into the guidebooks. The former Buddhist priest who owns it, presides over shoeless diners huddled cross-legged on pillows on the shiny wood floors around low tables covered completely with small dishes of treasures from the mountainsides, garden, and oceans. Sixteen courses of pancakes, greens, acorn dumplings, yam noodles, seaweed soup, pickles, tempura-like fried vegetables, fern fronds, and sweets are served together. Some of the courses are actually multiple dishes, raising the total to about twenty-five individual tastes, smells, and textures. For the curious, each dish is described on the menu. Incredible.

Vigoron The national dish of Nicaragua is a cabbage and tomato slaw/ salad topped with crisp fried pieces of pork skin, fried chicharrones, and potato-like pieces of boiled yuca.

W

Wontons 1954, age 15. How extraordinary wontons seemed at the time! I got a summer job in Lower Manhattan's financial district and spent all my non-working hours exploring. Chinatown was within walking distance and the Hong Fat Company on Mott Street became my shared favorite destination along with the Fulton Fish Market and an importer warehouse, Eagle Bag and Burlap Company.

At Hong Fat, I sat in the back where I could watch a pair of women turn a two-foot-high mound of pink chopped filling and stacks of thin dough rounds into hundreds of wontons. A bowl of wonton soup with about ten wontons in it cost 50 cents. On alternate visits, I ate pork lo mein instead. Both were so large that I could only consume one or the other. For 60 cents, one could buy a dozen uncooked wontons to go. To my chagrin, the Health Department put the kibosh on the sale of uncooked wontons a few years later. Since the advent of pre-made wonton wrappers in markets throughout the world, preparation has become a breeze. To construct your own wonton, place an individual wrapper in front of you with the powdery (cornstarch) side down. Cover the wrappers-in-waiting with a moist tea towel so they don't become dry and brittle. To assemble, set the diamond-shaped wrapper with a corner near you. Place a small scoop of filling just inside the corner. Fold away from you point first, until the folded tube becomes the base of a triangle below the unfolded portion. Leaving the top peak alone, bring the other two points together using a dab of egg white as glue.

For the filling, mince together ground pork, shrimp meat, water chestnuts, black mushrooms, and bamboo shoots. For every cupful add a teaspoon each of cornstarch and rice wine, a half teaspoon of salt or soy sauce, a pinch of white pepper, and a pinch of sugar. Mix well. I like to add a little minced ginger, a few drops of seasoned sesame oil, and finely diced garlic chive. Other options include finely chopped cilantro, watercress and/or green onion, a pinch of five spice powder, a little MSG, chopped scallops, or shredded crab meat. It is best to boil the wontons separately from the soup for a few minutes to cook off the surface cornstarch. Then they can be added to the soup for about five or six more minutes of simmering to cook the ingredients. Overcooking will excessively soften and fragment the wrappers. The soup itself usually is loaded with any combination of green vegetables and meats – including bok choy, carrots, bamboo shoots, mushrooms, roast pork slices, shrimp and chicken. For convenience, you can freeze uncooked wontons, wrappers, and filling for several weeks and proceed when you have a new batch of soup.

X

Xiaolongbao Soup dumplings. Humility lessons and Mandarin lessons had been the same for me. Aha. I knew that xia was the word for shrimp and bao was a leavened fluffy rice flour bun. So the only part missing was the olong in the middle of an obvious bun filled with shrimp. Olong turned out to be the name of a dozen businesses from home appliance sales to hair grafting, but no edible olong, just hundreds of references to oolong tea. Head slightly bowed and spirit a little dampened, I learned that xiaolongbao are dumplings with soup inside. They are shiny, thinner-skinned dumplings filled with pork or crab plus mitten crab roe, originally from the Shanghai suburb of Nanxiang. The flour is slightly leavened so the skin is thicker and less translucent than most dumplings, but it is obviously thinner and more translucent than bao buns. It is a tasty tweener. More confusion from the giant soup filled xiaolongbao that you may see people eating from a bowl with a ceramic spoon or sucking the soup through a small hole in the top of the dumpling with a large straw. They come in a host of sizes, but the smaller ones are considered the best. Savory filling, delicate wrapper, and hot broth just out of the steamer, wow! Great mouthful. Because the dough is only slightly leavened, it more nearly resembles jiaozi, dumplings.

How do they get the soup inside? Right up there with the sailing ship in the bottle and the falling snow in the crystal ball, soup-filled dumplings raise the question, "How did they get it in there?" In San Francisco, Shanghai, and Ho Chi Min City, they did it the same way. The dough for these xiaolongbao receives a filling of minced pork often with added shrimp or crabmeat and a solid chunk of chilled aspic. Collagen rich broth transformed into gelatinous soup jelly enters the wrapper as a jiggly solid before boiling or steaming. The fist-sized bao closes with a top twist like a Hershey kiss and goes gently into a steamer. When the aspic melts, heats, and the skin finishes steaming, the server gently transfers the pastry bag of hot soup into a bowl. Diners either nibble off the top and attack the soup with a spoon or large straw or they simply deconstruct the soup dumpling into the bowl. Nice combination of fun and flavors.

There are literally dozens of places to get them in Shanghai, and they are not strangers to myriad night markets and food streets all over PRC and ROC. A large excellent quality chain of XLB (xiaolongbao) purveyors originated in Taipei and spread throughout Asia and to New York, Los Angeles, and the San Francisco Bay Area. Its name is Din Tai Fung. The original location received a Michelin star. Its claims to fame are that the XLB have precisely 18 creases in the top curl and the wrapper is as thin as it gets and still maintains its leak-proof integrity. This chain is a sure bet for quality from Sydney to Singapore to New York. There will always be a line. Although I commend their business model, professionally trained accommodating staff, and product, there are many other XLB makers serving soup dumplings of all kinds with tastier pork balls, more flavorful soup, and more options for less money. We celebrated Joan's birthday two years ago at the original location of din Tai Fung in Taipei.

XO Sauce XO sauce is a spicy condiment made of dried scallops, shrimp, onions, garlic, and chili oil. Add it to tofu, fried rice, dim sum, or really anything that could use a kick of spice. You are most likely to encounter it in Hong Kong and neighboring Guangdong Province. It has only been around for the past few decades.

Y

Yakitori is a sweet tangy serving of marinated and skewered chicken pieces interspersed with vegetables, gingko nuts, and chicken livers. The marinade combines honey, ginger, soy sauce, mirin, black pepper, optional cayenne, and optional wasabi. Yakitori-ya, small shops all over Japan, serve skewers to go or to eat in with a variety of chicken parts from thigh to breast to gizzard to liver to tail to choose from. By comparison, Americanized yakitori venues serve bland skewers of breast of chicken seasoned with a little salt and sweet, but no kick.

Young Jackfruit Curry The tree that yields jackfruit, the jack tree, grows very well in the tropics at or near sea level. In Brazil, it grows so well, that it is considered an invasive species. The fruit is the largest in the world of those that grow on a tree, reaching more than a hundred pounds. Large jack trees can produce hundreds of fruit each year. On our small farm in Costa Rica, we are up about 2500 feet above sea level, less than ideal for jack trees. Our one jack tree gives us only about 8-10 fruit per year, each weighing around 50 pounds. The unripe fruit, called young jackfruit is currently very popular among vegetarians and vegans because of its meat-like texture and mild taste – vegan steak. When the fruit ripens, it becomes sweet enough to transform into desserts. Its banana, mango, apple flavor does well in custards, cakes, and puddings.

It is so popular that jackfruit has become the national fruit of Bangladesh and Sri Lanka, and the state fruit of the Indian states of Kerala and Tamil Nadu. Canned and frozen versions supplant the fresh fruit in urban centers and when it is off season (dry season).

The comforting popular young jackfruit curry of Sri Lanka cooks the unripe flesh in coconut milk seasoned with black pepper, cardamom, cinnamon, curry leaves, curry powder, garlic, pandan leaf (screwpine), red onion, sambal, and tamarind paste. It is served with naan, roti, or rice. The seeds are edible and have been likened to Brazil nuts or chestnuts.

Young tender leaves may be used as a green vegetable.

In the rest of South Asia and virtually everywhere else in the tropical girdle that circumscribes the equator, jackfruit appears in stews, curries, soups desserts, jams and candies.

Yuca Oh the confusion over the one "C" yuca and the two "C" yucca! In so many books they are used interchangeably, but they are very different. Yucca is related to all the other southwestern desert euphorbias including century plants, aloe, and the agaves - source of tequila, mescal and pulque, Mexican alcoholic brews. Although seeds, flowers and fruit may be edible, they have nothing in common with the potato-like starchy root with one "C" yuca. That root thinly sliced, fried, and salted yields a pleasant alternative to potato chips.

It is also a mainstay in the weekend root vegetable stew called olla de carne.

Z

Zi Mahu This wonderfully nutty, sweet, smooth-as-velvet soup surprises all first-timers. A very popular dessert in South China, it varies from jet black to gunmetal gray and usually comes without decorated surface. The ingredients are sugar, black sesame seed powder, and milk, thickened by rice flour. The name on Chinese menus is zi mahu, translated to English as black sesame seed soup.

Ziti is a tube-shaped pasta that is commonly served with light sauces or baked in casseroles. Baked ziti with sausage is probably as much American as Italian, but creamy ziti Florentine is indeed a Tuscan original. The pasta al dente, spinach, ricotta, diced scallions, basil, lemon zest, olive oil, and a sprinkling of parsley and Parmesan are all that it takes.

Zongzi is a traditional Chinese rice dish made of glutinous rice stuffed with different fillings and wrapped in bamboo leaves, generally of the species Indocalamus tessellatus, sometimes with other large flat leaves. They are cooked by steaming or boiling. Zongzi take center stage during the Dragon Boat Festival in China.

Zuppa Inglese is an Italian dessert that mimics a mini English trifle. It alternates layers of lemon scented egg custard with either sponge cake or lady fingers, chocolate pastry cream, and an herbal liqueur. The liqueur is not part of any trifle recipe I have ever seen. It gives the sponge layers a vivid scarlet color and herbal flavor. The verb zuppare actually means to dip into liquid, to dunk.

Hence the name reflects the red dousing, not soup. When I tried to order it once in Parma where it is popular, the waiter brought me gelato with a flavor of the same name. He changed it.

Index for foods not listed alphabetically.

Is It Jook Yet?

Fava bean stew — Foul madamas
Fava bean and fennel seed soup — Maccu

Filipino curry offal stew — Kare-kare
Four happy meatballs — Lion's head meatballs
French fries with cheese curds and gravy — Poutine

Fried chicken — Ayam goreng
Fried pork belly — Stegt flæsk
Fried pork cutlet and onions over rice — Katsu donburi

Gai lan — Chinese broccoli
Guinea pig — Cuy
Ham and cheese sandwich — Croque Monsieur
Ham hock stew — Garbure
Holishkes — Cabbage rolls
Injeira — Doro wat
Indian spiced dal bhat — Khichdi
Italian dessert mimics mini English trifle — Zuppa Inglese

Italian egg drop and parmesan soup — Stracciatella

Jewish wontons — Kreplach
Joloff — Chicken-in-the-pot (African)
Jordanian muglaba — Upside down
Karfiolleves — Paprika-spiced cauliflower soup
Kitchen sink stew — Cozido a Portuguesa
Kosovo skinless sausage — Qebapa
Kumpir — Jacket potatoes
Lamb, pork, or veal shank — Haxe
Latin American stuffed veal breast — Matahambre

Lebanese flatbread spiced with za'atar — Man'oushe za'atar

Lentils and rice — Dal bhat
Mac & cheese — Cacio e pepe, (Älplermagronen)

Mamaliga	Grits
Mandu	Dumplings
Mashed potatoes and cheese	Aligot
Meatballs	Albondigas
Minestrone	Asheh reshteh
Moroccan pigeon pie	B'steeya
Mutton stuffed pastry tubes	Chopone-choptwo
Myanmar fish noodle soup	Mohinga
Old clothes	Ropa Viejo
Pakistani lamb and bone marrow stew	Nihari
Pap	Grits
Persian kuku	Frittata
Pirohy	Ukrainian varenyky in Canada
Poached eggs in spicy tomato sauce	Shakshuka
Polpette	Albondigas
Pork skin, yuca, cabbage slaw salad	Vigoron
Puerto Rican smashed plantains	Mofongo
Red bean and rice porridge	Patjuk
Rice coated pork balls	Pearl balls
Serviettenknödel	Dumplings
Shanghai soup dumplings	Xiaolongbao
Sicilian caviar	Bottarga
Sicilian rice balls	Aranchini.
Skate wings in brown butter	Raie au beurre noir
Skopjie fermented stuffed cabbage leaves	Sarma
Small stuffed eggplants, lamb, feta	Papoutsakia
Smoked duck	Bebek betutu
Smoked haddock	Finnan haddie
Soft cheese and raw onion	Handkäse mit Musik
Southern rice and black-eyed peas	Hoppin John

Is It Jook Yet?

Spaetzle	Dunplings
Stuffed leg or boned shoulder of lamb	Colonial Goose
Stuffed savory rocoto pepper	Rocoto relleno
Tako-yaki	Octopus dumplings
Thickened pancake stuffed with savories	Pupusas
Tibetan yak meat dumplings	Momos
Tiger bites pig	Taiwanese hamburger
Two sided hot pot	Lover's hot pot
Vegan Southern Indian fluffy pancake	Uthappami
Vietnamese spring rolls	Cha gio

The End

About the author:

Books by Lenny Karpman:

1) *Chana's Legacy*
   Co-author with Charles Karpman, family history
2) *Noni, Baloney, Puddin' & Pie*
   Anthology of non-fiction travel stories
3) *First You Boil a Chicken*
   Worldwide description of dishes made with chicken broth or chicken soup.
4) *Voy, the Russian Word for "Wow!"*
   Historical Novel based on *Chana's Legacy*
5) *Feasting and Foraging in Costa Rica*
   Costa Rican Cuisine and Countrywide Restaurant Reviews
6) *The Food Bridge to Everywhere*
   Memoir
7) *Innards Sanctum, Offal Sanctorum*
   Guide to preparing and eating organ meats
8) *Feasting in Costa Rica's Central Valley*
   Update of number 5
9) *Foods That Confuse and Amuse*
   Collection and explanation of bizarre and/or confusing international food names.
10) *Fabulous Regional Foods in China*
    Non-fiction exploration of 40 regional food styles in China and American faccimiles.
11) *Is it Jook Yet?*
    International Comfort Food
12) *Forever Honey*
    Novel about lost love and grief. Release pending.

Anthology Contributions:

1)   Costa Rican Kaleidoscope
2)   Best Travel Writing 2005
3)   Venturing in Ireland
4)   Wandering in Costa Rica

Restaurant Reviewer:

Pacific Sun, California
A. M. Costa Rica

Editor:

San Francisco Medicine
Chanticleer

Contributor:

American Heart Journal, American Journal of Cardiology, Chanticlear, Circulation, Conversely, Dallas Morning News, Jewish Magazine, Journal of the American Medical Association, Marin Independent Journal, Newark Star Ledger, Pacific Sun, PanGuia, Pittsburgh Post - Gazette, Salon, San Francisco Examiner, San Francisco Medicine, Tico Times, Travelers' Tales, Troika, and more.